yes

ALEXANDER MUNZEL

TECHNICAL SOFTWARE INC.
RICHMOND
1999

By The Same Author:
B-611 – WAY OUT THERE

Published by:
TECHNICAL SOFTWARE INC.
#9 - 6600 Lucas Road
Richmond, B.C. V7C 4T1
Canada

Printed in Canada by:
HEMLOCK PRINTERS LTD.

ISBN 0-9672566-0-7

FOR GRETA

Look up—no—way up
where the stars twinkle at you,
all at once, all together, all at you.
Can you hear the tingle in their twinkle?
Can you feel that tingle from their twinkle?
Can you hear them trying to sing to you?
Know that when I am near you no longer
I shall try to sing to your heart
from way up there.
I shall try to sing over and over,
again and again,
about how so very happy I was
to have been allowed to have known you.

ACKNOWLEDGMENTS

I must confess more than gratitude to my devoted editor, Susan Erb. Without her help this book wouldn't have been possible. And to Barbara Green-McDonald for some fine English points.

♣ CONTENTS ♣

yes

♣ CHAPTER 1 ♣

All slang is metaphor, and all metaphor is poetry.

—G.K. Chesterton

"Yeah, slang is poetry, people poetry, and it's powerful, powerful when it talks."

"It talks?"

"It talks. And—in time—gets stuck in wisdom. And when it talks to your heart, it sounds like music. It sings."

"I don't understand what you mean. I believe in poetry…but just a bit. It's such a private thing."

"I understand what you mean by *just a bit*. Poetry isn't the most important thing in life. True. Many things are more important."

"What's in the envelope, Alexander?"

"Just some faded pictures and things I promised to show John."

"So…how long have you known him?"

"A few months."

"And he's supposed to be your best friend?"

"Yeah. That's how I feel about him."

"I don't understand."

"We've been friends for over forty years. But if you count the actual hours and days we've spent together, it would add up to just a few months…maybe."

"Then how can he be your best friend?"

"Because he was a big part of me—still is."

"Why?"

"I don't know. Maybe, we're alike somehow. That's probably it. I know he's a better chess player, but he'd never admit it. That's just the way he is. I think he's a better man than I am. Wait 'til you meet him. You'll like him. He's a good listener too. He doesn't say much. He's busy thinking most of the time. He smiles a lot, and cracks jokes whenever he gets an opening. That's John. You'll see for yourself. He'll be waiting at the gate.

"He and Estelle have a cabin in upstate New York where he's taking us today. It's way out in the boonies. During the War of 1812, the Americans made a stand at the creek that runs through his place. It's really something. Like it has some sort of magic in it. It's hard to describe how I feel about it. The last time I was there…"

At The Stream
I stood at its edge
and let its cold water
splash over my feet.

Its rushing wildness
stampedes down the land,
picking up strength,
forcing its way
over and under
and past and through,
heading down
to who knows where.

It's overpowering.
I felt it could grab me,
somehow,
and take me with it,
if it wanted,

making me part of it.

"It was almost frightening."

"Amazing. Sounds like you're more interested in seeing the creek than you are John."

"No, I want to see John mostly, but I do love that stream."

"What about Estelle?"

"You'll meet her too."

The plane released us. Greta and I stood among the sluggish mass of searching passengers in the high-ceilinged airport in Laval, where post-Easter travelers with winter-white faces pushed nervously, trying to get past us and jostling us while we stood in their way looking for...

John
There he was—
waiting at the gate,
with a baggage cart,
a welcoming smile,
and laughing eyes,
with a distinguished-looking bald head,
and a solid body,
his hands secured in the pockets
of a well-worn brown leather jacket.

"John, you look great. I'm so glad to see you." We hugged each other hard. From a glance at his eyes, I saw how much he approved of Greta. They kissed like old friends.

"Good flight?"

"Yes, thanks."

From out of nowhere, an old memory surfaced—John's old saying, "Make good vibes." Where had that come from?

"My car's right over there."

The Buick was like John, compact, in good shape, clean. As soon as we got in, he reached under the seat and pulled out an odd-shaped checkered hat.

"What have you got there, John?"

It was the ugliest hat I'd ever seen, an oversized soft floppy thing. No wonder he kept it under the seat. He smiled as he put it on for us. It covered one side of his face and hung down, almost touching his shoulder. We all laughed. He knew how he looked.

"Gee, John, Greta can't see your face, and all I see is your nose."

"Yeah, Estelle thinks I'd get arrested if the cops saw me wearing it. She hates it. But I like it, so I wear it anyway when she's not with me."

I silently agreed with Estelle.

"Didn't your dad have a blue car like this?"

"Yeah, it was blue, but it was a Plymouth."

"Greta, the first time I met John's dad, I instantly knew he would never berate me. I could see it in his face. And he was always the same—cheerful. That's what I remember most. When we met, I'd call out, 'General' and he'd shout, 'A-ten-shun,' with a grin on his face. Then I'd salute, 'Yes sir, my General,' and that's how we'd pick up with each where we'd left off.

"John's mother I called *Madam*. She knew I said it with my heart, and she liked it. She had a special way of cheering me up when I needed it most. She was tiny. She'd bend down to check me over from the floor up. She'd move closer and look at me with her deep bitter-sweet-chocolate eyes, and laugh right in my face, laugh like hell with her whole body, then thunder, *'Donner, Blitz und Hagel!* What's the matter with you? Cheer up, Tom! Cheer up!' She only did it when I was really down, instantly making me feel it was just plain stupid to be down at all. She never elbowed herself into my heart affairs though. Never.

"They were the greatest, funniest folks I ever knew. And kind. Once they took me in for almost a year. They lived in a Panabode house and raised purebred boxers. They were those rare people who gave more to life than they took. But all that was a long time ago."

We were still sitting in the parking lot. John put hat back under the seat and started the car.

"How are your sisters, John?"

"The youngest is fine and the oldest died a while ago. And Ada lives alone. She's okay."

"What do you mean by *okay*?"

"Well, after what happened."

"What?"

"Her house caught fire, but the firemen couldn't find her little girl. When they told Ada, she went nuts and ran back into the burning house but couldn't find her either. Later they found her under her bed, all black. Ada has finally made peace with it, but she'll never get over it."

"How awful. I always liked Ada."

There was silence in the car as John drove along a winding country road.

"John, where are you going? I seem to remember we took a freeway last time."

"I'm taking the back way to show you some old stone houses that were built by English Loyalists who came to Canada from the States before 1812. This area was British then. At the same time, the French and pro-Americans left Canada, slipping into the States, settling near where our cabin is. When we get there, I'll show you where the Yankees made cannonballs in 1812, right at my creek."

John drove past occasional farmhouses among the miles of spring-green fields and large bare trees. He lapsed into silence. Knowing him, I knew he was thinking about something he was going to tell us. I glanced at him periodically to see if I was right, watching for the grin that signaled the start of a story. Nothing. So…

I Enjoyed The Rolling Landscape
Open fields in tender green velvet,
alternating with

two-story brick houses
nestled in groves of tall trees.
The road wound around the hills,
rising and falling.
My hands rested loosely on my lap
as my head swung here and there.
I let the sway of the car move my body…
totally at ease.

"Alexander, look at those old brick houses. They're lovely, so well kept, gardens and all. They look happy, as if the people living in them are happy. They remind me of the houses we saw in New England on our drive down the East Coast years ago."

"Yes, but look at the outhouses. They go with them too. Do they still use outhouses here, John?"

"I doubt it."

John grinned. Here it comes.

"Those outhouses remind me of something I did one crazy Halloween in Alberta when I was just a kid. Want to hear it?"

"Sure. I know it'll be funny, coming from you."

"Let's see. I think I was fourteen. A bunch of us kids went out in the country at night to settle a score with a mean old farmer. We figured Halloween and settling an old score went well together. And we had a plan. On the way, we discussed the details. For our plan to work, he had to come out of his house and walk directly into our trap. We hid behind his dilapidated outhouse and waited and waited for him to come out. We were getting mighty cold, shivering, crouched close together, but we were young, so we stuck it out. To tell you the truth, we weren't just cold, we were scared. Partly because it was dark, but mostly we were afraid of him and of being caught."

John started laughing, likely reliving the scenes to come.

"Finally, out he came—straight at us. He walked quickly, probably because of the cold, but we were afraid maybe he'd seen us. The closer he came, the more scared we got. We put our heads down, not daring to look as he entered the outhouse.

We heard the door squeak, his steps on the wood floor, the rustle of clothing, and a soft plopping—our signal to trap him. We knew he was sitting with his pants down, so he couldn't come after us right away if we messed up. We looked at one another and grinned, kicking one another with our elbows, trying not to laugh. But somebody giggled which caused us all to burst out laughing, and then the farmer started hollering. At the sound of paper rustling, we pumped up our undersized muscles, barely able to heave the outhouse up, up, higher and higher, until it tipped in a ghost-like slow sway and crashed down onto the hard ground. Now he was locked in with his own shit, so to speak, nose down on the heart-cut-out door. And us yelling and laughing.

"Within seconds, realization set in. We were shocked at what we'd done. We stood in disbelief that turned quickly to fear, which made us run faster and faster as he hollered louder and louder. We knew he was alive, and that as soon as he got out, he'd be after us as fast as he could go, and furious. We ran most of the way home."

Still laughing, John looked at me to see how I'd enjoyed his story. I was still laughing. Greta just shook her head, grinning.

"Didn't you see if the farmer got out?"

"No, hell no. We had to get away. We never looked back. We never found out how he got out but knew he would eventually. I know we shouldn't have done it, but at the time it seemed like the right thing to do. I have to tell you that was the best Halloween I ever had."

"I never thought you'd do something like that."

"Well, times were different."

I glanced at Greta who was smiling.

"John, your story reminds me of something that happened to me one year when I was an architect working for the Canadian government. I went to Fort Chipewyan to take over a nursing home from the contractor. The night before *takeover*, the contractor pumped me full of whisky. After a few hours sleep in a slapped-together, poorly heated hotel belonging to a

Chinaman, I had to go. I looked for a bathroom along the corridor of the so-called hotel, walking up and down twice. No bathroom anywhere, so I knew there had to be an outhouse—out in the dark where it was forty below zero. I was in a hurry by then, so I ran outside in my long johns."

"Did you find it?"

"Yes, but the door was locked. I panicked. The padlock was tiny, no bigger than your thumbnail. I pulled on it, but it didn't give. I was getting colder and madder and felt like going right there, but I knew the Chinaman would see the frozen pee the next morning and figure out it must have been me—because of the amount I'd had to drink at the hotel bar that night. Being the Government representative, it wouldn't be good PR. I figured I'd better get the key.

By the time I got the owner out of bed, I was jumping from one leg to the other. When he finally handed me the key, I shot outside into the wind, shaking with cold, trying to find the tiny hole in the lock with the even tinier key. My shivering made it impossible. I was left out in the cold, as they say, and then some. So I did what I had to, right then and there, then took the key back, and thanked him for it. The next morning I saw the yellow in the white showing itself to anyone who passed by."

I looked at Greta, to see how she took to what was a man's story. She smiled at me. I asked myself if I could risk the good vibes in the car by encouraging John to tell another story he'd told me once.

"John, tell Greta the story about the time you decided to get even, waiting until hell froze over to do it. Remember? You said it was damn cold in front of Lee's Drugstore, at Twenty-fourth and Second in Edmonton."

"Oh yeah. You tell it Alex."

"No, it happened to you. You tell it better, John."

"Okay. This happened in Edmonton in the late thirties when I was in my teens. I had a weekend job delivering prescriptions for Lee's Drugstore. Saturdays I had to clean the windows and the black marble entrance, summer or winter. I hated it most in the winter, especially when it was forty below. It's damn hard work shining black marble when it's that cold."

"It's hard to do anything when it's that cold, Greta. John's right."

"Well, my fussy boss liked to show off his black marble. Saturdays were the busiest, so that's when the marble had to be at its shiniest. And every Saturday, just after I finished polishing and rubbing the marble, some damn dog came along and peed on it. It always seemed to happen when I was out delivering prescriptions, as if the bastard knew. People coming in the store would tell my boss about the pee on his marble, just doing him a favor. Well, they weren't doing me any favor. I had to clean it and shine it all over again—in the bitterly cold wind. It was always windy on that corner in winter.

"The dog always peed in the same spot. After a while I figured out which dog it was. I hated that dog with a vengeance, and finally I was driven to a plan for revenge. I'd fix that dog, once and for all. I was furious. My mind was mad and hot, so I went for a plan with lots of power. I fastened a copper plate onto the spot where the dog always peed, wired it to a car battery inside and waited. One day, sure enough, along came the dog and did it again. The instant the yellow stream hit the plate, I connected the wires to the battery, and that did it! When I heard the loud yelp, I ran out of the store just in time to see the dog running away as fast as he could on the slippery ice. I knew he'd never be back."

John laughed as he wiped tears from his cheeks with the back of his hand.

"You know, you can weld steel with the charge from a battery. It must have given that dog a heck of a jolt."

"I know it now, but I didn't then. I couldn't do it today, but in those days it was okay—smart even—for a kid to outwit the odds against him."

Greta and I laughed.

"That story reminds me of another one."

"Is it short? We're almost at the U.S. border."

"It's short. In 1952 I worked for the Q.N.S.& L. Railway, helping survey a new rail line that was needed to *'haul iron ore by fifty-four.'* I'd just arrived at camp and my boss and I were working late, so trying to impress on me how tough life was out in the bush, he told me a story about a Chinese cook.

"The tough and rough and ready boys in camp had played jokes on the cook for almost a year, trying to add some fun to the long hard days to relieve their boredom. They nailed his boots to the wooden tent floor, tied knots in his socks, and, when they were high, they'd teasingly sing:

'Ching Chong China man, sitting on a rail,
'long came a white man an' chopped off his tail.'

"At Christmas time, feeling remorseful, they told Chang they were sorry about the jokes they'd pulled on him all year. They'd now decided to turn over a new leaf and stop the rough jokes. They felt real bad, they told him, smiling at each other. Chang said nothing. Maybe he didn't believe them and maybe he figured this was just one more of their jokes. After they'd eaten their usual meal of soup, bread, steaks, and dessert—the same meal he'd fixed faithfully all year long—they went up to him and apologized individually, to make sure he'd believe them.

"Chang smiled, thanked them, bowed, smiled some more and, after thinking for a while, said, 'Okay. You pull no jokes on Chang. Okay. Chang happy. Now Chang promise not to pee in soup no more. Now we all happy.' "

"That's awful, Alexander!"

"Yeah, Alex. That was a little crude to tell Greta. I wouldn't tell that to Estelle."

♣ CHAPTER 2 ♣

"We're at the border." John had stopped the car.

The first thing I saw was an officer's belly at the open window. He was wearing a beautifully ornate pistol in a silver-riveted belt. His enlarged face suddenly appeared as he leaned down into the car and poked his head through the window. He wore that *knowing look.* His circulating eyes looked at us, closing in on my eyes looking at him. He looked around the whole inside, with tight-lipped determination set on his authoritarian-looking mouth. Then he looked straight at John.

"Where're you going?"

"To my cabin near Plattsburg."

I could tell by the slight twitch of his tight lips that John's aloof, accent-free reply had gotten him through the border. Now he looked at Greta and I, wanting to know more. His neck appeared to be sitting on the windowsill, disembodied; his head tilted sideways. It looked to me as if he kept his merry eye on Greta and his mean one on me. The mean one seemed to move his tight lips.

"Where're you from?" His voice was like his eyes—sneaky, insinuating.

"Vancouver," I meekly replied.

His lips tightened some more, likely having picked up on my accent.

"Where were you born?"

"Moscow."

His face tensed. I knew I'd shocked him.

"Moscow, Russia?"

"Yes, sir." I saw a vision of myself with my hands up.

"Nationality?"

"Canadian."

He must have questioned my meek-voiced answer. He demanded my papers, glanced at them, looked at me, thought authoritarian-like, paused, and ended with a big wave of his arm, telling us to move on.

On our way again, now in upstate New York, John looked at me for quite a while, saying nothing, then, "Alex, at first, I thought you were up to your usual tricks, just pulling that officer's leg. That guy was tough. And he knew his stuff. If you'd lied to him, and then he saw from your papers you weren't born in Moscow, we'd all have been in a lot of trouble. I didn't know you were born in Russia."

"Alexander is Russian, John."

"No, I'm not."

"How come you were born there?"

"Because my dad had been given a job with Junkers Aircraft in Moscow where the Germans were secretly building airplanes. That was in 1925. He was delighted, not only because he could see his Jewish mother there, but also because he would have a chance to get her out of jail where she was incarcerated for having supported the Czar's government with a pledge of a 100,000 gold rubles. And he succeeded, aided by his speaking fluent Russian from having lived most of his childhood in Russia."

"I see why Greta says you're Russian."

"It isn't exactly right. I'm not Russian, even though I do have a Russian birth certificate. I'm part this and that: a bit Jewish, a bit German, a bit Russian, and what else, I don't know. I'll show you pictures of some of my relatives from Russia later. They're in this envelope. One's of a great-great uncle who served as a physician in the Russian army, a colonel, during the war with Japan in 1905."

"How did you get out of Russia into Germany?"

"I was so young when we left that I don't know. And I never asked."

"Being a Russian-born kid in Nazi Germany with a Jewish grandmother must have caused problems for you."

"Yes, very much so—though no one knew about my grandmother."

"I remember you telling me once that your dad served in the German forces during World War I. Am I remembering right?"

"Yes, he was an observer in the German air force. He flew in German planes over enemy territory to map out French artillery positions. When directly over the target, he'd shoot colored flares as a signal to the waiting German ground artillery. One time his flare pistol accidentally went off from under his pants. He was sitting on it to avoid doing just that. Not only did the flare give the wrong-colored signal, but even worse, it shot through the canvas-covered fuselage, barely missing the fuel tank. Word about it spread among the pilots, so they wouldn't take him up after that until he showed them his flare pistol with a walking stick inserted through the barrel to prove it wasn't loaded. He figured he was the only guy in the German air force to fly with a walking stick.

"The more stories he told, the more I understood his *tongue-in-cheek* claim that the Germans had lost the war because of soldiers like him. Like his story about the time he took over a French-occupied farmhouse with a unit of eight men. He'd cased the house from the woods, carefully, but had taken way too long as far as his shivering men were concerned. They wanted to get inside to get warm. So he went for the daring approach with his legs spread like an old western gunfighter, shooting from Lugers in each hand, trying to force a French response. Nothing, so they hurried into the farmhouse and headed down to the cellar to look for some wine to warm up with. Then all hell broke loose. The French artillery began pounding the place. His men crouched together on a bench, sitting across from Dad. As the shelling continued and got heavier, the men glared at him—their anger growing. They blamed his wild shooting for alerting the French artillery. 'The men were mighty angry at me,' he'd told me. He knew they'd never follow him again. That was my dad in the war."

"He sounds like my dad, always trying something that didn't quite work out like he planned. We're coming up to a place I'd like to stop at if you're interested. It's a truck stop that has some of the best lemon pie I've ever tasted. Estelle likes the paper-thin crust. Okay with you?"

"Sure. Let's stop."

An array of metal-monster trucks with gleaming, polished chrome partially blocked our view of an old wood building with a weathered sign on the roof, *Mary's*.

"This looks like the kind of place where the waitress asks, 'What's it gonna be?' and you answer, 'What kind hav'ya got?' Then she gives you a rundown of their fresh homemade pies and you finish with, 'Make it apple and a coffee.' "

"You sound like a truck driver."

As we entered the cafe, John held the squeaky screen door open, grinning at us, watching our faces. My eyes circled the room in total surprise, trying to take it all in at once. I was delighted, feeling as if I'd seen it before.

"Greta, this place is fabulous, right out of the fifties."

I began pointing out details, explaining how it all worked—the lunch counter with its swivel stools and the row of high-backed booths along the wall.

"The only thing missing is the jukebox that sat on each table. After feeding it a nickel, a record from the stack flopped down and the needle would sing your favorite hit, songs like *Goodnight Irene* or *Sentimental Journey*. Do you remember those songs, John? And the times?"

"I sure do."

Animated by what we remembered of them, John and I began laughing, moving our arms and feet to show what good times those were. I started to sing.

"Oh no, Alexander, please don't."

I couldn't stop myself. "They try to tell us we're too young, too young to really be in love…"

"Uh...the truckers are looking at you."

"Sorry."

We were still standing in the middle of the place, still looking.

"Those were quite the times. Those old songs are going through my whole body now, bringing back feelings from years ago. I feel some of what I felt then—what it felt like being the age I was, how I felt about the world, the feeling of well-being I had. Nothing could stop me then. Funny."

"Alex, I think that feeling comes with the hungry desire for life you have when you're young, when you want so badly to be part of life, no, when you want it, all of it, and you want it all at once."

"Yeah, I think you're right."

I continued my description to Greta. "Each table had a bottle of ketchup, a sugar jar, salt and pepper shakers, and a napkin dispenser, all sitting beside the juke box. You had to check out the salt and sugar dispensers to be sure some joker hadn't switched the contents, causing you to sugar your eggs or salt your coffee.

"A counter like that one standing there was the heart of the place. A neatly dressed waitress would stand behind the lunch counter, waiting to sell you *the goods* if you let her. The counters were real busy. At the soda fountain, a *jerk* would be busy filling foot-high soda cups with scoops of ice cream, mixed fruit, syrup, and a straw. And the glass display case behind the counter was filled with homemade fresh pies. Every cafe had its own *specialty of the house*. Pie and a cup of coffee was what most people ordered. You always got free coffee refills. See those twin coffee urns? One's to fill the customers' cups and the other's to make fresh coffee; it's always on the go. There was happy and practical eating at those counters.

"Greta, see that foot rail along the bottom of the counter. That's the *real McCoy*. Every counter had to have a foot rail. I can't believe what I see here. Everything is exactly the way I remember it. See that waitress behind the register. In front of her, under the glass countertop, there's an assortment of candy and gum. You're supposed to spend your change on it when you pay your bill, to look past your change to the sweets tempting your eyes, to want something more. Smart, isn't it?

"And the waitress wore an apron to identify herself. You called *Missy* to get service. She usually had two voices: a soft one, to get all the orders she could get out of you, and a harsh one for the cook to get the orders filled, quick-like. The harsh one generally helped serve a quick meal to her good-tipping customers. She trained them to come back and choose her tables so that she'd be sure to get their good tips. For the specially chosen customers she would give more of herself—insinuating promises to the old ones and, perhaps, a joke to the young.

"The only place in the world you'll find these kinds of cafes is in the U.S. and Canada. When you sit at the counter, you can leave your hat on while you eat—like those guys—put your elbows on the counter and eat with just a fork in your balled fist. You could ask the stranger next to you where he'd come from, where he was heading, and why and what he was doing in town. There was no offense in it. People asked, 'What's your racket?' It's the American way: feeling free to ask anything you wanted...almost anything. And you could tell your neighbors all. Darn right. And some would tell you more than you wanted to hear. It's like a second home for some people. It felt homey to me back then, a second home during those first few years I lived in Canada."

I was memory-moved by this place, reminding me of the fifties, making me feel younger. Odd.

"Let's sit down and order."

"Good idea."

"I spent a lot of time in a place like this when I first came to Canada in 1951. Those were some of my happiest moments then. That was in Guelph."

"I didn't know you lived in Guelph."

"Yeah, I went there from Germany, pretending to be a plasterer."

"How come?"

"It's a long story. I'll tell you about it sometime."

We all ordered lemon pie and coffee. It came quickly.

"That pie looks real good, John."

I slowly scooped up a large spoonful, looking at it closely before I tasted it. It was tart and sweet and smooth and crisp—all at the same time—a palette of sensations, a wonderful combination of flavors and texture. My tongue moved the pie off the spoon, pushing it up and down as if to make it last, holding it, then moving it back and forth slowly. One spoonful followed another. Wonderful heaping spoonfuls, soon gone. It was everything John said it would be.

Enjoying the taste from the past, I sat, satiated, my brain signaling it was time to rest. I pushed the clean plate away with my right thumb, flipped up my cap, leaned back, and looked around once more—for old time's sake—dessert for my emotions.

"This pie would have cost ten cents in the fifties. I made eighty-nine cents an hour. Everything seemed to be worth more then. Not like today when I can't help feeling I'm being taken when I buy anything."

"That must have been during the Korean war?"

"It was, but I wasn't aware of it. What happened on the other side of the world wasn't part of my world. The people I lived with, their ways, their homes—that was my world. It's all clearly etched in my mind."

♣ CHAPTER 3 ♣

As John drove, the only sound in the car was the hum of the wheels on the pavement. The road rose and fell gently, in harmony with the contours of the land. We passed through stretches of sparse timber and semi-green grass in a gently rolling countryside. I looked past John's head, beyond the car's hood to the pavement, and ahead to the end of the road. It looked like it went to the end of the world—on and on and on—in a straight line.

Unexpectedly, John turned off the highway onto a gravel road. He pointed at a shack, waving his right arm up and down as he turned with his left, "See that place? It belongs to a third generation welfare family, living in apparent poverty. Notice, I said *apparent*?"

"It looks like a poor man's shack, one of those helpless poor who make a fraction less than they need to survive."

"Don't believe it. They own all the land around here, hundreds and hundreds of acres. And draw welfare checks. They have the *know-how*. Our system has gone soft, soft in the belly where the money is. It allows more and more shysters to cheat and con the government. They pay no taxes, they lie, and they rat on everybody around here, even on the old man who owns the run-down grocery store down towards Plattsburg. Our government is too lazy to check things out. Too many people aren't honest anymore. If they think they can get away with something, they do."

The shack was covered with randomly attached sheets of weathered plywood with holes for windows and smoke rose from its crooked chimney. Piles of green firewood stood heaped beside the door, which was ajar. Two shiny red motorbikes blocked the door, not fitting into the picture at all. None of us said anything.

Again, unexpectedly, John turned off the road. We were there. We drove through a stand of thin birch trees with black and white curls of bark hanging in peels along their trunks. I imagined how smooth the peeled trunk would feel. The lawn looked like a park, dotted here and there with piles of neatly gathered dead branches.

"Someone labored in love here, John. Was it you?"

"Yeah, I do all the work on the place."

"I like the way your driveway cuts through the green lawn with two strips of gravel for the wheels of your car. Smart. Greta, listen. Can you hear the stream calling? I can't wait to show it to you."

"Sounds like you like my little creek, Alex."

"I do, John. I love it. I'm crazy about it actually, especially now that it's spring and it's so powerful as it stampedes along, spraying as it goes. There I go again, Greta. John, when I told her about it earlier, I went on and on."

"There's Estelle, waiting for us, standing on the porch."

Estelle stood with her legs apart, her arms spread wide and her hands resting firmly on top of the railing, showing her position. She looked as if she was the boss here, smiling with smart, dark eyes, looking down on us all. Closer, she looked friendly, but frail, maybe exhausted from cleaning the cottage. She was at the age when smooth, velvety skin droops and becomes flabby, something she concealed with her dress. She gave me the impression that she knew how to do things right and was in control of her surroundings. It would be her way around here. I wondered how we measured up as she looked us over to see how we'd fit into her world. She was a large-framed woman, giving the distinct expression that she was her own person, one who could stand her ground.

When we went up the steps to greet her, I sensed that she was a bit uneasy. Maybe because she was meeting Greta for the first time and she wanted to make sure she made a good impression on her. We smiled at each other. I imagined her whispering to John, "I hope they like me." We exchanged pleasantries for long minutes on the porch. John just watched. Then Estelle invited us in, just as the sun began to go down.

We followed, with some excitement, continuing to get to know her by her explanations of things in the cottage. She showed us a bit of herself, revealing some of her personality by how she'd arranged the cabin. John had done a lot of work since I'd been here last, building the whole cabin, step by step, with much love and time. Small windows let subdued daylight into the dark cozy spaces, spaces that were filled with well-worn upholstered easy chairs and leftover tables covered with bric-a-brac. It gave a sense of being stuffed, in a comfortable way—a reflection of Estelle's personality perhaps.

We followed Estelle into the kitchen. It was cluttered with a collection of gadgets on the counters, practical things to make do and make with. I could imagine Estelle working here, even if it was just a good excuse not to do anything else, a place she was happy in. It was dimly lit by a window that revealed a stand of birch growing so tightly together that they stole most of the natural light.

We followed her down a hall and past the open door of a compact bathroom, with Estelle commenting here on how John watches the money he spends. The end of the hall opened into an oversized living room that had dark wooden beams in the ceiling, and walls of bright tongue-and-groove decking that ran vertically down to the floor, except for one wall, which was floor-to-ceiling windows. A few branches from alder and birch trees brushed against the windows as if stretching into the room.

A majestic potbelly stove sat ready to warm the room and

make it cozy. I remembered watching John light a fire in it once before, latching the door to control the draft, adjusting it just so with a cast-iron chock, a treasured one-winged eagle.

After feeding twigs and odd pieces of wood into the belly of the stove, John started a fire. He knew exactly when to put the chock in place. Through the reflection in the windows I watched the fire quickly engulf the twigs. They burst into flames, throwing dancing lights around the cabin as they crackled and snapped—a comforting sound.

There was a plain table for everyday eating. It was partly set for dinner. I could see John and Estelle's comfortable armchairs pulled up to the table. Guests, like us, had to slide along a hard wooden bench with their backs to the window.

Estelle continued the tour, leading us back towards the entry and up to our room in the attic. We climbed a steep ladder-like stair that had Estelle huffing and puffing by the time we got to the top. Then she left us to it. There were two rooms with white sloping walls that were filled with four well-used beds, covered with clean sheets, and some cast-off chairs. Just right for a few days stay.

I stood still and listened. I could hear the stream. It drew me out onto the balcony. I rested my hands on the railing, feeling its peeling paint under my palms. I took a deep breath of the air coming up from the stream and let my eyes embrace all that I saw. I could hear splashing, gurgling sounds, somehow joyful. I could just make out the water—partially lit by the light from our room—flowing over sheets of shale. The light threw my shadow almost to the edge of the water.

I remembered how the singing waters had teased my soul summers ago, inspiring me to write poetry to the one with me now. I wished I could find the poem I'd written for her. I hung onto the railing, letting my senses become saturated.

Back inside, with the sound buffered, I realized how small the sparsely furnished room actually was. There were some neatly laid-out business papers and magazines that I suspected John wanted me to read so that we could talk about them later.

It reflected John's way of doing things—thoughtful, tactful, and to the point.

I looked out to the balcony, around the room, and then at Greta, trying to store it all in my memory. Our eyes met. She caressed my hand, letting her fingers glide down mine, then suddenly grabbed me by the hand, laughing. She pulled me up and down the steep stairs where John had warmed the entryway. He clicked the stove door shut and smiled, looking the way I remembered him most often. Then pointed us to some easy chairs.

"Please. Sit down. I just poured Estelle a sherry. Greta, would you like one?"

"That would be nice, John."

"Alex?"

"Whiskey on the rocks, please."

Estelle was leaning back in her oversized chair, stuffed amongst some colorful cushions with her arms on the armrests. By her face and how she sat, she showed that her world was at peace. Her place in that chair was the center of her world. She could keep her hands on everything from there, including anything out of reach, by asking John to get it. She could sit in that chair and not have to stand on her feet. I saw now what was conspicuous about her. She needed to have space around her, always. I could see it plainly as she sat there. It gave her a sense of power. She radiated some sort of force around her. She demanded attention and got it. She glanced past me to Greta—studying her—then smiling at her.

"Greta, how did you meet Alexander?"

"Alexander, will you tell Estelle and John how we met, please? You remember it better than I do."

"I told John all that a long time ago. Do you remember, John?"

"Yes. You told me a lot about her when you were here last. Was it three years now?"

"Yeah, I was really depressed. I sat out on some rock in the middle of your stream, trying to be closer to Greta by being close to nature, searching for some inner peace. I was going through an emotional upheaval with her. The stream seemed to understand. It's different today—with Greta and me and the stream. Did you ever tell Estelle about us?"

"Hell no! I thought you expected me to keep it just between us. You'd better tell Estelle what she wants to know."

I sucked on a piece of ice with the whiskey in my mouth, closed my eyes and wondered how to start my story.

"Estelle, I think I need to go back a few years before we met so that you'll understand how much meeting her meant to me."

"Sure, I'd love to hear it."

♣ CHAPTER 4 ♣

My mother and father separated when I was very young. I must have been five or so when I first became aware of it. They'd left my brother and me in a public children's home. My earliest memory there is of planting radish seeds with one of the nurses. Every morning, I'd run out to the garden and lay down with my face inches away from the radishes and my ear pressed to the dirt as I checked to see how much they'd grown from the day before, measuring the whites with my eyes.

Not long after that I was sent—by whom I don't know—to live with my father in Kassel. We lived alone—in one room—two sad, lonely figures without my mother in our days, so we took the train to Berlin to ask my mother to reconsider living with us. I was covered by a blanket with my knees pulled up touching my tummy to make me look smaller than I was so that I could travel free. To convince the conductor I was a toddler, Dad had put my thumb into my mouth.

We rang the bell to my mother's luxurious apartment building in an affluent neighborhood and were let into a large spacious lobby with an open spiral staircase. My mother looked down from the third floor to see who it was and what we wanted. We started our plea, asking her to come to Kassel to live with us. She told us to get out. At once!

To console ourselves, we spent the money saved on my ticket

to see a magician, something I'd always wanted to do. I was excited. When he dared anyone from the audience to remain seated on the chairs on stage, I had to be one of those *anyones* to test whether he was for real or he was trying to fool us all. *Abracadabra* and the seat of the chair turned into a hot plate, getting rid of all the other curious ones, but not me—not with my determination to show him up. Another *abracadabra* and my bottom felt like it was on fire, but I stayed put as the audience broke into waves of laughter. That was my signal to leave the hot seat. I'd made my point. The poor magician; he'd tried so hard.

When Dad and I had returned to Kassel, he started with Fieseler Aircraft and I with my scooter. At Fieseler he guided the development of struts and wings for a plane called a *Fieseler Storch*, the slowest observer plane of its time. He was away all day, every day, so my scooter became the most important thing in my life. During the summer I used it to explore the city; I loved visiting the markets, watching and listening to the goings-on of the people. Other times I pedaled two hours just to meet Dad when he got off work, to make him happy, to see him smile when he saw me. He rarely smiled. And though I tried everything to make him smile, to make him happy, deep down I was a quiet boy, an introvert. It took years for me to come out of my shell.

With the start of school in the fall, my lengthy explorations pretty well ended. I spent my lunch money on extra pencils, pencil sharpeners, and other unnecessary items I *had* to have. One day that too ended. When Dad asked what I'd bought for lunch, I told him pancakes. But there weren't any pancakes on the menu where I ate. Furthermore, the restaurant owner told him I hadn't been around for some time. I got the belt for lying. To me it was punishment for my hunger to have what I needed—shiny trinkets—more than food.

On weekends I had to go with Dad out into the country. We usually took the train to a place just distant enough to take us all day to walk back. While we walked through the thick, dark forests looking for mushrooms, at times he would tell me about parts of his childhood, mostly about his life in Russia, near Odessa, where he'd lived with his Jewish mother and sometimes played in his grandmother's music store, *Meyer's*, where he remembered a woman in tears rushing into the store to tell his grandmother that her husband, his grandfather, had dropped dead while singing on stage after his friend had whispered from behind the curtain, "I'm sorry, but I can't repay the money I owe you, so I will just have to kill myself." Most thought the idea of his friend killing himself must have caused his death. My dad thought otherwise, knowing his grandmother. His grandfather was more likely overcome with fear of not knowing how to tell his wife that he'd again taken money from her private safe, this time a large sum, to lend to his friend who, ironically, never did take his own life.

When he wasn't telling stories, he would show me things in the forest or make things for me—a bow and arrow or a whistle—that I could play with on the long walk back.

On weekdays, Dad left early, before I was awake. Occasionally I played hooky, roaming the city on my scooter, wandering down sidewalks and alleys, and looking for places and people I hadn't already seen.

With my father preoccupied and all that freedom, I soon got used to doing things my own way. One thing I wanted to do was sleep all night with my clothes on. That would be doing things my way. I asked many times. One day—I was nine—Dad surprised me by saying *yes*. I woke up to find a tall stern policeman standing over my bed. I thought I was being arrested for sleeping with my clothes on. It must be against the law since nobody did it. He told me to get up at once and follow him.

Dad was at work. I was terrified. I just knew I was being taken to prison. I followed the policeman out to the street, out of our humble room. A second shock! He ordered me towards two strangers. One, I thought, just might be my mother. The man with her I'd never seen before. He was leaning against a big car, in itself a rarity. The policeman ordered me in. I pulled back, crying, digging in my heels, and begging to talk to my father. They took me to a public phone where I whined my dad's ear full, telling him what was happening, making him cry too, something I'd never known him to do. Finally he told me that the court, in its wisdom, had given me to my mother. I had no choice but to go. Totally confused, I obeyed, feeling like a piece of baggage being shipped to some destiny I didn't know, crying my way to a city called Berlin, sitting in the back seat of my mother's car wondering why.

It didn't take me long to learn that I was a pawn in her power struggle with Dad. She didn't want me. She just didn't want Dad to have me, the last piece of love he had. I remained a piece of luggage, more unwanted as time went on. She'd already chosen the sunshine of her life, my younger brother, when they'd *divided lots*. Being hurt, it wasn't hard for me to pick a fight with him as soon as I arrived. He wasn't there long. My mother's favorite was soon sent off to an elite boarding school.

In Berlin, I felt like a possession in her shiny world. It was a glittering cage that sparkled with artificiality. The first thing she did, the very first day, was change my name from my father's name—Alexander—to Hermann, and then dress me in all new clothes. I felt like someone else, turned inside out.

From that very moment my life changed forever. With that she'd given birth to a rebel—to one who dared.

I began resisting everything in my mother's world, even though I didn't understand why—not only her world, but the whole world around me. I rebelled against the clothes she knit for me—short pants and suspenders and jackets with monstrous white bow ties. Heaven knows when she had time to knit them. She gave her love the way she knew best, but I didn't understand that at the time. Today I can't help feeling sad about such misplaced and misunderstood love.

Typical of my growing rebellious ways was an incident that happened a few years later at a time when food and clothing were rationed; oranges were plentiful, but coal and butter and eggs were scarce. People wore suits made of wooden cellulose fiber, and swastika flags were hung from every house and apartment on Hitler's birthday and any other Nazi holiday.

On one of those days my mother had invited a number of influential people for dinner. After dinner she called me into the dining room to present myself, as was customary. I said my good evening, turned, and was on my way out when she asked if I'd bought the raincoat I'd been sent out for that day. Indeed I had. After much searching in many stores, the only raincoat I could find, and lucky at that, was one far too big for my skinny body, so when my mother told me to show off the coat, what I saw was a long row of faces along the table all laughing at me. I felt like a clown. I was humiliated and stood stone-faced. My mother, trying to *save face*, ordered me to smile and excuse myself—at once. I looked at her with the same stony expression. After an awkward moment, she instructed my generally kind stepfather to slap the smile out of me. He asked in his kind way that I do what my mother asked. I shook my head *no*, then felt a sharp slap on my cheek. Again he asked if I would do as asked. Again I shook my head. The other cheek stung. It went on until my stepfather stamped his foot, turned, and—embarrassed—sat down with the onlookers while I stood smirking at the now serious faces. That very moment taught me how to cope with life in the future by encouraging me to dare to go my own way and not be afraid of what lay ahead, just to dare.

My mother was the one who put bread on the table, while my stepfather, whom I'd learned to love and admire, muddled through from one day to the next. He was an artist, through and through. He avoided problems by not getting involved in controversy. He never carried anything in his hands except a short pencil used for composing music at the piano. By combining their abilities, they created *Frontbuehnen*, state stage shows for German soldiers that were part of the army theater. Later the shows were politically controlled by both the Gestapo and the Nazis. Both powerhouses wanted absolute control over her *Frontbuehnen*. Both had to approve the sketches, the music, and the locations for the shows. My mother must have been very courageous in dealing with both the Nazis and Dr. Soandsos at the cultural department of the Gestapo, while at the same time safeguarding her private relationships with Jewish families.

She risked everything by staying married to my stepfather, whose mother was Jewish, by employing Jews who claimed not to be—like my stepfather's cousin, Mrs. Rothman, her trusted accountant throughout the war years—and by occasionally welcoming Jews in rare clandestine visits, arranged by her friend Mr. Levy, a Jew and former banker. She later told me that during the last months of the war she'd hidden him in her apartment attic in Berlin before he emigrated to the States.

She seemed fearless. I had the impression that she stood up well against the very world she worked within. She surrounded herself with artists, frequent visitors to her apartment. I remember a Danish journalist and hobby composer named Rechnezar, with a shepherd dog, and Jens Kronika, a Danish newspaper reporter who masqueraded as an English army captain following the war. She knew powerful people who'd reigned during the Weimar Republic, prior to Hitler, as well as Nazis who had come to power. She dealt with them all right up to the end of the war, and after the war, she had contacts within the new power structure, the British Intelligence Service, stationed in Hannover.

With all that going on around her, and having the uncommon ability to paddle in the murky political stream, day after day, my mother just wasn't able to be a mother to me. She never had time for me. I could never get close to her, nor did I want to understand her, and maybe she didn't want to understand me either, so I kept to myself and looked forward to leaving her world as soon as I could—for good.

For the most part I was sad, a sensitive child by nature. I was quiet and depressed, both at home and at school. I didn't put in much effort at school, so I got poor marks. I played out on the streets as much as I could to avoid the lengthening shadows at home. I felt overburdened in a world of artificial values and phony ideals, a world that demanded that I give up my identity to become a nobody.

I had no friends at school. They shunned me after learning I'd been born in Russia, which made no sense to me. I had one friend my own age, Wolfgang Lauboeck. He was shunned by the boys in the neighborhood even more than I was because he was a Jew. He didn't go to school. He had a private tutor at home. He had a loving, Jewish mother who was gracious to all visitors and, at times, chattered away with me, something my own mother didn't do, teasing me once about marrying her little daughter someday.

Despite her cheerful manner, she carried a heavy burden of worry for her brother, who lived with them, waiting for the day he'd be picked up and deported to a concentration camp. He spent his time painting abstracts—circles of dark color that reflected his last days of disappearing into a *black hole*, of being pulled into a vortex he was powerless to resist.

The other friends I had were grownups, people I admired and who were generous with their time, like Mr. Arnheim, who was always willing to listen to any kind of nonsense I spouted, changing it into some kind of wisdom for me. Some weekends I sat with him and his hunting friends in a lodge with his dachshund on my lap and listened to their hunting tales and wondrous stories they swapped, spellbound.

Then one day my stepfather told me I couldn't visit him again. He was no more. He'd killed himself because the Gestapo had forbidden him to ever see his gentile girlfriend again. His was my first funeral, my first friend to die. I watched from a distance as the casket was lowered to the sound of a hunter's French horn. Fearing Gestapo agents, my stepfather and I had hidden behind a large fir tree to listen and to say a last good-bye.

I was depressed for days. I wandered through the city, ending up at my stepfather's mother's place. I called her *Schatzi*, "sweetheart." She was Lisa to everyone else. Her maiden name was Palma. She lived in a dark too-large apartment, stuffed with old things and framed in dark heavy curtains. I told her what had happened. She nodded, saying nothing.

Eventually, to get my mind on something else, she gestured towards her parrot. The poor thing was sitting on top of the dining room door, as naked as a plucked chicken, no feathers at all. He made a loud racket as soon as we looked at him, probably remembering his former feathered days, when he used to dive down onto unsuspecting passers-by. It made me laugh to see him there. Just what she'd hoped for.

Schatzi was the cheerful type, always consoling, someone who made you smile. To an eleven-year-old like me she was more—she was a pushover, someone to pull pranks on. Once she took me to dinner in a respectable dining room with overly put-on service. I sat across from her, neat and straight, my hands on the edge of the formally set white linen-covered table. She liked me to sit that way, and I was happy to play it her way. The room was filled with silent, elegantly dressed people.

Killing time, waiting for the meal to come, I thought this was just the right situation to try something I'd just perfected—burping at will, so I gave the specious situation a wholesome burp, excusing myself politely at once, of course, while the guests at the nearby tables looked disdainfully in our direction. Schatzi, not I, had to meet their eyes. That was the best part. And I enjoyed repeating it a couple more times, each time excusing myself, at once, overly polite.

Her son, my stepfather, was a softy too, an extra kind man. I have much to thank him for. Once, when ordered by my reigning mother to give me the belt—for what I forget, but I'm sure I had it coming—he handled it by motioning me with a stern face—for my mother's benefit—to follow him to the bathroom. Once inside, he smiled as he took a large bath towel from the rack and told me to howl on the count of three, as loud as I could. On three I did, and he hit the towel as hard as he could. I couldn't believe my good luck. But it worked really well. Mother and he and I, especially, were all content afterwards.

His way of finding peaceful approaches and solutions to awkward problems made me love him forevermore. He was my model for bypassing trouble. He had a way of turning into a cloud when trouble came his way, by becoming invisible, by ignoring insults, and by talking about something else. Later in life I found this a good way of keeping my emotions under control while treating people with common sense.

Whenever I asked his advice, in the end he would add, "You can do it. Don't worry. You'll find a way." That's what he always concluded with, nothing more. It was his way of encouraging me to solve my own problems. He laid a good foundation for my *kid* soul to grow on, doing tough things in a pleasant, easy-going way. It's from him I learned kindness, and a lot of wisdom too.

A postcard addressed to me arrived in Berlin—almost a year late. It had been sent first to my father's address. The card told me to report at once to a meeting of the *Jungvolk*, a Nazi organization for boys ten to fourteen. I looked forward to it. I'd heard they went camping and made campfires and had lots of fun.

I reported eagerly the next Saturday. We gathered to form a new group, a few dozen boys. We were ordered to stand in rows and march around the streets. The next Saturday was the same. But marching didn't interest me. I wanted to sleep overnight in tents, deep in the forest, and sit beside a campfire. At the end of the second day, I asked one of the leaders about the camping. He made it clear my job was to become an obedient soldier. There was no tenting! I had to learn to march in columns, and—most of all—learn to follow orders. That wasn't for me. Me? An obedient soldier? But I was only eleven and didn't know how to get out of it.

So I dared to not go back. That simple. And I never went again. And nobody seemed to notice. To my surprise nothing was said for a number of weeks, until my mother, a truly influential business lady, empowered by the important people she knew, called me into the living room. She was enraged, not unusual when things around her went wrong. She asked why I hadn't gone to the *Jungvolk* meetings. I told her. She waved a letter from the *Reichsjugendfuehreramt* in my face, demanding I rejoin at once. I told her I wouldn't. She slapped my face left and right. It didn't hurt enough to make me change my mind. At the same time she screamed my slapped ears full of values I didn't understand, like how my refusal to join would ruin the family name, and more importantly, cause serious consequences for the whole family. I had to rejoin or else. That was final.

I was sent to my room, grounded for a week. It didn't change my mind. Nothing would have changed my mind by then—nothing. It got worse for us both. She got more threatening letters, and I got more slappings and house arrests. After a few more times, my mother gave up on me and handed the letters from the *Reichsjugendfuehreramt* to her old flame Dr. Soroff, requesting his advice and help, and that was the end of it.

Dr. Soroff was an assistant to Rudolf Hess. He'd already opened doors in the Nazi establishment for her *Frontbuehnen*, that is up to 1941. That year he was arrested and sent to a concentration camp for not divulging Hess's escape by parachute over Britain. By contrast, Martin Bormann, another of Hess's assistants, had reported it to Hitler immediately and was rewarded with a promotion as Hitler's direct assistant. Later Dr. Soroff served in a *Strafbattalion*, where he lost an arm clearing a Russian minefield.

The loss of my mother's old flame didn't affect her *Frontbuehnen* business, judging from bits of conversation I overheard through the wall that separated my bedroom from the dining room. The discussions and laughter continued unchanged at the dinner parties she gave for certain factions of Berlin's society. By 1941 she had all the contacts she needed, and she used them well.

Both the Nazis and the SS tried to control the shows for their own clandestine purposes. She dealt with them eye-to-eye, two political factions constantly at loggerheads, each other's biggest enemy. She played one against the other. Both knew of her contacts with the other and recognized that she was daring enough to make use of them both. On behalf of the SS, she once attempted to take Goebbels to court for some indecent act in the *UFA*, the German Hollywood. She knew they tolerated her only because it was wartime. She knew either could eliminate her when it was over. Many years later she told me about an attempt on her life in Sans Souci Park at Potsdam during the final weeks of the war.

♣ CHAPTER 5 ♣

"Greta, was your life touched by Nazis?"

"Yes, Estelle. I especially remember an incident that scared me to death when I was only ten. Every morning on my way to school, I passed a house that had a beautiful tiny window with snow-white curtains embroidered with roses. I loved looking at it, but on this particular morning the curtains were missing. I stopped, staring, when suddenly a kitchen stove flew out through the window into the street, pieces raining down like a comet—spitting glowing coals. I ran screaming until I was far enough away to chance looking back. Brown-uniformed Nazis were forcing furniture through the tiny window, throwing it down to the sidewalk. I changed my route to school after that."

"It's hard to believe."

"It was so frightening. I didn't understand what was happening."

"It must have been awful. I guess you saw lots of scary things. Was your city ever bombed? What was the name of it?"

"Krefeld, Estelle. Yes, I'll never forget some of those nights. By the time I was twelve, we had to hide in the cellar every night. One night I snuck out. I wanted to see for myself what the enemy bombers looked like. It was unforgettable. Rows and rows of planes, like huge black clouds, filled the sky, their drone making the ground vibrate. They flew in and out of the clouds, chased by gigantic searchlights and anti-aircraft tracers, their bombs falling in rows. At times the ground shook violently.

It was eerie, standing alone in the dark, surrounded by distant explosions and the fires from falling bombs; yet, at the same time, it was exciting. Eventually the black clouds moved on, having scared everyone including me, as I stood watching, fascinated, unable to move, my feet vibrating. It was strange, hard to describe."

"Why did the ground vibrate?"

"From the noise of the hundreds of planes in the air. The vibration of the motors pushes the air towards the ground with enough force to cause it to vibrate."

"Thanks John. Greta, weren't you scared one of the bombs would fall on you?"

"I didn't think of it. They were in the distance, so in my child's world, I felt safe, but I don't think I would have stayed there if they'd come very close. Another night I saw a tall church engulfed in flames from bottom to top, its flames licking high into the sky, a tall red tail streaming upwards, exploding, spitting, and its roar drowning out the drone of the planes. I was hypnotized by the brightness of the fire, by the strange wind coming from it, and by its desperate sound, as if the monstrous red cloud was in pain, going up to God.

"The next year I was nowhere near the bombing. The German authorities, fearing for the safety of the children in the cities, shipped whole schools out into the countryside, both teachers and students. I was sent to a little resort town in German-occupied Czechoslovakia called Trencin."

"What about you, Alex? Were you sent away?"

"Yes, Berlin was being bombed too. My school was first sent to Zakopane in the Polish mountains, until late spring 1941. Then we were moved by bus over the mountains to Trencin, where Greta was, and moved into a gray three-storied building. The rooms had high ceilings and creaky floors. I remember the sound my hobnailed shoes made walking across the floor. The hobnails made the leather soles last longer. Every day we marched off to school, but I don't remember anything about the school itself. On the way we marched past the building Greta's school lived in."

"Finally you get to Greta."

"Sorry it took so long, Estelle."

"It's okay."

"Even though we just walked past their building—you know the way boys and girls are—we soon found out about each other—where everyone was from, our daily schedules—and before long the girls were waiting for us. Of course, we did all we could to get their attention. We had to make contact somehow, we being boys and they being girls. We waved, shouted, and hollered at each other, the girls hanging out the windows like grapes, encouraging us to keep it up. Soon we found a way to pass notes up to the girls who'd caught our eye. We wrote notes on small pieces of paper that we licked, rolled tightly, folded into *V*'s, then shot up towards the windows with rubber bands. Most ended up on the sidewalk, but the girls stole out later to retrieve them, likely giggling at our *love notes*.

"As the days passed most of the boys had sent up notes, except me. I wasn't interested. I just watched the goings-on. None of the girls had caught my attention. I was footloose, fancy-free, and happy to stay that way. I was barely fourteen."

"Years later I told Alex what was going on in the girls' building at the time."

"That I want to hear, Greta."

"I shared a room with three older girls. We all enjoyed watching the boys march by, strutting and calling out to us. My roommates giggled, pointing out which ones had caught their eye, waving at them. They asked me which one was mine. I didn't have one but was afraid of being teased if they found out, so I hastily pointed at the smartest-dressed, a boy wearing a tie and a sun-colored jacket with narrow blue vertical stripes—Alexander. That's how he became my boyfriend without even knowing me, without being any closer to me than from the window to the street."

"Then you picked him. That's not how I had imagined you two meeting, you being so pretty."

"But that's how it happened, Estelle. I didn't know anything about him. I bit my nails, until we finally met a week later at an official get-together of our two schools. My roommates, suspecting I'd fibbed, put me to the test by getting me to stand in front of Alexander, so they could watch our first meeting."

* * *

Meeting Greta
I remember it still.
She was like an angel
fallen from heaven.
I'd been hit by lightning.
Here stood a ravishingly beautiful girl,
just inches away,
an awkward situation
for two shy people.
We didn't know anymore
than to smile at each other.

The girls standing around
giggled and stared.
I figured, "So what?
Girls giggle a lot for no reason anyhow."
More girls joined in
and the giggles got louder.
I still didn't care.
I was busy thinking,
"She is so pretty."
She sent off vibes of innocence,
of promises to come.

I still have a picture of her in her school uniform—white blouse, blue skirt, white knee socks, and buckled shoes—wearing her dark hair up in braided loops tied with an oversized white ribbon.

We didn't see each other for what seemed like a wretchedly long time to me. I was…

Under Her Spell
Greta, nothing but Greta,
was on my mind all day,
every day,
the afterglow of meeting an angel.
My feelings spun through my mind
like a carousel.
Pictures of her whirled through my head:
her deep turquoise eyes looking at me.
I'd left my old world behind.
Classic Greek became more Greek than before.
The teacher's voice came from far away.
When he questioned me in class,
I couldn't hear him.
I was too busy remembering
Greta's voice.

Only one thing mattered to me: when could, when would I see her again?

Finally it happened—at a competition between our schools—a game of *Voelkerball*. That's a German word meaning *the folk's ball game*. It's played with a ten-pound medicine ball. I was the last player left in the boy's square and Greta, the last girl, on their side. My classmates hollered at me to get on with it—"hit her out." I delayed as long as I could, but in the end I bowed to peer pressure, and with a heavy heart, I hit her out.

We'd won, but I'd lost. Bye-bye Greta. I figured I'd lost her for good, hitting her out in a game that didn't matter to me at all.

I joined the *rubber-band brigade*, begging Greta to forgive me, better yet, to see me. I kept at it until finally she threw down a note, surprisingly accepting my apology. Yes, she understood.

And yes, she agreed to meet me in the park to talk—even though it was strictly forbidden for girls and boys to meet in private. I was overjoyed. Although I was concerned about the consequences she might face if found out, I soon forgot about that as I imagined seeing her again, and getting to know her, and maybe even holding her hand. As the time approached, I wondered if she'd show up.

She was there. My mind danced, my heart pumped wildly, and my blood rushed, throbbing, through my head.

We strolled along the sandy paths under the giant trees in the park. We talked like grownups, yet we were so shy, so young. My heart danced and skipped through the park. Trembling hearts held our hands together. Through her hand, I could feel her in my heart.

As we walked, I pointed up. "Look at that funny cloud. It's a sheep with three legs." She smiled. As we talked some more, I began to reveal my feelings. I told her about the first poem I'd written when...

I Was Feeling Very Disheartened
I went to see the trees,
to sit down next to them,
to heal my wounded soul,
by being among them,
by being still like them.

Greta wondered if I'd made it up because I'd been hurt. I admitted I had. I'd escaped to the woods to lick my wounds, had found a stump to sit on, and, after a while, noticed how still the trees were. I felt as if they were looking down on me, soothing my hurt soul, telling me to go on. My world at school had just fallen apart.

We'd read some Nazi prose in class that stated that a person belonged where he was born. When class ended, my incited classmates taunted me for being born in Moscow, beat me up, and told me to go back to Moscow and not to come back to class. But the trees had told me to go back and act as if nothing had happened, to keep going, and to survive this situation the same way I'd survived being born with the umbilical cord wrapped around my neck three times. So my dad told me.

Greta and I felt that being together was our destiny. We talked and talked—sharing secrets and private memories.

Greta told me about a dear uncle who was arrested by the SS and taken to a concentration camp near Berlin for no reason at all, except that he was Jewish. After some months in camp, he bought his way out and came to say good-bye to Greta's family before escaping to Holland. They were surprised, thinking he was still imprisoned, to see him standing on the doorstep, tanned, as if he'd been on vacation. He laughingly explained that he'd gotten the tan in the camp by leaning against a barrack wall every minute the sun was out. It made him feel good, and had helped keep alive his hope of getting back home, where he would explain his long absence as a vacation somewhere in the sun.

He got to Holland safely and survived by painting and selling his pictures on the street. Many years later she learned that everything had gone fine for him, until some righteous Dutchman gave him away, sending him to Auschwitz where he was gassed.

When I look back to that day in the park, I'm amazed by how much we told each other, how much we felt for each other. I told her how I'd kept to myself at home—being a rebel. We even talked about death and not allowing anything to come between us, ever. We were kids, just little kids.

Without warning, our schools were ordered home. At the beginning of fall 1941 we were returned to our bombed-out cities, Greta to Krefeld and I to Berlin—worlds apart.

For weeks the Nazis had grouped their troops en masse in occupied Poland and Czechoslovakia for a surprise attack on Russia. All the civilians within the supply corridor leading to Russia had been herded out. That had included us.

I have no memory of the trip home. Suddenly I was back in

Berlin where everything seemed foreign. Each day I asked myself what I was doing there. My life seemed to be over. I was lost, back in a city where I had no one to talk to, no Greta. I missed everything about her—her face, her gestures, and her laughter.

Oh dear Greta
I'm in an inanimate state
in my body,
even more,
in my soul.
My soul longs for you.
It will never end.

Today I am alone.
There is no park with you.
I long so much for your hand,
your innocent hand
that I would know from all others,
the one I was at one with.

I want your hand.
Please.

♣ CHAPTER 6 ♣

A severe winter in 1941 saved Moscow from the German troops, troops who months ago had hastened Greta and me out of Trencin. That year, winter blanketed Berlin in snow and ice, freezing the rows and rows of now flattened houses on streets that just two years before had been filled with warm homes, stately old trees, and lively people going about their business. Now people lived in drafty rooms, some as cold inside as out.

I saw people on the *S-Bahn*, the fast train around Berlin, sitting slumped together, faces worn out by the war, staring sightlessly as the train made its way between bombed-out buildings with missing walls and rooms now open to prying eyes. Nobody bothered to look. And nobody noticed the girl get on the train—except me.

In sharp contrast to the rest, her face was animated, alive. She stood near the door, erect, composed, inches from the safety railing the rest clung to as the train swayed along its tracks. Not her. She stood straight, taking the sways, radiating a private pride, an inner strength, and a beauty distinct from the rest. I was spellbound by her: a goddess, standing unnoticed. She wore a yellow Star of David on a fine black coat.

I moved closer, to speak. Perhaps I could help. No. I didn't dare. I was a shy fourteen-year-old who didn't talk to girls, especially older ones, and for sure, not to one wearing a Star of

David. My heart wanted to, but fear held my tongue. I was afraid a *sightless one* would see and report me for breaking the law—one of those *good* Germans, law-abiding people trained to report lawbreakers. And talking to a marked Jew was against the law. She got off while I continued with my thoughts in turmoil. I stood silent, sending her good-byes and good wishes with my mind. But I never forgot her and can still see her clearly to this day.

Being at that age that questioned everything, I wondered what sort of life and hopes she might have left. Why did she wear the Star? How diabolical. What evil genius made anyone whose parents or grandparents were Jewish pay a fee for the cloth star—a holy symbol to them—then made them wear it to try to degrade them in the eyes of those who didn't?

I wouldn't have worn one. Hell no. I would have gotten out of it, somehow. Those who wore it—there were millions—had more courage, more character than I felt I had. I questioned those at home. "Did I have to wear a star too since my grandmother was a Jew, and why a star?" I rubbed against them with my questions, embarrassing them; they felt too insecure in their world to discuss such things with me. They evaded my questions. I meant trouble for them, trouble to be avoided. In the end I didn't trust them for not answering me. Finally, I trusted no one, not my mother, my stepfather, no one. Their world denied me the freedom to think for myself. I now had to think freely in secret.

I had more and more questions but no answers. I looked for answers that would give me ways to live, rules to go by, to seek a course that seemed more right to me.

I started at the library, finding people to read about who'd found their own course, freethinkers. I read a lot of philosophy, including Voltaire and numerous old fables, looking for wisdom hidden there by the old Greeks. I struggled to find what I sensed was right, never forgetting the girl with the Star of David. I tried to think things through, risking a course I'd kept secret, a course I didn't know for sure to be right. I asked no one. It was tough.

Months of happy hours reading in the libraries punished me with poor grades at school.

But suddenly, in a new wartime strategy, boys my age at school were assigned to serve in the German air force, as *Flackhelfer*, helpers in the anti-aircraft units around Berlin. We lived and went to school in barren underground shelters, near the batteries. During the day, teachers came by bike to hold school, and at night, we were part of the fireworks, shooting at enemy bombers we could hear—but not see—flying over our batteries.

Our class of about fifteen boys had to man the 10.5 cm guns. We were assigned, three to a gun, to set the gun's directions and distances. One checked the vertical angle and a second the horizontal angle, lining up crosshairs to the illuminated angles that were being sent to the gun electronically by the command post. The third used a key to set the distance to the enemy bombers on a dial located on the shells that were carried in by Russian prisoners, huge shells. By then my heart would be racing as I anticipated what was coming. All twenty-four guns went off together in one tremendous earthshaking thunderous racket that was terrifying.

During those nights and days, Greta and I wrote to each other often. I wrote letters filled with new poems and outpourings of love. She answered in shy cursive handwriting. How I waited for her letters!

In the winter of 1942, I turned sixteen and was now required to report to the *Arbeitsdienst*, a service required of all young men at sixteen, to dig ditches and to build roads with shovels and songs. To shovel with a song! I was determined not to shovel or sing. I had to find a way out of this.

The first night I couldn't sleep. I tossed and turned trying to figure out what I could do to weasel out of this one. Then I thought of something. And dared to try it. I got up at four in the morning, dressed quietly, slipped out of my barrack and went over to the one where the corporals and sergeants slept. I fired up their stove, swept their floor, and quietly returned to my bunk. The next morning I got up again and when I arrived, just as I'd gambled, one of the sergeants, a rotund, lazy-looking figure with a mustache, asked if I'd like to look after his warehouse and office—warm it up early in the morning, clean up, count and sort uniforms, and do whatever other chores needed doing. Would I? "Oh, yes, sir!"

So I didn't have to march or stand in line or dig or sing like the hundreds of others working outside in the cold. My cushy job lasted the whole six months of my duty, occasionally leading to boredom until I reminded myself, by looking out the window, to put boredom back in its box. Sometimes the cook came by, begging for socks or underwear, in return for butter or whatever he could spare from the kitchen.

By the spring of 1943 Hitler had lost his duel with Stalin at Stalingrad. And I got new orders, this time from my mother. I was to report to her bookkeeper Helga Rothman in Vienna, where her sister, also Jewish, was secretly living with her. Helly, as we called her, had arranged travel service by train. I traveled from Vienna to Prague by first class sleeping car. On arrival, a waiting chauffeur whisked me to the Ambassador Hotel to join my mother and her entourage. Such service was unheard of in those days. It made me uneasy.

I was shocked to see how royally my mother and her protégés lived. My mother, queen of the *Frontbuehnen*, had rented the entire second floor of the Ambassador Hotel for her office. From there she directed her ensembles, actors, and musicians along the front lines and hinterlands of Naziland, lands stretching throughout parts of Europe. She lived in a luxurious apartment, each room was exquisitely furnished in different antique periods—Baroque, Rococo, Biedermeier—and overlooked the beautiful fourteenth century Charles Bridge that spanned the Vlatava River; the ancient town of Hradcany sat in the distance. It was too much for me to take in.

From the moment I arrived, I despised being part of her life style and the opulent surroundings. The extravagance was in stark contrast to the six-month stint I'd just served. My inner gut wanted out. Fast. But I didn't know how.

One day my stepfather took me along to his tailor where he had to try on a new suit. Before the Czech tailor let us in, he demanded tea. It struck me as strange when my stepfather handed over the tea, as I hadn't realized he was carrying it. No tea, no suit. While my stepfather went with the tailor for his fitting, the tailor's wife kept me company in her kitchen. She was the wholesome-looking motherly type, someone to hang your hat on. With her apron and smile, her plump arms and breasts, and her kindly face, I soon found myself telling her everything.

I told her how and why I didn't belong in Prague. I wanted to go out on my own in the world, to find myself, to see what was right for me. She nodded a hundred times, saying nothing as I talked. When I had finished, she smiled and babbled in her German, pointing west, *"Gen se. Jaa, gen se."* "Go there. Yes, go there." I knew then I'd dare to take her advice.

I nodded yes and smiled—smiling inside too—as I hugged her good-bye. Back in the luxury of the hotel I kept my mouth shut, but early the next morning I set out to take a train to Berlin. I was surprised. It worked. No one stopped or questioned me, a sixteen-year-old. But the minute I arrived at the station in Berlin, I felt like someone who shouldn't be there. I worried that people were looking at me all the time, as if they knew I didn't belong there. I was alone, at last, for the first time in my life—just the way I wanted it.

The nights were lonely, but the days were filled with a kind of lively rootless enjoyment. I walked around the first few days, trying to plan out what to do. I knew I'd better get used to the feeling of sadness that came from being alone, and learn to live with it. It was a feeling that stayed with me for decades.

I was simply overwhelmed by what I saw as I roamed the city day after day. Each day brought new challenges, seemingly insurmountable until I solved them, only to be followed by something else the next day. From each I learned how to better cope with the next—and gradually became accustomed to being alone. In time I learned to fear female arms and to never stay very long in one place. Being with someone could become a comfortable habit—being held by arms—that could put me to bed without my even being aware of it.

I needed a job. Finally, I went looking for Mrs. Fabian, an old friend of my mother's, a lady who'd once told me to come to see her "if I ever needed her." Initially, I had hesitated because I feared she meant *sex*, so it took a couple of weeks before I dared to take a chance with her.

In a high-ceilinged living room, filled with old pictures and heavy curtains, she welcomed me in a half-open nightgown, stunningly beautiful and sensuous looking. She flattered and complimented me for being so grown up and so good-looking, dangerously good looking to women, and opened her nightgown a bit more, watching for my reaction to an offering I didn't want, while I told her about the tailor's wife and my immediate hopes. In the end she admired what I was doing, my efforts to find my own way in the world, and agreed to help.

Many years later she confessed her *offer* was what I'd suspected, but she also admitted that my mother had saved me in the end. Knowing my mother's high moral standards and her political clout, she feared what might happen to her if my mother found out. Mrs. Fabian and her husband also saved a number of Jews, not only losing a lot of money in the process, but endangering their own lives as well. They knew a lot of people in Berlin, those who belonged to their political way of thinking and those who didn't. The shades of political identities—generally passive, but easily disguised within the membranous layers of the interwoven social structures of cosmopolitan Berlin—were easy to hide. Even the Nazis couldn't penetrate its murky, complex layers to ferret out dissidents, to cleanse the city of Jews totally. I knew dozens of Jews who quietly survived Nazism.

Mrs. Fabian got me a job, counting and measuring plumbing pipes, including room and board with the owner, a Polish lady, who was soon like a mother to me, and also active in the passive resistance. Every day after school, I counted, measured, and recorded the coming and going of pipes.

For the rest of that year I counted pipes and my blessings—until my mother appeared. She'd discovered my whereabouts somehow. And this time she asked—didn't command—me to meet her in the Blue Room of the Friedrichstrasse Hotel. I obliged. The essence of the meeting wasn't "How was I doing?" but that "It wasn't dignified for a son of hers to work." She wanted me to quit, offering me a generous amount of money, much more than what I earned counting pipes. In the end she went back to Prague, wearing a beautiful, daringly oversized hat, while I kept my job and began receiving a ration card in my own name. Finally, I'd won my freedom. I was standing on my own two feet. But not for long.

In a few short weeks a draft notice arrived, ordering me to join the army. My ration card had precipitated the draft order, thanks to the thorough German war machinery. I decided to dare repeating what I'd done years before. I ignored the order. Exactly one month later, a second draft order arrived with a warning that I'd be treated as a deserter if I didn't report at once. And I knew what happened to deserters. They were shot on the spot and left lying in the open—as a lesson to others. I hated even the thought of being in the army, so I knew I had to move, and leave my newly won Polish mother. The day the third order arrived, I left. Grim days were to follow.

I was now a deserter in the eyes of the law. What should I do? I knew of Jewish boys living and hiding in the rubble of bombed-out houses. There were dozens of them from the Jewish school at the Hamburgerstrasse, pawing through the refuse, rootless and hiding. They got ID's from the dead bodies they located by smell under the piles of rocks and bricks, staying one step ahead of the law through the help of a Rabbi from their old school. That wasn't for me.

I went to see the elderly father of my Jewish hunting friend, Mr. Arnheim, whom I'd seen being buried. Dr. Arnheim lived a hermit-like existence in a cabin near Berlin. I could be a hermit if I had to. He took me in, not knowing my problem. He'd abandoned practicing his Jewish beliefs to stay alive. He kept from being bored by translating old Greek stories, keeping sane in an insane world. Greek letters hewn into a huge rock—*Oi antropoi skia tou ouronaou estin*—greeted anyone visiting his cabin. "Mankind is the shadow of heaven."

During late oil-lamp hours he told me stories. About Socrates, who thought one had to know oneself to know anything. About Diogenes, who'd been admired by Alexander the Great and, upon meeting, had told Diogenes he'd grant him anything he wished. In response the sunbathing Diogenes had begged him kindly to get out of the way of his sun. Fascinating stories.

I began to get nervous about letting my old friend harbor me, a deserter, and knew I should move on, so I told him my situation. Did he think I should report to the army or try hiding in the rubble to ultimately end up living like a rat? After a long look into my eyes, he told me to report to the army. Why? He couldn't explain it. He, not I, ended up in tears when I left. He knew I was going into hell. I didn't.

The face of the army captain I dared to report to looked more and more put out as he glanced at the three-month-old deadline on my draft notice. His voice was rigid, disapproving. "Too bad you reported so late, two months too late. I'm afraid that puts your case out of my hands. We are obliged to send you to the Gestapo. I'll be back."

I sat on my hands and waited and waited in a small room. Just a tiny window and I. I watched the sun set, probably my last. Hours passed. The sun was long gone. I became used to the dark, alone with my fear of what was to come. I stared at the closed door, at a small shaft of light at the bottom, at the dust balls making shadows along the floor. I waited for a sudden burst of light. I heard a metallic click. Light poured in around the black silhouette outlined in the doorway, the captain.

Hope rushed forward. A good feeling washed over me when I saw that the captain was alone. Or maybe it was the way he opened the door and stood there. He commanded that I be taken to a *Strafbattalion* in Potsdam. No Gestapo. Unaware I'd been holding my breath, I exhaled with relief, and wondered what that order meant.

It was late when I got to Potsdam. From the outside I saw a high, dilapidated brickworks without bars on any of its tiny windows. The inside looked like a large brickyard. The next morning I was told I'd been placed with cripples and simulators, men who didn't want to serve in the army, so faked disabilities—dragging legs, crouching to affect crooked backs, stiff necks, crippled limbs, and senility. That first morning I heard a man screaming. Guards who thought he was faking his disability had broken his arm. I felt degraded to my very core.

The first days were confusing: disorganized marching, standing in place for hours, orders that elicited muttered responses from lunatics, and misunderstood orders that resulted in crisscrossed marching. Crackpots having fun? I wondered—were these people for real or were they fake? Most of the day we cleaned. We cleaned everything possible, everyday, twice or more, over and over. Some were ordered to use their own toothbrush. Most men were friendly to each other. Some sang and hummed all the time. One Viennese hunchback always sang sentimental songs. He had kind eyes. Watching the good in people was the only good I saw in that place.

By the summer of 1944, I'd spent a few months in the brickyard. One guard, a war-weary lieutenant, covered with scars from his wounds, limping, and seemingly in disgrace for some reason I never found out, took me aside and said he'd been watching me. He'd concluded I didn't belong there, so he'd wielded some of his remaining influence to arrange for me to be sent to another unit. I didn't understand what he meant, but within a few days I was moved.

The new unit, in Frankfurt at the Oder, was a mixed group of men—some cured simulators, some discreet gays. After the first day one called me his little *up-and-down*. I didn't know what he meant. I thought he was being friendly; the others looked at me, wondering. He gave me some chocolate that first day. I felt he wanted something, but I didn't know what.

On July 20th, 1944, in the early morning darkness, our unit was ordered to march to Berlin. We were issued WWI rifles and three bullets each. Three bullets? What good was that? We marched all day in the heat. In the evening, there were new orders. Turn around and march back. Days later we learned that our unit was supposed to have kept civil order for a new government forming in Berlin. It was rumored that our commanding officer was in with General Staufenberg who'd planned to assassinate Hitler. It ended in a fiasco.

By this time I was all of seventeen. I was given two day's leave, so I went to visit the only person on my mind. I traveled all night to visit Greta at school. I presented myself to her principal as a cousin visiting from far away. To my surprise he gave her permission to stroll in the park with me.

We hadn't seen each other for three years. The years fell away. We were holding hands again, at last. Happiness bubbled up and spilled over into our laughter and joy at just being together. We still felt the magic. Little did we know how long we'd have to remember that feeling before we'd see each other again.

A few months later I was sent to a regular army camp in Zelenzig, today called Sulecin, in Poland. My new assignment was to service and clean lethal mines used in military exercises—a dangerous job.

Early in the cold January of 1945, our unit was ordered to march over a hundred miles to Berlin. I carried a big box of detonators in my knapsack over the icy roads. For every two steps forward, I slipped one back. The first night I fell into the straw, comatose, my feet hurting so badly they felt as if they'd burst inside my boots. For the next two days all I remembered was staring at the back of the man in front of me, going forward step by step, sliding back, plodding on, numb, exhausted. We passed through one village after another, three the first day, until they all looked alike. My feet got worse. By nightfall my body was relieved to be able to lie down. Darkness meant relief.

Each day was the same: villages—more frequent as we moved west—the back of the man in front of me, and my throbbing, burning feet. Hardly anyone spoke. We just tried to survive. As the long shadows of late afternoon arrived, I'd begin looking for signs of a village with straw. Sooner or later a village would come, always with straw. At night I stared at my boots; my feet were clamped inside leather vices that I didn't take off for fear of not being able to get them back on over my swollen feet the next morning. Mornings brought another pain—gnawing hunger.

One morning the red-haired boy who marched to my right told me he couldn't take it any more. I could have his ration. I didn't take it. I was glad to see him marching beside me as we set out. Some hours later he slipped out of the row. "Probably going to pee," I thought, as he jumped into the ditch. I heard a gunshot and looked back. He lay slumped in the ditch with his rifle in his mouth. It had happened so fast. We were commanded to just march on. I couldn't help thinking about kids being willing to die so easily, ready to waste their only life, while the old ones who don't want to die find ways to hang on.

It must have been a week of slipping on ice before we arrived at a dark horizon of smoke. Under that smoke was Berlin. At a village on the southeast outskirts of the city, we were given the task of defending Berlin against the Russian tanks that were already on their way. But for now we were to rest.

The first night we looked for food in the cold winter fields and deserted houses. We found a few potatoes on an empty barge and fried them until they whispered in the pan. After a few days I'd recovered enough to look for a pretty girl in the village. I found one too, mine for the evening. She leaned up against a tree trunk and told me we could make love this way. I couldn't figure out how, so she wasn't interested in seeing me the next night.

During the next few days we dug foxholes all day in the frozen soil—deathtraps, where Russian tanks could drop hand grenades through trapdoors in their floors. The following days we hacked endless tank ditches and barriers in the frozen ground. There was an air of desperation among us kids. The few old soldiers around remained stern-faced, silent, doing little. They gave no answers for why we were doing what we were, for how these holes could stop enormous tanks.

In the distance, out of Berlin, smoke from tall pipes spewed straight up—a cold day. I thought about walking away from it all. But how? I would be caught. There were checkpoints everywhere—*Feldwache*, over-zealous watchers—surrounding Berlin. It wasn't even regular wartime anymore, not like it had been the year before when I had served in the *Arbeitsdienst*. Now it was panic. The days were senseless.

We'd hardly finished digging when we were shipped by truck to a complex of gray barracks in Potsdam in the dark—secretly. From the minute we arrived, I felt tension in the air. The next morning I knew why. Outside the barrack entrances, frozen bodies lay in the snow, each wearing a sign reading, "I was a traitor."

"Why?" we asked each other. "What had they done?" We were terrified, fear that grew day-by-day, fear we'd be next. More and more bodies appeared at the entrances, always early in the morning. It was eerie. One morning it was a buddy of mine, an easy-going kid who'd joked with me over the damnable situation we were in, always with a smile on his face. I asked myself if the fear we could be next was supposed to make us more willing to follow insane orders. It did.

Hitler had given that order to put the fear of hell into us, preparing us kids to save the country through his next order: bring the new, heavy Russian tanks moving toward Berlin to a swift and severe stop—through the magic of both us and anti-tank grenades. Thus, he ordered the formation of the *1st Tank Destroyer Division*. Years after the war, I read what Guderian, a famous German tank general had written about our unit:

> *"The Russians were gaining increased momentum as they became aware of the growing weakness of the*

> *German frontline. Their tank forces assumed bolder tactics. Hitler therefore ordered, on January 26th, 1945, the setting up of the 1st Tank Destroyer Division. This division was to consist of bicycle companies, equipped with anti-tank grenades and were, in this fashion, to stop the heavier Russian tanks. This division was to be committed company by company. It was too bad about the men involved."*

A master sergeant called for me, questioning how well I'd known a certain frozen traitor in the snow. Guessing what lay behind his questions, I denied that I'd known him. He stared at me, drilling me with his eyes, then gave me my new assignment—laying mines behind the Russian line. I had to prove myself at the Russian front. Behind it! I'd just turned eighteen.

♣ CHAPTER 7 ♣

"Alexander, what about you and Greta? That's what I'm waiting for, but now it's time to put supper on."

Estelle eased her big body slowly up out of her chair. "Greta, would you like to keep me company in the kitchen?"

"I'd love to, Estelle."

In the kitchen the girls talked. It sounded like jabbering. The sounds faded as I thought about what I'd relived, talking for hours about my past, now feeling weary. A familiar clinking noise brought me back to the room. John was feeding the stove. The sound of the girls' jabbering in the kitchen came back. I could hear them shoving things around. It sounded as if they were *playing* supper, not making it, having fun doing whatever it was. I watched John adjust the one-winged eagle chock. Who knows why he kept that broken thing. I didn't.

"I see you looking at my chock. It's an old one. It was already broken when my mother gave it to me. I don't know what happened to it, but I'm attached to it, and it still works."

John screeched open the stove door, feeding rustling paper and dried sticks inside. Seconds later I heard the rushing sound of the fire coming back to life, and the clack of the door closing. John's sigh was drowned out by the wild crackling of the flames that warmed everything around them. I was amazed at how quickly the stove warmed the whole room, including me.

The lights from the room illuminated the trees outside. The limbs of the trees—alder and birch—had grown into each other from trunks that stood tightly together along a long-abandoned streambed.

"Did you build this room by yourself, John?"

"Yes. Actually, I had a lot of trouble getting those beams through customs from Canada."

"This room has that special feeling of being homemade. It feels good just being in it."

"Thanks."

Estelle called us to supper, her voice coming through the walls and doors. When she hollered a second time, I wondered if walls were vibrating.

"Coming."

I followed John. We had roast beef with Idaho potatoes and a colorful salad. It hit the spot after the long wearing hours. A cake with whipped cream and a bottle of Spanish wine finished the meal off.

"Great dinner, Estelle. How did you do that so fast?"

"Nothing to it, Alexander. Let's have a port. Then I want to hear how you met Greta again."

"It's a long road until I meet Greta again. I'm sorry. But that's how it happened."

"Well, I don't mind, as long as I'm comfortable, so carry on. Tell us your story. John, fill Alexander's glass. Make it a good one."

John poured another whiskey to help ease me back into my story. I hoped she wouldn't be bored by what came before I met Greta again. I took a sip and smiled at her.

* * *

The *1st Tank Destroyer Division* was formed in Potsdam and stationed near Dresden. I had orders to pick up a box of detonator caps with my bike. On the way back I stopped to rest. It was noon. As I lay on the grass enjoying the sun, a group of English soldiers came along. I was petrified. I stood up. They weren't armed. Frankly, they looked as if they were out walking in the woods for the fun of it, as if it was normal for them to be walking around inside Germany while it was at war with their country, with their hands in their pockets and scarves tied leisurely around their necks. An amazing sight. Then, to my relief, I saw a tiny German, round like a ball, following behind. I sat back down. He seemed glad to see me and sat down alongside me, waving his gentlemen prisoners to do likewise.

"I'm moving these prisoners to a camp near Dresden, a few miles from here."

I nodded. He couldn't wait to tell me his war experiences as a medic. They sounded like exaggerations and lies, one after another, but I nodded politely. Then I noticed the special holster on his belt, deep maroon, a general's holster. I figured it must hold an exquisite handgun, probably stolen from a dying general. Medics didn't normally carry guns, but he was on special duty, moving prisoners. That explained the rifle in his possession, but not the general's gun. I couldn't have stopped him talking if I'd wanted to. He was too busy telling me what a hero he was. Apparently listening, I nodded whenever he gave me a chance, but my attention was on that maroon holster. It fascinated me. I wanted to see the gun inside. Better yet, to have it.

Lying on the grass, I noticed a smooth flat stone nearby, just the right shape and size to fit into the holster. Within reach of my left hand. It seemed to talk to me, "Why don't you put me into that holster? I'm a perfect fit. Why do you think I'm lying here? I was just waiting for you."

I wondered what my chances would be to pull it off successfully. My eyes went from the rock to the holster, back and forth. I kept the medic talking, asking a bunch of questions, while I picked up the rock in my left hand, put it playfully into my right, then slowly dropped it onto the ground. I opened the holster carefully, inching the gun out, watching his eyes for any signs of awareness. I slipped the gun into my pocket, then gently slid the rock into the holster and closed it, smiling casually at him as well as at his prisoners, whom I hadn't really been paying attention to in my concentration to get his pistol. Alarmed, I saw open-mouthed astonishment on some who'd watched the whole thing. I glared at them fiercely, signaling that they'd better keep their mouths shut. I got some scared smiles in return. Now I watched every move by both them and the medic. I realized I'd better get on my way, fast. I casually excused myself to the medic, thanked him for his interesting stories, wished him a good journey, jumped on my bike and fled, pedaling hard, not caring a damn what happened between him and his prisoners.

I never looked back. The air rushed past my face as I pedaled furiously, fearing the medic might be after me. I was anxious to get far enough away to see what I had. With no one in sight, I stopped the bike to take a look. What a beauty! I studied it slowly, from all angles, checked the chamber, the artistic engraving and felt its smoothness. A masterpiece. Then I realized what I'd done. It was something treasonable, something awful. I'd better take it back. No! It was too late. I had to keep it. I began pedaling again, still fearing the medic was after me.

By now I'd begun to feel guilty. Then I laughed, my dark soul smiling as I imagined the changing face of the medic as he pulled his gun out in front of his prisoners—who would already be geared up for laughter knowing the medic would discover a rock in his hand. If the rock had been as round as the medic's ball-like figure, it wouldn't have fit into the holster and I would never have been tempted. Maybe it was fate. Maybe the gun was meant to save my life, not his.

* * *

"Hold it a minute, Alex. Do you expect us to believe that? That is the most far-fetched story I've ever heard."

"Maybe so John. But it's true."

* * *

It was also the day I met the redhead. As I started to ride

past her, I saw that she was a robust-looking girl, about my age. She had a cupid-like figure. Wow! I slowed my pace to hers, pedaling as close to her side as I could, the gun in my pocket now completely forgotten. I kept her talking, making her laugh, hoping for only one thing, the chance to grab her tight and maybe more. Talking as we rode along, I realized we were both hungry for sex. Afterwards, I said no more than good-bye, feeling sleazy, leaving her to her fate with the Russian soldiers already on their way.

I pushed hard towards camp, more to get away from myself, thinking about what a rotten thing I'd just done. I damned myself, keeping my eyes on the dirt road ahead, as the day turned to dusk. After riding for a while in the dark, the dirt ahead of me reddened. Strange. There was a reddish tint coloring the sky behind me—blood red. I sped on. At camp I learned that Dresden was in flames, the place I'd just come from. British phosphate bombs had turned the city into a roaring inferno, incinerating a few hundred thousand women and children—obliterating the whole city in one night.

That same day, February 13th, 1945, we heard that fifty Russian tanks had crossed the German front line at the Neisse river, sixty miles north of us, rolling towards Hitler's headquarters in Berlin and precipitating dark days ahead.

One cold evening a few days later, I was at work, sitting on an ammunition keg in an old shack, surrounded by dozens of anti-tank mines that I'd fitted with detonator caps, when an old soldier passed by the open door. His hands were curled around the peniform bowl of his smoking pipe. I asked him if he really kept his hands warm that way. He said it helped, so I got a pipe like it. True enough, smoking it, holding my hands around its bowl, gave my hands comfort. It was a pleasure to hold it, at times reminding me of the cupid-like figure of the redhead. I didn't know why.

My job was to insert detonators into mines for the others to carry out exercises and play hero with. From the safety of my perch on the powder keg I watched stupidity march by. Kids, wearing oversized hand-me-down uniforms, marched off to play war in fields of cold mud. They were ordered around like idiots, running up and down hills in their gas masks, as imaginary tanks rolled over them in dugouts, attacking the tanks with makeshift bazookas, dummy anti-tank mines, and with some of my real ones. I often watched them march back at day's end, kid-soldiers, bodies slumped with fatigue from wallowing in the mud, now dragging themselves home.

Home was a deserted three-story factory. Through the large open windows I watched them come into their rooms and throw themselves down on straw mattresses, all of them in unison, their automatic rifles clattering into piles on oversized tables. Then silence, until a sergeant arrived, making them jump up to clean their rifles and sing while doing it. I could hear their singing, put on, as they cleaned weapons meant to kill.

One night I watched a kid clean his rifle with the magazine still attached. When he removed the cover plate, exposing the firing mechanism, he accidentally brushed it with his cleaning cloth, thereby releasing a spray of bullets that emptied the magazine through the ceiling and table of the floor above. Kid-soldiers screamed and scattered, but fortunately no one was hurt.

I wondered about these kids, kids who were the very core of the so-called *1st Tank Destroyer Division*. Along with the other units spread out along the length of the west side of the Neisse River, the entire division was being readied to cross the river into Russian-occupied territory to seek out and destroy large Russian tanks with bazookas and mines. We were to move quickly, hit without warning, and leave swiftly—a sneak attack. Hitler was throwing thousands of us kids against thousands of tanks.

Each unit was led by a battle-experienced lieutenant. We were to keep in touch with each other as well as a *Fieseler Storch* observer plane—which was to spot the tanks to direct us to them by radio. One of us carried the radio pack. My job was to handle the lethal detonators that were to be attached to mines hidden in a pre-stocked underground bunker behind the Russian line: a bunker filled not only with mines, but hand grenades, bazookas, ammunition, guns, and rations. At last everything was in place. The order came.

♣ CHAPTER 8 ♣

We started out under a half-moon. With the help of silent old soldiers, we crossed the river in rubber dinghies overloaded with fearful kids and our metal toys—each with a bazooka and anti-tank mines, and most carrying automatic rifles and hand grenades. Ice floes bumped against rubber in a mysterious, glittering moonlight. We wore camouflaged down-filled military fatigues, sneakers, and backpacks filled with ammunition, rations, and a little whiskey.

After being dumped on the enemy side, I was filled with a sense of gloom. We wormed our way up the icy snow-covered banks, then under some nearby trees and bushes where we lay shivering. We waited for the Russians to wake up and start shooting, giving away their positions. We lay in silence, cloaked in the disguise of the dark moonlight shadows under the trees. Soon a barrage of shots hit high in the trees—too high, the way night shots usually are. With no response to their gunfire, the fireworks subsided. Then a Vlasso soldier in Russian uniform—a Russian fighting with the Germans, who knew the lay of the land—guided us through possible mine fields, past the Russians, over open muskeg, and into the forest beyond where darkness provided cover. There he left us to our fate.

On we prowled, like cats, our bodies bent, tiptoeing slowly, step by step, along a path in single file, expecting Russians behind every tree. Hours of listening and looking for the enemy tested the limits of our young bodies. We were relieved to see morning come, so we could hide. We lay on the icy ground, camouflaging ourselves with a cover of loose leaves and snow. Comatose, we slept off the exhaustion of the first night, ready to move again when darkness returned.

That first day in hiding, I listened for any kind of sound, waiting in fear for something I didn't want to hear—someone coming—as I lay helpless under the leaves. I hoped death would come quickly during this mission. My situation didn't seem all that different from my friend in Potsdam who'd been shot and left with the sign labeling him as a traitor. At least he got it over with quickly. I feared dying slowly. With that thought, exhausted, I fell asleep.

I woke sometime later during the day. I was ready to go. I wondered how long until dark, our second night of looking for Russians. Maybe we wouldn't find any tanks. Maybe they'd find us first. That was more likely. It was their territory. I'd seen Russians before—prisoners—but these men would be armed. The end could come in just minutes, face-to-face, hand-to-hand, boys against men. I had no rifle, just the jackknife from Dad that I had used for wiring detonators, and the general's pistol hidden in my back pocket, loaded and waiting, just in case. That I didn't dare show anyone, not just because I'd stolen it, but because I feared being suspected of having killed some general to get it.

Night came. Having slept off our exhaustion, we were ready to go with the moon, our best friend, scared we might actually find some tanks. Sneaking along a path under the trees, I imagined, again and again, Russian tanks just ahead. I knew we wouldn't see them until we were right on top of them. They'd be hidden behind bushes or dug deep into the ground to protect them from a direct hit.

The lieutenant signaled for us to stop. At dawn our spy-plane had signaled the location of a battery of anti-aircraft guns. We should be close. Two other ten-kid units were to join us in surprising the Russians. We listened for their arrival, waiting, quiet, until short flashlight signals brought us together. We were closer to the Russians than we thought. We touched our way through the dark to the gun battery, then froze at the sight of it, waiting, hoping we hadn't been noticed. We waited a while longer, on edge, while the three lieutenants worked out a plan.

Finally, one signaled us to let loose with the blinding back-lights from the bazookas. We waited long seconds in the eerie silence that followed, until the shells exploded on the Russians—more noise than effect. That signaled the attack: the sound of spirited, courageous yelling from the kid-soldiers mixed with the noise from their automatic rifles as they went for the Russian men. Kids against men. I tossed a few hand grenades. Sporadic rifle fire answered, but in minutes, it was over. That was it. We'd surprised them and captured a battery of anti-aircraft guns, some vehicles, and dugouts filled with Russian men, who slowly rose, transformed into silhouettes with their hands up, standing in ground-touching coats. A few escaped into the forest. But no tanks.

Now my job started. Along with two others who had my job in the other units, we attached anti-tank mines to formerly German anti-aircraft guns and makeshift vehicles, filled them with whatever Russian ammunition and guns we'd collected, poured canisters of their own gasoline onto them, then lit the fuses and left as quickly as we'd come. Hit and run. One unit took the prisoners off somewhere. We headed back into the forest, where the sounds from a series of explosions told me I'd carried out my part of the attack.

Although it was still dark, we hurried to get well hidden in the underbrush before the Russians came searching for us in the morning light. We covered our tracks with sticks and twigs and hid under leaves, waiting. It was still. Time went slowly. At daylight I began to listen for Russians probing the underbrush with their extra long bayonets. Nothing. I imagined that being pierced by a bayonet would be a slow way to die, like pulsating between life and death, like a hand opening and closing, strength coming and going, until, after a long struggle, the hand could no longer make a fist. Life at its end. Somehow, I finally slept.

When night came, we pushed through the forest to find our hidden supply bunker. Once found, we opened it carefully and crawled in. We were amazed by how much was there—food and water, mines and bazookas—all waiting to be found by anyone. We organized what we needed and waited out the day inside. That day I slept well.

By the next night I had no idea where we were. The moon helped light the way pointed out by the lieutenant, with him thinking we would, and me fearing we could, find some Russian tanks. We found nothing that night, or the next few nights. One night we came to a road where I laid a few mines here and there in the middle of the road and suspended some hand grenades—wired to trees on both sides—at a height calculated to collide with the radiators of any passing Russian trucks.

About the ninth night, I knew something was up. I could feel it. The lieutenant had news from the spotter plane that we were to attack a suspected Russian headquarters, joining other units nearby. We walked until almost dawn where the others were waiting. Within minutes all hell broke loose—bazooka flashes, loud German hurrahs, gunfire, explosions, and hand-to-hand battles—all taking place outside a shack surrounded by vehicles. Just as suddenly as it had started, it was over. A deathly silence fell over what the night tried to hide, followed by groans and cries of pain. Russians in long coats stood with their hands up amid a cluster of partially damaged vehicles. I went to work—laying mines, fastening grenades, and pouring canisters of gasoline over everything, burnable or not. After I'd finished and returned to the lieutenant, I learned that we'd captured a general and his staff. They'd already been marched off towards the German line by another unit. I wondered how they could possibly get through the Russian line alive.

Our unit, with one slightly wounded, sneaked quickly into the forest, trying to cover our tracks on the way, and spent the day resting. I listened from beneath the brush and snow and woke up to darkness. They hadn't found us.

At nightfall we went on again. We saw no Russians that night. By daybreak we were tired, hungry and thirsty, and back hiding under the leaves. The next night we looked for our bunker. We were lost and worn out, so we rested during what was left of the night. I was out as soon as I hit the ground.

I woke up at daylight, just as the lieutenant returned. He'd found the bunker. Revived by food and drink and re-armed with as many bazookas as we could carry, we went looking for Russians again. It was a good night for me. We didn't find any.

Another day, as I lay under the brush and leaves waiting for daylight to fade, a bug crawled along a tiny twig on my face, then stopped in front of my eyes. Up close it looked like a monster. I didn't dare wipe it away and disturb my leafy camouflage. We played dead as we waited for the Russians to come searching. I willed myself to see nothing, to hear nothing. It must have worked. I dozed off. When I woke up, I was stiff from the cold. Melting snow lay on my face.

Thoughts from the past filled my mind, mistakes I'd made, time I'd wasted—wasted the wrong way. Wasting time the right way was okay, like when I used to sit in old gentleman Kronika's elegant apartment that was stuffed with things from cultures from around the world. His collection filled every nook and cranny, things he'd collected on his travels as a Danish reporter. They cloaked the dark room with an air of mystery, making it exciting to listen to what he knew about the world outside, each piece having its own story. I knew he was gay. How I knew, I forget. I felt safe with him though. He was the kind of gentleman who never showed his emotions. I sensed that he was aware of how childishly I walked along the edge of his world—dangerous to me, yet exciting.

Now I was in a different world, under wet leaves, and too young to die. I fell asleep again for a while, then woke from the cold, my muscles aching. I watched my mind go places again. My thoughts went in waves, being thrown off first one thing, then landing on another. Some things I hadn't thought about before, and some I didn't want to think about—like my mother. My memories of her weren't happy ones, but I thanked her now in my mind. My thanking her would probably surprise anyone who knew how poorly we got along. But I thanked her just the same. She'd given me life, a chance to learn and to dream, even right now, at this moment, as I lay thinking of her under the leaves.

Night came. Time to go on our way again by using the leftover twilight to follow along a grassy cut in the forest. I'd had enough of this war, but there was no way out, nothing to do but stick it out. Word was whispered back that there were Russians ahead, apparently waiting for us.

We stopped, waiting, looking into the black silence ahead. Nothing. We came to a creek with a plank lain across it as a footbridge. It looked like a Russian trap. On the lieutenant's signal, we fired our bazookas. Meant for tanks initially, now they were for our survival. Our hurrahs and automatic rifle fire cut into the dark as we jumped across the creek, running right into some Russians we hadn't seen. I raced behind the hurrahs, instinctively running along the open cut as fast as I could, daring the burst of Russian machine-gun bullets. I ran like hell trying to outrun the gunfire, on towards an open field, not knowing why. Some of the kids followed. It was a swamp. We had to step quickly on the soggy soil. Our sneakers filled with water. We literally had to walk on water.

We regrouped after crossing. There were only six of us left. One stood stiff, helpless. His head seemed oddly shaped, with something gray hanging out. He noticed me staring at it. He smiled at me, as if embarrassed, and handed me his automatic rifle and his magazines, reluctantly, slowly. The lieutenant nodded. We all realized the seriousness of his situation and moved to do what we could. We pressed his brain back in, gently, covered it with clean leaves to keep it moist, and bandaged him up. He didn't speak; he just stared ahead and stood quietly, like a good horse being harnessed. His motionless face reflected silent stoicism. His face has stayed with me to this day. He'd been hit by a Russian dumdum bullet. He was the best of us.

One kid murmured, "It's too bad. He's of no use to us now. We sure could use him to get out of the jam we're in. At least he can walk, so he won't hold us up much." His comment bothered me but this wasn't the time or place for me to say more. I looked around at who'd made it this time and wondered who'd be missing at the next count.

The lieutenant ordered me to go out a few hundred feet ahead of the group, heading west along a trail towards the German line. That meant I was the patsy, the first one shot at to warn the group behind.

Now alone in the dark forest, I stalked Russians with my first automatic in the war, my trigger finger ready, thinking about how different it was between the nights and the days, of being the hunter, not the hunted. While being hunted I worried about all the horrible things that could happen to me, but when I was the hunter, I had only one thought—to kill first. For hours I imagined Russians behind every tree. Finally I heard something—the faint sound of an accordion. I stopped, waiting for the others to catch up. We'd come to a Russian camp we had to get past. Six kids and a lieutenant.

The lieutenant told one of the boys to give me the last bazooka. Whoever was behind me was motioned away before I could fire. I knew how it worked but had never fired one. I pulled the safety pin, fired, dropped the empty pipe, and before the shell even hit the ground, I'd jumped up to follow the lieutenant who was running straight at the Russians along a road, the second enemy road we crossed that night. As I ran behind him, I emptied my automatic at where I imagined Russians to be in the dark. They returned sporadic fire. Then a machine-gun salvo burst from my right, mowing down everything in its path. Everything. I headed left towards the forest, over soft green patches and crunching snow—its noise telling me I was still alive, still running. Seconds filled with tiny events. Bullets chased anything running. I ran towards a swamp, across its miry ground, and on towards some bushes. Flat on my face, I lay in the wet and cold, waiting for the others.

I counted—five and the lieutenant. One didn't make it.

Back to the forest. Daybreak again. We knew the procedure: covering our tracks, then underbrush and leaves covering us. My thoughts wavered between hope and despair. The Russians we'd passed would come after us for sure. I feared going insane, confined, waiting, emotional yet motionless, thinking of life and death, wanting the one but afraid of getting the other. I thought about dying, about how little I'd done in my short life, nothing really. One's supposed to die when one becomes tired of it all, weak in body, unable to continue. That's what nature intended. But not this, a kid, me, now.

Under the leaves I worried about what I couldn't see. I heard indistinct voices and shaving-like sounds. Slowly, very slowly, the sounds became distinct, bayonets slicing into the frozen ground. It came from my right. I sensed the distance—a few hundred yards. No more. My heart pounded; my mind panicked. This was it. My index finger cramped around the trigger of the automatic lying along my right leg. I waited for the sound of a shot to signal that I should start shooting. More shaving sounds. Crunching footsteps in the hard snow. I was ready. Then shouts. Apparently a command for the shaving sounds to move in another direction. Footsteps faded into the sounds of the forest. If even one of us had moved, it would have been the end of us all. The silence grew; even the forest grew quieter. Slowly my body came back, back to its place. A sense of mortality weighed down on me—like unwilling sleep.

When I opened my eyes, daylight was fading. Darkness had come in slowly. We dared to whisper to each other, getting gradually louder, protected by the darkness. We decided to stay one more day where they'd already looked for us. It seemed safest. The kid with half a brain was still with us. Not a word from him. It was unbelievable that he was still alive, yet so still.

We ate and drank at dusk, taking our time. As I lay in the dark, random thoughts swirled through my head, fragments of memories. I remembered watching a flock of birds eating cherries in a tree a long time ago. I was no more than ten or eleven. The birds ate the cherries as if they belonged to them. If I could have asked the cherries, I'm sure they would have answered that they were glad to be eaten by the birds and become droppings that started new trees. The owner of the trees thought otherwise. He handed me a rifle. When I took my first shot at the tree, I was surprised to see a bird fall, a mistake. It couldn't have been me who shot it, me who'd never even held a rifle before. I picked the bird up. It was warm in my hand, but dead. I buried it and handed the gun back, leaving the cherries for the birds.

I wondered if the other kids around me were having similar thoughts. Damn. I'm going to die before I have a chance to live, just like that bird. A year ago I never even gave death a thought. Why had they sent us young ones out to hide under leaves? Suddenly I knew. It was easy to convince us to listen and follow orders because we were so young, brought up to listen and do as we were told. That was it. Old men listened to orders with doubt in their minds, doubts arising from memories they'd collected listening to leaders who had turned out to be wrong before.

I thought about home. I wondered how my mother was doing in Prague. She sure wasn't hiding under a pile of leaves all day. She'd be at her usual. She always seemed so sure of herself. She had self-discipline coming out of her bones, rubbing off on those around her. She never gave up once she started something. And wherever she was, there was action. That was how she gave to others. She had everything under control. Always. If something didn't turn out the way she wanted it, she gave it all her attention, with material gifts if need be. She gave generously. Often. No, too often.

I remembered her kissing me generously when I was very, very small. I could still feel it. I could remember the sound of her faint voice singing sweet songs to me. Later the songs turned into shoves. There was always a loving shove on my back, along with a kiss from her, pushing me in the direction she wanted me to go. That push held another message, a reminder to stand up straight, with poise, to produce an effect. She believed in stature. She never showed it when she was discouraged. She taught me to tell everybody that everything was great, even if I was down. She taught that to everyone she cared about. The smart ones didn't listen. I thought I was smart. I tried not to listen to her ways.

Thinking about that made me smile. I enjoyed thinking about having stood up to her, to such power of determination and independence. She was strong. She needed no one. And asked no one for help, ever. I still wondered how I'd been strong enough to stand up to her, but I did it by doing things my way. But what was my way, really? One thing was for sure. I needed to learn not to judge too quickly. And how to be humble. But how do I learn that? How do I learn what is good? Albert Einstein is good, a good *mensch*. Too good. I'd read that in books. It must be true because I had read it. I admired his humility. He didn't seem arrogant. I'm arrogant. Why? Maybe to protect myself because I'm weak. Or am I arrogant because I'm young, because I haven't much to stand up with against those stronger than me, those like my mother?

Voices came again, indistinguishable. Sounds floated in from a distance. I heard grunts, maybe from the effort of shoving steel into the frozen ground. I listened, hard. Slowly the sounds faded. Danger seemed to fade with them. I stopped trying to hold my breath. It was silent the rest of the day. I'd kept my eyes closed the whole time. My body was stiff from the long tense hours in the snow. I knew my legs were there, but I couldn't feel them. I slept again.

The following night we continued towards the German front along a path in the forest. Two kept watch on the wounded kid, somehow still alive. The lieutenant ordered me to take my automatic and go a few hundred feet out ahead—bait again. I sensed we weren't that many miles from the front. I knew I would run into Russians near the front, this time alone.

I turned the visor of my cap inside to make it look Russian.

Alone on the trail I stumbled noisily along, playing the drunk, cursing in Russian, the same words over and over, with my index finger on the trigger, senses alert. My ears, more than my eyes, tried to decipher any movement, however slight. After hours alone in the lead, I felt abandoned. The others were so far behind I couldn't hear or see them any more.

I changed from a noisy, careless drunk to a silent one, walking on the snow-poor edges of the path to reduce the crunching sounds. When I accidentally snapped a twig, I covered the sound by cursing in Russian.

Unexpectedly I came out onto a meadow, shimmering in the slight moonlight. I froze and listened. There had to be Russians nearby. It was all open. I couldn't believe my luck so far, not having heard or seen anything of them. My senses combed the meadow and the edges of the forest beyond it for the slightest signs of anything. Nothing. To get across the meadow I first had to climb a ten-foot-high mesh fence. It looked Russian-made. I could see no way around it except to climb over it. It was tough going. I was sure they'd hear me climbing. I'd get shot and be left hanging on the fence. But it was still quiet after I'd quickly dropped down onto the other side.

Now I had to cross the open meadow, easy prey in the moonlight. I ran, fearing sudden fire from a Russian machine gun. Breathing hard, I sank down in relief, once more under cover in the forest. Now I watched the six who'd watched me cross the meadow. Still no shots. They didn't climb over the fence though; they'd found a hole in it and crawled under. Well, hell. All that time, I'd thought I'd been sent out ahead because I was the smart one.

The lieutenant took over the lead. That meant trouble was coming. He whispered, gesturing that the Russians were within talking distance. We moved cautiously, in slow motion, one step at a time, often standing still to listen for long minutes. I made out the sounds of ice scraping and grinding, moving along in the floes of the river. We were back where we'd started. It seemed a lifetime ago.

Suddenly right in our path, in the shadows of the bushes, a dark figure rose out of the bare ground, a Russian standing up in his foxhole, growing larger, becoming a huge man. The lieutenant leapt at him, instantaneously shoving his fist deep into his mouth to prevent him from yelling for help. When the Russian giant bent down for his rifle, he pulled the lieutenant and his fist down with him. I quickly crouched down beside the lieutenant, swinging my gunstock at the Russian's skull. The stock broke in two as the Russian stood up again, rifle in hand, struggling to shoot, groaning with the fist in his mouth. My mind made my hand reach for my jackknife, as if in a trance. I opened it slowly, as if I had all the time in the world, and watched my hand saw back and forth below the lieutenant's hand, as if someone else was doing it. The knife disappeared into the giant's neck. He flailed with his rifle, twisting his body, splattering his blood onto my face, onto my hands, my clothes, everything. His body slumped to the ground like a heavy sack, releasing the lieutenant's bloodied hand. Behind us, the other kids stood—frozen. I looked at their shocked faces—bloodguilt. One life for six.

We disappeared down the bank to the river, unnoticed, unscarred, alive. I became aware of how soaked in blood I was by a wet feeling on my skin. Down at the river's edge, we stood with our backs to the water, exposed, lined up like clay pigeons waiting for Russian dumdums to tear us apart. Behind us, the ice sheets moved lazily, twisting, turning—an eerie sound in a stillness that let us live a little longer. Now we had no more to give except the wait for our final end.

At daybreak we knew, sooner or later, a Russian would come down the bank to scoop up a bucket of water. And that would be it. They would kill us all.

In my mind our only chance was for someone to cross the river to wake the Germans for help. In the early morning twilight, I persuaded myself, then the lieutenant that I should go for help. It didn't take much courage to jump into the river to trade this place of certain death for a slim chance of survival.

Within seconds in the icy water, although my skin felt good to be cleansed of foreign blood, I was yanked under by the weight of my water-soaked down overalls. I clawed my way back along the river bottom to the bank and went up for air, then stripped down to my underwear and jumped back in, glad I hadn't given myself time to think about what I was doing. Ice cut into my face and hands, but I was so numb from the cold that I couldn't feel myself bleeding. I swam as hard as I could, splashing, swallowing ice water, frantically aiming for the opposite bank. Sporadic bullets hit the water around me, German bullets. Water sprayed into the air. I swam harder. The German shots were soon answered by Russian ones. I was being fired on from both sides. What had I gotten myself into?

Somehow I got to the far bank without being hit, and clung to a bare slender root from a willow growing out of the bank. Hidden in shadow, I felt safe under the tree's dark branches, out of sight from both sides. I held on, getting my wind back. I wanted to stay, knowing that the worst was yet to come—a German minefield ahead on the bank. How could I avoid the network of invisible trip wires? I couldn't.

Fear kept me hanging onto the root until the freezing water began to numb my body. The freezing water meant certain death, within minutes; the minefield ahead was a maybe, maybe dying or losing a leg or two. What choice was there? I chose to go on—the most logical, yet the hardest. Some line of hogwash flashed through my mind, "Only if you put your life on the line will it be given to you."

I scrambled up the steep bank and began to run, running as fast as my numb legs could go and as far as they could take me, not bothering to look for the thin trip wires. A figure appeared in the dark, and pointed his rifle at me, yelling for me to stop or be shot. I didn't stop and he shot. Missed. I couldn't believe my luck. A split second of exhilaration came over me, a strange joy, as if I'd been given a new life in that very instant after he could—he really should—have killed me. Then I saw him. He was old. I ran faster, straight at him, hoping to reach him before he could fire again, and this time not miss. I stood right in his face. He pointed his rifle at my chest, ready to shoot. I started yelling, giving him hell for shooting at me, spouting everything my mouth and bewildered mind could think of. I soon realized that I'd shocked the old soldier—appearing like a white ghost in my white underwear and coming at him from the Russian side. I raised my hands like a prisoner, freezing in the slight breeze, wanting to get out of the cold.

He prodded me towards a knoll with the end of his barrel, mumbling, *"Freies Deutschland,"* that I was a spy without a uniform. He wasn't going to be fooled. I must be one of those German men who'd gone over to the Russians, who still wore a German army uniform but with a *Freies Deutschland* insignia. I'd be shot as a deserter. He was sure. He marched me down into a bunker, filled with candlelight and astonished faces, half asleep. They woke the commander up. Now I could talk to reason, get help for the others, and get warm.

I told the commander why I was there, about our unit operating behind the Russian line. I explained everything. His mouth opened in disbelief. Silence. I looked around for support. None of them believed me. They conferred with each other, occasionally looking over at me, as they discussed what to do. In the end they cranked up the phone to call a higher level of authority. A long discussion took place before the commander broke into a smile, then explained to the rest that it was true—everything that I'd told them was true.

Legitimized, their looks changed to admiration. They hurried to find a blanket, something stale to eat and a strong shot of liquor. I crawled into myself, huddled under a blanket, holding my hands over a candle until someone smelled burning meat. My hands were so frozen that I'd burned them without feeling it. My mind wasn't on my hands, but on the kids I'd left on the bank.

The next night I learned that, right after I'd left, a Russian had come down the bank to get water and discovered them. Minutes later they were gunned down. Only two survived—the lieutenant and the one missing half his brain. The bodies of the others were retrieved in a dinghy by a rescue party that night. The following morning I stood looking over them as they lay on the ground like logs in the mud, so young, so still. The one near death was delivered to the medics and given a medal to die with.

I'd cut that Russian's throat for them—in vain. Now I had to live with the memory of a Russian face struggling for air, for life, almost surviving until I'd changed his destiny. I'd made it with my body unscarred, but with my mind and soul scarred forever—like a cancer that will be buried with my flesh and bones.

♣ CHAPTER 9 ♣

On January 26th, 1945, Hitler had prophesized halting the thousands of Russian tanks heading towards his headquarters in Berlin with the thousands of children he'd conscripted into the bizarrely named *1st Tank Destroyer Division.* By the *Ides of March* the entire division had been committed, company by company. I've never heard of even one tank being destroyed by it. Fifty Russian T34 tanks had already crossed the Neisse by February 13th, tanks our division was supposed to have halted. By the end of March, thousands more of their tanks were regrouped east of the Neisse, ready to roll towards Berlin.

The few of us left from the original thousands were put up in abandoned homes west of the Neisse to recuperate. We were young, so we recovered quickly. In a few days we regrouped on an open meadow in front of a colonel. He asked some—me being one—to step forward. I was stricken with fear, wondering what punishment was to come, then shocked to find myself decorated with the Iron Cross, 2nd Class, and a *Nahkampf Spange*, and promoted from Private to Corporal. The colonel said our heroism had been reported to Hitler during a daily briefing, providing some cheer to the otherwise dismal atmosphere at his headquarters. I went back to my group, embarrassed. It wasn't what I'd sought. I was just a kid trying to survive. I'd done nothing more than survive, daring to take risks, not from choice, but from knowing of no other way.

I was now assigned as a regular member to what was left of the *1st Tank Destroyer Division*, issued a bike with two bazookas strapped to it, and sent to seek out Russian tanks—though this time not behind the front line. We were sent to an empty village that straddled the Neisse, now cut in half by a blown-up bridge. On the other side the Russians were regrouping with their T34's. We didn't want to see or find them. We held our breath, hoping they would stay where they were.

We were nervous, like animals before a storm. Loose shingles rattled and open doors banged as the occasional gust of wind blew through the abandoned buildings in the village, now temporarily shared with the Russians who watched us from their side of the river. Around us the land was deserted, given up by the villagers who'd left it for us to fight over.

We sneaked through the empty buildings scrounging for something to eat or drink, maybe an overlooked bottle of wine. One day we found some rabbits in hutches; then we noticed Russian soldiers on their side doing just what we were. We watched each other cautiously, but neither of us shot. After that we were more alert, keeping our heads up and eyes peeled, while we searched in the buildings for something to eat. Hunger made us risk scavenging, no different than rats.

After too many days we were finally relieved, and we, ourselves, relieved to be heading south to look for tanks—old tanks we were told—at a place where the Russians had come across the river. Off on our bikes, with two bazookas tied to the front fork and an automatic slung on our back, we followed a winding footpath for a good day's ride, nearing the spot where the tanks were supposed to be hidden when, suddenly, a wild-looking bunch of Russians, a few feet from the path, stormed towards us, yelling and swinging outdated rifles with bayonets. We threw ourselves off the bikes, in a long single row, and, bewildered, we ran in zigzag patterns, seeking refuge in a stand of beech trees a few hundred feet away.

I raced from one man-thick-sized trunk to another. Worn out, gasping for air, I slumped behind a big tree to return fire and discovered that two scruffy-looking Russians were scavenging through my knapsack, through everything that was holy to me, including my picture of Greta, the only thing I had left of her. Then, as if by command, the whole bunch of them swarmed over the rest of the spoils we'd left, giving me a chance to look behind me. There was nobody there. The rest had been chased to a safe distance farther away, leaving me there alone. That was all I needed. While the scavengers were busy, I chanced bolting, running again in zigzags as bullets zinged past my head, making it to where the others were hiding in a thicket of pines.

Looking back every now and then as we slowly walked away from what had just happened, I started to shake, overcome by the attack on us. One minute we were looking for tanks, old ones they said, the next, we were running for our lives. I was getting bitter, thinking about how senseless it all was—the whole idea of kids against tanks. The orders given us were getting worse, like the whole war, worse by the day. And I had nothing left from my past to hold close—no picture of Greta.

Defeated, we straggled away from the Russians into the arms of some busybodies, an SS unit, preparing to attack the wild-lookers who'd just stripped us. The SS would do what we'd failed to do—search and destroy the Russian tanks hidden in a nearby gully, and do it with an armored vehicle equipped with a two-centimeter, four-barreled, anti-aircraft gun and a stove pipe covered with canvas to make it look like a canon—all intended to make their armored vehicle resemble a tank. It was ludicrous. I wanted no more of it. I sneaked slowly past them, anxious to avoid being pulled into their upcoming battle.

I felt like a thief as I snuck away, but I figured it made more sense than what they were doing—making a pretend tank. I walked west along a winding road through the forest until I ran into an SS checkpoint around one bend where they were waiting for guys like me. Pointing their guns at me, they yelled at me to turn around and go back where I'd come from—to fight for the *Fuehrer*. Remembering the sight of my buddy, lying in the snow with the traitor's sign on his chest, made me utter some excuses and quickly obey, taking long strides on my way back until out of their sight. Then I took my time, walking slowly, hoping the SS battle would be over before I got there.

As luck would have it, I met up with my old lieutenant. Asking no questions, he took me to the headquarters of what was left of our division for a new assignment. He introduced me to the chief who was in the midst of a bunch of officers, some appearing to be grandfathers, all quietly murmuring. The chief waved me off busy-like, without looking at me, ordering me to bodyguard duty for the officers roaming around outside headquarters. I was to stand guard with the others and perform odd errands.

After a few days of guard duty, I was assigned my first errand: to take some information about a certain reconsolidation of the German front line to the officers on the fighting line. I got the location of the latest front line configuration from a large wall map pinned in red. About an hour's bike ride on pavement, the front line crossed the paved road, just past a transmission building on the left.

After I'd pedaled the hour without seeing a single soul, I began to doubt where I was. I got off the bike so that I could react more quickly if something happened. I'd already learned that lesson. I pushed the bike along the pavement, watching the left side for the transmission building. Bareheaded and wearing my military fatigues, I'd walked for only a few minutes before bullets whizzed past my ears. In one motion I threw my bike in the ditch and myself past it, making for a thicket of tight pine bushes, snaking across pine needles that worked under my sleeves to prickle my arms. I lay in the silence, slowly easing forward, becoming aware of the pine-needle scent and the sound of my heartbeat. A few pine needles moved ever so slightly from the rapid rise and fall of my chest.

I searched with my eyes and ears. What was around me? Nothing. I was becoming confused. Who'd shot at me? It must have come from close by. Where was the front line? I hadn't seen anyone. Where was the fighting, where was the damn war going on? And where in the hell was the transmission building?

I wormed myself forward, towards some light under the thicket. Through a window-like opening, the sun glared into my eyes, blinding me but, at the same time, warming my face, making it feel good. Gradually I saw the gray-green of a large meadow, at least a thousand yards across. At the edges, in the low trees were dots here and there. They moved, dark brown figures clad in coats to the ground. Russians! Bullets hissed over my head, penetrating the thin tree trunks around me, small woodpecker-sized holes becoming fist-sized exits. Russian dumdums!

They were trying to get me with dumdums—bullets filed at their tips to split on impact that left fist-sized exits—which were forbidden by Geneva Convention.

I was both furious and scared. Those bastards! I aimed at the long-coats, emptying my whole magazine. I smiled as I watched them hit the ground for cover. But I knew I was in trouble now.

I wiggled into a slight depression in the pine bed to wait. Nothing. More silence. Then I heard soft clopping sounds from the forest across the road. Horses. I made out some mounted Cossacks situated just inside the cover of some dark trees across the road. I'd slipped a new magazine into my automatic, which left three on my belt. I counted eight across the road. I had enough to take them all down. I held my breath, hoping they hadn't seen me. I waited. I saw their faces turned in my direction. They sat on their horses, apparently waiting for me to make the first move. The one in front, wearing a tall fur hat, gestured with his *Kalashnikov* at me, talking Russian. I stayed put, trigger-ready. Seconds passed. They were still looking at me, waiting, as if they weren't afraid of me. I was ready for them.

The leader opened his Cossack jacket, revealing a German medal-plastered uniform, then rumbled in raw German, "We Vlasso soldiers. We spy for German army. We help you. We know you not Russky. You in Russky land. Russky sniper shoot you. He watches now. We must make you prisoner. You not come, Russky sniper shoot you. You keep gun and bike. We put you with horses. We show you how walk back to German army."

More seconds. I figured I had to chance it. It sounded legit. After I'd figured out that they were taking a chance with me too, with me and my trigger-ready automatic, I nodded agreement. I crawled out from under the brush, got my bike, and got in between the horses, hoping the apparent sniper would buy what he saw, me being taken prisoner. I held the bike with my left hand and the rifle with my right, with my finger tight on the trigger in case they tried anything. They could easily shoot me in the head from the back, but if they did, I'd try to take some of them with me. I'd force myself to stay alive long enough to do it. I kept pace between their tall horses, trotting, with the tight formation surrounding me, along a trail.

As the minutes passed and I was still alive, I began to feel safer. It looked as if I'd made the right choice. After an hour in the forest, we came to a large clearing that opened out onto a knoll of gently rolling land, sunshine, and a gruesome spectacle. Hundreds of Russian bodies lay scattered over the knoll, killed in fierce fighting, to judge from how they lay. It must have happened many days ago; their bodies were starting to smell. An abandoned tank sat at the bottom of the knoll. Silence and sunlight.

The Cossacks had stopped. I turned to the leader as he spoke, "You safe now. Trail to German army, that way." As he lifted his arm to point towards the bottom of the knoll, my gun arm moved, ready for whatever his outstretched arm was to mean. I thanked him, then asked him the whereabouts of the transmission station on the paved road.

He laughed, showing no front teeth, "Kaput, yesterday."

And I had one more question I'd been pondering. "How could you tell I was German? I'm wearing camouflaged fatigues, no uniform, and no cap, so how could you tell?"

"You walk like German, not like Russian. We watch you

long time."

He grinned, giving a quiet command in Russian. I threw my bike to the ground and pointed my automatic at them, only to watch as their horses turned back. They didn't see me wave a good-bye with the rifle. The forest had already taken them in.

Later I found out that the Vlasso troops were named after Vlasso Andrejewitsch, a Russian general taken prisoner by the Germans. Because Stalin had decreed that any Russian officer taken prisoner would be shot upon returning to Russia, Vlasso chose to fight for the Nazis, recruiting forlorn Russian prisoners into two divisions of Vlasso troops. Some were Cossacks, like those who had rescued me.

I felt queasy, as if standing in an open cemetery. No wind; nothing moving. I was nervous as I started down the knoll among the dead, worrying that one might still be alive, playing dead, waiting to shoot anything German. I scanned quickly, left and right, not wanting to look too closely, but alert for anything that moved. I made my way towards the tank, sidestepping the corpses, lifting my bike here and there. The tank looked German by its shape. It looked bigger to me now as I stood up close to it, and even more dangerous. Even though it was incapacitated, it still looked menacing, a monster in steel with awesome power. But like everything else, it was still. It had a kettle welded to its rear, making it wood-fired and steam-driven, allowing it to crawl maybe a mile at a time. Spotted and softened with rust, it was a goner. A monster of a corpse. German.

By the time I got back, headquarters already knew everything I could tell them about the transmission building and the rest, all except for my encounter with the Cossacks, which met with some skeptical looks.

There were no errands for me to run after that, Cossacks and all, notwithstanding. I was assigned to guard the entrance of headquarters. I barred unauthorized entry with my firing finger on my automatic, a Luger on my belt, the general's handgun hidden in my back pocket, a grenade in each pocket, and my fatal jackknife, my last resource. I was ready to meet danger and death as best I knew how, over-armed.

Guarding headquarters provided me with idle weeks, weeks of ho-hum events, with time to listen to what went on inside as I wondered about what lay ahead. I tried to overhear some of the hushed conversations inside, making out an occasional word here and there, but not enough to piece together what was happening. Then one day it changed, the voices were louder, happier, as if something wonderful had happened. A bespectacled Lieutenant Tanz passing my guard post whispered, "The Russians are fighting inside Berlin."

It was like being hit by a rock. As the shock wore off, I became elated. I felt I had a chance for life maybe. Maybe I could shed my conviction of certain death, and my damn arsenal with it. As I stood guard, I started thinking about the future, quietly hoping to have one. Along with the rest of the kids I'd served with, we were toughened through our unwanted experiences behind Russian lines where we'd risked our lives. Maybe having had to risk it all would help us meet the challenges to come in a new world after the war, one we didn't yet know. And any new world would surely need risk-takers. And hadn't we learned that! Maybe one day, when no longer kids, we'd look back at what we'd endured and recognize that we'd gained inner strength from it all, that it had given us an edge. Maybe. Who knows.

♣ CHAPTER 10 ♣

The war was going to be over soon. It was in the air. Rumors were rampant. Some new: "Most of Germany was already Russian" or "The Americans were fighting the Russians, Germans with the Americans." Some old: "Hitler was dead." That I'd heard before, many times, as if by repeating it often enough, the rumormongers could make it come true. For more than a week no commands were sent to the front line. There was nothing anywhere to stop the Russians.

Then it happened. After an unforgettable warm sunny day, on the evening of May 1st, 1945, the war was over! We were told to go home, to what was left of home. Everyone was on his own. I was invited to go with the officers at headquarters, who had organized a convoy of a dozen thrown-together vehicles and a lone armored vehicle to slip past the Russians quickly, moving south into mountainous Czechoslovakia.

As the snake of vehicles moved into the second night, with each place in the convoy filled with silent men, scared ones, mostly officers, we passed Zittau sometime in the night, then crawled up the mountains towards partisan-held Varnsdorf. We were worried we'd be ambushed in the village, so we took a dirt road around it. It's a good thing we did. Sitting in the last vehicle, sucking dust, I could hear explosions and gunfire in the village. I just hoped our tires would hold up against the rocks and the deep ruts in the road.

The convoy rolled on through empty land to Decin. In town we saw our first Czech flags hanging out open windows. The streets were deserted, as if waiting for something new to come, anything but us. Sporadic gunfire and occasional shots came from some of the higher windows where the Czech flags fluttered. We kept going, ignoring the shots, speeding through the town straight towards the Elbe River, trying to cross the only bridge ahead of the Russians. The elderly officers didn't see anything. They'd ducked down—keeping their faces to the floor. At the bridge the column stopped. Word snaked back, from the head to the tail, telling us to stay put, not to worry. Though Czech partisans held the bridge, some of our soldiers would take care of it shortly. It took a good hour for a handful of our soldiers to clear the bridge. It cost the column two dead. We hurried across, fearing an ambush or explosives, racing on along dusty roads, and keeping an eye out for partisans. We were in their territory, maybe soon to become Russian. The column stopped slowly, like a train coming into a station, with a feeling of finality, this being the last stop. And it was. The senior officers had decided it was no longer safe to travel in a column. We dispersed into small groups on foot, walking our way west.

Some of the grandfatherly officers begged me to take them along in return for a share of their hard rye bread. "To join me, a kid?" I asked myself. They had to be kidding, no, desperate. I was puzzled, but in the end I figured, why not? Now I was in charge of the officers who'd seen no more of the war than the papers on their desks. Now they had to follow my instructions to the letter—where and when to go or rest, all without comment or question—as they had been trained to do for years already.

We went west, towards old Germany, using the same tactics I'd learned behind the Russian line, of sleeping during the day and marching at night, and I shared their bread. All we needed to find each night was water. And that was easy because there were plenty of creeks in the semi-mountainous land. The old men followed as best they could, clumsily, but they followed nevertheless, following my instructions. We worked our way past a village the first night.

The next night, towards dawn, we approached the outskirts of Usti where a group of women ran towards us, crying, waving their arms, and shouting in German that the city was controlled by 300 partisans sent by the new Czech government to execute anyone who looked German. They'd burned ancestral German homes, robbed and raped, then had chased anyone still alive to a bridge, forcing them to jump into the Elbe River, fifty feet below. Those who didn't drown were machine-gunned. They'd killed hundreds of Germans. The two-thirds population of German descent was to be rooted out forever. Any Czechs who'd tried to stop the massacre had been killed along with them.

We could do no more than to nod and sympathize. The sun rose. We had to move on to find somewhere to hide. Thanks to the women, we stayed far north of the town. At night we continued west towards the German border in the mountains. As daylight appeared we looked for somewhere to hide, but wherever we found bushes, they were already filled with German soldiers. There were so many of us now, and as more and more men appeared in the fields, we changed our tactics—moving in the daylight.

At a self-designated resting place for the masses of German soldiers, a Russian KGB officer on a German motorbike waited, telling everyone, "Be smart. Take the train to *madja*, to mother. It's waiting just a couple of hour's away."

He was persuasive. Some took his advice. My old grandfathers worried, whispering, "Don't trust him. Pass on the friendly offer. Likely that train is going to forced labor camps somewhere in Siberia."

The encounter with the KGB convinced us to begin traveling at night again. That night we avoided three villages filled with barking dogs, skirting around them. The terrain changed from flat fields to rolling high country, so the next night we climbed higher, walking above the villages. At daybreak, in the distance, we could see not hundreds, but thousands and thousands of straggling German soldiers marching across fields. By dusk the flow had increased. We joined the tens of thousands, sleeping with them wherever we could at night, then moving on at dawn, now marching openly. That day the old officers thanked me and we parted, lost in the masses. We were less than a couple days from the German border in the mountains.

More and more men appeared in the open fields, far too many for the now-plugged roads. I was in the midst of men moving like a lazy river's delta a mile wide, like locusts swarming over open grazing lands, all heading towards the mountain pass near Steinbach.

We went silently, strangers, some too old, most too young, but each of us battle-weary, beaten, broken in spirit, and ragged—beggars bound by a common undercurrent of desperation, facing a nothing future. There was nothing left for these once brave, battle-ready men, betrayed by those who'd suddenly faded away.

We passed isolated groups of Russian anti-aircraft batteries, the men there singing and dancing. They'd won. They ignored us.

As I marched through trampled fields of once-fertile soil, one among hundreds of thousands of defeated German soldiers, I feared I'd be checked by Russians for hidden weapons, so I took out the prized pistol I'd never fired—yet looked at a hundred times—reluctantly disassembled it, taking my time to look at each part, and part by part, dropped the pieces in the field, unnoticed, to be trampled by the thousands coming behind me. And in doing so, I somehow felt I had freed myself of what had happened in the land behind me in the east.

On May 9th, the day German forces officially surrendered, I arrived in Steinbach, a German village. I said good-bye to the war. Back on German soil I dared beg for water, hoping too for some bread to eat. I found water, bread, and even brief shelter with an elderly woman, who told me straight out that she was a communist, and what's more she hoped the Russians would come soon. "What an idealist! What a wish!" I thought, but she let me rest on a bench in front of her house in the warm sun, so I kept my mouth shut. It was like heaven. I felt safe enough to close my eyes.

I fell asleep, waking with the taste of a kiss on my mouth. Was it a kiss? I didn't know. I'd dreamed it most likely. Back from my trip through hell, lying on the bench, an angel face bent over me, kissed my mouth, and smiled. She was real; her name was Maria. I noticed the communist woman eyeing us, as only mothers do, immediately reminding me of another communist woman, Pilar, watching over her Maria in Hemingway's *For Whom The Bell Tolls*. Our story, however, ended differently. In spite of her mother's watchfulness and the many soldiers coming and going from her house, Maria and I, desperate for each other, found a way—on a thick bed of pine needles, the sun our only witness. I longed to stay longer, but the next day Maria insisted that I take her brother's suit and bike to find my way home. Sweet Maria.

I rode for miles down a mountainous road through an endless forest, until a lone American soldier, the first I'd ever seen, stopped me. He was a picture—except for the *white* gamashes over his boots. "White? Gamashes? On a young soldier?" I asked myself. I was shocked. My grandpa used to wear them for dancing—black ones. It struck me funny. I couldn't keep myself from starting to grin, but his scowling face kept me from laughing. I quickly sobered when I saw the anger in his face, and how big he was. I slipped off the bike and stood at an obedient distance, trying to calm him, letting him wave his rifle at me. I figured he was just scared, trying to act tough. And maybe his patience had been worn thin by the mass of German soldiers who must have come ahead of me. He patted me down, looking for weapons. I had none. He let me pass, mumbling something I suspected was a curse.

Fearing he might call me back, I pedaled away as fast as I could, inhaling the scent of trees, wonderful trees. I was suddenly aware of how intoxicating the smells in a forest are. Overcome with happiness, I began singing to the trees, singing my way west. I felt free. Safe and free. Free to plan what I was going to do. And I knew what. I was going to see Greta, not my mother or father or anyone else.

I came to the Autobahn, which headed straight west. I rode past villages and towns that showed no signs of life. I got off the highway to find something to eat but got only water, so I returned to the smooth pavement where biking was easy and fun. I saw hundreds of others biking west with me. Where had all those bikes come from? I was one among thousands upon thousands of the once-uniformed, hoping to get safely past the endless convoys of American tanks and trucks, which were heading east towards the Russians. The trucks were filled with gum-chewing Americans, legs dangling out, who eyed us as they passed by, no doubt hoping to find some girls among us.

I biked day and night to get to Greta more quickly. My bike was like a part of my body now. In the early dawn it took me off the Autobahn to look for something to eat and drink, carrying a stomach desperate for a piece of dry bread. I'd learned that to get it I had to knock on doors in the village very early, ahead of all the others seeking the same. Most doors stayed closed, the inside still and silent, the people behind them listening. I had to knock at ten doors before a scared face might appear so that I could ask for water. Ten more doors got bread. Well-fed barking dogs tied near the doors meant don't bother. The village churches were empty, their bells silent.

Between villages I often pedaled along dirt roads, past deserted weed-filled fields. I saw no more German uniforms, just men in civilian clothes, most often disguised as farm workers, carrying a sickle, a wooden rake, a shovel, or bag of hay, and some even pushing wheelbarrows, but all heading west. I saw one fellow wearing a bowler, holding a wreath and a sad face to go with it, mourning his way west.

I saw American tanks with rubber tracks speeding east on the Autobahn, columns and columns of tanks. When a familiar face passed by on a bike, I recognized Eberhard Tanz, the young lieutenant from headquarters, one of those who'd never seen action in the war. He sat kind of stiff on his bike, as stiff as I remembered him walking in and out of headquarters, wearing bug-eyed gas-mask glasses that made him look funny—somehow approachable, so I thought, "What the heck—maybe we can go west together." So I caught up with him. Having someone to travel with made the days more fun.

We decided to head for his aunt's in Apfelstaedt—our energy spent in getting there—where we were welcomed by an elderly aunt, Frieda Tantz, a large-framed woman who dressed all in black, her hands gnarled with arthritis. She was alone, except for her farm hand, a confessed communist—another idealist—who was sticking around waiting for the Russian army to arrive. We planned to stay until just before they arrived, to eat and rest and to help out a little on the farm. It worked out fine.

One evening as Eberhard and I sat quietly playing chess in the living room, the windows shattered! Shards rained down on our chessboard as gun barrels poked in through the broken glass. American MP's smashed open the door and rushed at us, guns pointed, yelling. Confused, we jumped up and put our hands behind our heads. It didn't calm things. They were wild, tough-acting, prodding us with their gun barrels out the door and onto their waiting truck, ordering us to sit on a folding bench.

From the opposite bench they watched us, jumpy and ready to shoot, as we bounced along, swaying as the truck swerved around the curves in the road, and finally stopped at a villa with a sign proclaiming it *CIA Headquarters*. We were herded into a cellar and watched through the night by a guard on the stairs.

Late the next morning they prodded us up the stairs to stand before an officer, sitting with his boots up on an empty desk. He and his soles eyed us together. He said nothing for an uncomfortably long time, then let loose with a barrage of questions about what unit we'd belonged to, what rank we were, and on and on along that vein. Suddenly he told us to take our shirts off. We asked why, fearing something was going to happen to us. Our *why* angered him. We obliged in slow motion. Now he demanded that we lift up our arms. He wasn't pointing a gun at us, so maybe he was kidding around with us in some American way. No. He meant it. He stepped closer. I could feel his breath on my underarm, his nose almost touching my skin. Then he stepped back, told us to put our arms down and get dressed. He gave no explanation for his strange inspection, but suggested that we should get ourselves discharge papers at an American prisoner of war camp near Würzburg. He half smiled, shook our hands, and then told one of his men to drive us back to the farm. We still had no idea why we'd been taken in.

Immediately after the war there were no newspapers. Rumors took their place. We heard that the Russians would be coming soon. Knowing we'd be moving on, I decided to visit my aunt at nearby Eisenach to see if she was all right. Her husband had just died. She wasn't a Nazi; indeed, she was a British subject. Her husband had been a cabinet minister in the Weimar Republic, the government prior to Hitler.

She was fine, she said, but told me in no uncertain terms that she wasn't happy to see me. I'd just wanted to see someone in my family, so I was kind of hurt at being brushed off. I learned later that as a British subject she'd received Red Cross food packages, which she'd hoarded in her cellar. Knowing all young men were hungry, she was afraid to let anyone find out and that anyone very much included me. It was all she had to survive on. Within less than an hour, I was pedaling back to the farm.

On the way back I ran into some freed Russian prisoners of war. They chased me up a hill, most likely to steal my bike. Being young I shot up the hill and was soon looking down on the out-of-breath Russians, cheekily waving at them and at the rocks they were throwing. At the time there were no cars or motorbikes and few bicycles. Most had to walk. I should be careful.

When they were out of sight, I returned to the busy road. Nearing the top of a hill, I heard brawling sounds. They grew louder and louder. It was a drunken bunch of men and women crowded into the back of an open-railed American army truck, and it was over-taking me. As they passed they showered me with fist-sized rocks and empty vodka bottles, missing—thanks to their drunken aim.

It took a while before I finally realized who they were. At first I was mad, but slowly it dawned on me that they were freed Russian prisoners returning to Russia. By the time the truck had become a speck in the distance I was feeling sorry for them. They seemed to be the biggest losers of all in this war. First they'd fought against the Nazis, who'd taken them prisoner. Then, because Stalin had decreed that all those taken prisoner were to be shot, they had defected to fight for the Germans. Now they'd lost the war fighting for the Germans and were being shipped back to Russia and would probably be shot on arrival. One of those on the truck could have been the Cossack who'd saved my life a few weeks ago. Was it just weeks ago? It already seemed like part of another time, another world.

Eberhard and I heard persistent rumors that the Americans would be leaving soon, handing the village over to the Russians stationed further east. Soldiers wearing a motley, mismatched collection of ragged uniforms would be arriving any day, riding in horse-drawn wagons. We knew it was time to go.

We said good-bye to the stooping figure of his aunt. She stood, old and bent, waving one of her gnarled hands, left alone with the communist farm hand, who'd caused our problem with the Americans—we'd discovered—by falsely reporting us as SS officers. As she watched us go, she had a blank look on her face as if she didn't really understand why we went, old Frieda Tantz from Apfelstaedt, standing at number 59 Hauptstrasse on July 2nd, 1945.

* * *

"Greta, did you meet any Russians during the war?"

"No, but after the war there were loose prisoners of war running around Krefeld. When I went out on my bike, I took a curtain rod to defend myself against them."

"A curtain rod? What kind of weapon was that?"

"I'd been warned that freed prisoners on stolen bikes were following local people on bikes, and knocking them down to steal more bikes. In my young mind I figured that I could use the rod to knock them down first. Lucky for me I never met any. I'm afraid I would have lost more than my bike."

* * *

"Eberhard and I made our way up the winding roads to the ancient village of Arnstadt, where Sebastian Bach had arrived a few hundred years before us. We pedaled over the round cobblestones and past Bach's church. I imagined him inside, playing the organ he'd built, the only organ ever built with actual bells and whistles. When we rode through the village's long narrow lanes, my mind saw him walking there long, long ago, his head filled with organ music. Unforgettable images and sensations!

We went on, passing through Coburg and in and out of stretches of forest. We rolled into Bamberg, then on to Würzburg. As we'd been told by the CIA officer, we reported to the guard at the mammoth gate of an American prisoner of war camp to get the necessary discharge papers, which would get us through the American army checkpoints stationed ahead of us on the road.

The camp was filled with thousands of German prisoners, fenced in by barbed wire, rolls and rolls of it, on open rolling land. Those in disguise, inevitably grinning as they entered, caused waves of laughter and whistling among the men lying and sitting around. They watched the never-ending show of arrivals—men disguised as anything but German soldiers. All those that I'd seen on the road, pretending to be farm hands, or mourners, or on business—all of them—were here, now hoping for the papers to go on with, to get home.

Eberhard and I caused no whistling, just blank looks. Our future now depended on the scrutiny of the CIA. The first day we were told that prisoners were given no canned food for fear that they'd make the tin into weapons, some claimed machine guns. That sounded like an American joke to me. It was more likely the canned food had been sold on the black market.

We finally learned what was behind the bizarre interrogation by the CIA officer who'd inspected our underarms. Members of the SS had their blood type tattooed under their arms, an SS secret we knew nothing about.

After a few days, Eberhard and I were released, our walking papers in hand. Back on our bikes, we continued west. Somehow from the endless ant-like trail of former soldiers ahead of us, we were passed along information about where and when to catch a freight train heading towards Frankfurt. From there rails went everywhere in Germany, including Krefeld—to Greta. The very method of passing information was a mystery to me. I never understood quite how it worked. But it did.

Eberhard and I got a ride on a steam engine, at the very front, between the elongated wings of the boiler. My right hand held onto some part of the engine while my left held onto my bike. As the engine cut through the lazy summer air, the wind stung my face forcing my eyes to close to a narrow squint. I could barely make out the open country. Tears flowed down my cheeks for the entire length of the country that had just lost the war.

When we arrived in Frankfurt, I wiped my eyes and cheeks and looked down from the engine, surprised at how high up we were. It looked as if all trains—trains pulling endless chains of freight cars, both full and empty—stopped here, going east, west, north, or south, to get fresh engines before going on.

Long rows of freight cars sat on rusty rails, some filled with precious goods for the American GI's, the victors. There were no passenger trains. We climbed into a freight car and sat on the edge, our legs dangling over, along with others like us. We were all strangers, forced together by a similar fate, now traveling on an unauthorized free rail service along its squealing, screeching tracks. We marked time by listening to rumors and jokes, waiting for the next train north.

Someone opened a freight door, a hand-width, just enough to spill green coffee beans from a knifed-open gunnysack into his cap, held beggar-style. Coffee beans, the gold of the black market, poured like water into his hat, spilling a lot onto the ground. Swarms of us ran for a share, our arms outstretched with our caps to catch even a few. As Eberhard and I ran towards the opened freight door, someone on the roof of a canvas-covered car threw down some wooden boxes that landed right in our arms. Back inside our waiting freight car, we looked at the labels on our catch. Eberhard had eight gallon-sized cans of sour cherries and I had eight cans of uncooked hash browns, all destined for an American canteen. We got some gunnybags and tied the treasures onto our bikes.

The whistle blew. The train nudged its way north with us hanging on, like bees on a hive, heading along the romantic Rhine valley lined with vineyards and castles on steep mountain slopes. It was a world forgotten by all of us. We watched with tired eyes, squinting to block out the dirt and dust in the wind, while we held tightly onto our caches and bikes. We soon got to Cologne, not far from Krefeld and Greta."

♣ CHAPTER 11 ♣

"Alex, your story is fascinating, but I'm getting hungry so I'll go make us a snack. Maybe Greta will keep me company. John, would you look after the drinks, please?"

"Yes, dear. So, Alex, did you see Greta then?"

"Yeah. If you're interested, I'll tell you about it later."

I glanced outside, seeing nighttime shadows cast by the tree limbs. I was glad for a pause in telling my story. Reliving it through the telling was exhausting. John seemed to sense it and left me alone with my thoughts.

A little while later he spoke, "Alex, it's sure nice to have you and Greta come visit us."

"John, I always enjoy your company. We're both glad to be here. With you, I feel free to talk about my past, and somehow, in telling it, to rid myself of some of the burden of it. It was an overwhelming experience, especially because I was so young at the time."

Estelle and Greta returned with a tray laden with cheese and crackers and grapes. John had mixed more drinks, so we sat down again at the long table to feed ourselves—the potbelly stove being fed on the side. We made pleasant conversation. The food and drink disappeared quickly. We were warm and full and it had gotten very late, but John and Estelle wanted to hear more.

* * *

When we'd reached Krefeld, Eberhard—realizing how high the emotional stakes were for me in going to see Greta—let me go alone to the two-story red brick house. As I got closer, my heart started pounding harder and harder. By the time I got to the door I could hardly breathe. I was scared and anxious, wondering if she'd be there, wondering mostly if she'd want to see me. I stood back from the door a few steps, on the walk, as I listened to the bell chime. I checked my clothes quickly, making sure the flaps of my pockets were neat, as if somehow that was critical.

I rang the bell once more, my hand less sure. The door opened just a crack—revealing the face of Greta's little sister, wanting to know who'd rung. She recognized me and disappeared, yelling loudly, "Greta!" Seconds passed.

Finally, there she stood. She stared for some time, then said, "Oh it's you! What a surprise!"

I mumbled, "Yes, me." What else could I say?

Then Greta said, "Mutti, guess who's here."

We smiled at each other, stunned to be standing face-to-face after so long.

Her mother arrived, peering around the half-open door, then gave me a somber look, one I'd mentally prepared myself to expect. I smiled at her as widely as I could, trying to promote my chance of being asked in. "Come on in, my boy."

I smiled some more and thanked her, moving gingerly like a cat, weighing each step, into the living room where her mother, with a wave of her hand, invited me to sit on a stiff chair. She'd make us a cup of *Ersatz* coffee. Before she went to the kitchen, she gave me a penetrating stare, as if telling me I'd better behave. Misbehaving wasn't what I was thinking of right then. It was her innuendo that I'd been invited to stay for only minutes, not hours, as I'd hoped. I understood her meaning of *a cup* all right. But I'd come so far. I was determined to stretch out my stay, somehow.

Greta and I—my hands between my knees—sat across from each other, smiling. We were overjoyed, almost embarrassed, at seeing each other.

At the end of the hall, a little boy peeked around the corner, wanting to know who the world had let in. I stood up and waved. He disappeared. I sat down on the couch next to Greta, glancing around, my hands folded. There was old silver around the room, crystal of all sorts, and linen on the table. Greta and I exchanged side-glances, looking shyly, sweetly, at each other, all under the indifferent eyes of a former Princess of Hessen who looked down from a portrait on the wall.

Greta was the brave one, starting the conversation, by telling me that she was glad to see I hadn't lost my legs. I thought she must have misspoken. I asked if she meant she was glad I hadn't lost something like my mind. But she looked at my legs. I followed her eyes down my legs, stretching them out and towards her. She explained that after I'd written about being at the Russian front, she'd visited a fortune teller who had told her she would see me soon but not to be shocked. She would have to be brave because I'd lost both my legs. I was embarrassed to think she'd been worried by such rubbish. I slapped my thigh hard, laughing loudly, too loudly, which Greta signaled to me by putting her forefinger to her lips. I whispered that my legs were in good shape and had traveled a lot of miles already just coming to see her. And they had to be good for a lot more because I had big plans.

Then I remembered: that day running across the minefield when the old soldier had shot at me. Could that have been when the fortuneteller was dangling Greta's ring over my picture?

Her mother appeared like a dark cloud, with the coffee and a small piece of Greta's birthday cake, meant for the following day, her birthday that I knew nothing about. I was embarrassed by not knowing about it, of having come to eat her cake without bringing a present for the next day. At the table we sat stiffly with our put-on-your-best-behavior formal manners while I secretly longed to escape with Greta to the garden for a few minutes of privacy. I could see the garden through the window—so inviting. Her mother, knowing young desires, held onto her daughter, prolonging the conversation with tittle-tattle, useless bits of nothing, as she droned on and on, aging us, until…

Finally We Got A Chance
to slip into the garden,
on the pretext of checking the peaches,
and whatever else had ripened in midsummer.
We held hands all the way
to the back of the garden
where flowers hid in the wild grass.
We lay under the peach tree,
to look and smile at each other,
alone at last.
I was remembering the first time
I held her hand,
those four long years ago in the park.
She held up a peach,
smiling,
enticing me to take Adam's bite.
I curled my body up to her,
to her peach,
feeling joy in the bite,
as the juice ran down my chin.

As Eve, she took my hand,
and led me to her sandbox,
her little girl's land of dreams,
filled no longer with sand,
but with sweet memories
she shared with me.
I loved hearing her tell
of finding colorful stones
in the garden path

when she was three,
and how she'd saved them for years,
jewels in a small tin bucket.

Our hearts grew softer.
When it grew dark,
I dared to ask her to sit on my lap,
surprised when she did.
I kissed her deeply,
as long as she let me,
her response echoing my feelings,
confessing nothing,
but feeling much.

We heard the military tattoo
of the American occupation troops,
the curfew telling all Germans
to get off their own streets,
her waiting mother's signal
to call us in.

Inside, we sat on the couch,
holding hands,
hanging on to what we'd felt in the garden.
Too soon,
her vigilant mother called it a day,
and I was left alone in the dark,
still thinking of Greta,
now asleep in her room
directly overhead.

At breakfast her mother's eyes signaled to me, again and again, that it was time for me to go. I guessed it meant that I wasn't wanted; I was far too carefree for her Greta. She soon confirmed what I'd surmised, telling me outright that I should go, go make something of myself. It was what I'd feared hearing from her the day before, and somehow secretly understood.

I thanked her for her advice, kissed her hand and left. Greta walked me to the road. I swung onto the familiar saddle of my bike with a feeling that it was where I belonged. From the bike I still held onto her hand, smiled, then let her hand glide out of mine as I moved off down the road. I pushed hard on the pedals, hearing the air rush past, as I realized that I had a long, long way to go before I'd fit into Greta's world, if ever at all.

A spot on the road became Eberhard, waiting. We now had to find a place to get food. I remembered my aunt's farm near Bremen. The fastest way there was by rail, on empty freight cars.

My aunt looked upon us as good fortune, some strong hands to work on her farm. It took only weeks to change her mind. Eberhard ate too much and labored too little. He had to go, she said. He left the next night, silently disappearing into the dark shadows. I followed the next morning, now with a dream to make something of myself, as Greta's mother said I should.

Part of my dream meant heading back towards Greta. First I went to see a man selling horses and pigs. I'd heard he'd take my saved-up ration cards for a horse, an old one, no good one to anyone but me. He traded me a dirty white Mongolian horse, half-wild, for my stack of ration cards—the second part of my dream. The pony was small in size but big on biting, especially when I tried to halter him. I called him Alex. After all, he'd apparently come from Russia the same as I. Now we had to find our way together to make my dream come true, to go into business somehow, but the what and how of it I had to figure out along the way to Krefeld.

The first problem was basic—and daily. Alex had his own idea of what direction we should take. I pedaled hard, pulling the stubborn horse along behind me, frequently looking skyward, begging for help. He couldn't ride the bike and, because of his small size, I couldn't ride him, so I had to tow him west. There was no other way.

It was slow, but I soon learned I had a worse problem—

finding a place for us to stay at night. Late each afternoon I'd start looking for a farmer who might let Alex graze on his land during the night. There weren't many farmers along the way who would. The few remaining ones were constantly bothered by others like me, begging for water and hoping for bread. Most times the door was slammed in my face before I could ask. I soon found out that it would have been easier to travel alone. The bike and I could have slept anywhere.

Then I discovered the worst problem of all, which happened every morning—catching my stubborn, quick-footed critter. I got more than exercise chasing after him with promises and the bridle in the early morning dew. Worse, I sympathized. Heaven knows how many hands had driven, beaten, pushed, and coaxed him all the way from Siberia to Germany before I took over. Here I was, a kid, without as much horse sense as the pony that outran me every morning and had a horselaugh while doing it.

After he was bridled, sometime later, we'd make a few miles, his clop, clop behind me as I dragged him along. The land was flat, but the flowers and high grass growing along the roadside tempted Alex to graze as I struggled to keep him moving in the…

Midsummer
Despite my problems
it was midsummer,
summer at its best.
The sun shone every day.
And I began to feel
that this was a very special time for me.
I was going where I wanted to go,
cumbersome as it was.
And I began to see things
along the roadside
in the grass and fields
that I hadn't noticed before.
In the end I fell in love

with the everyday sun,
with Alex, and with life.

After a few days I met a band of Gypsies camping along the edge of the road. They eyed my horse first, then me, coming towards us with dark looks, meant to make us stay put. They zeroed in on Alex as if he belonged to them, checking his teeth and legs. Then my bike, acting as if I'd stolen it from them. They circled us. For some reason they liked what they saw and began to smile, gesturing. I had to barter with them. Or else. Would I trade the horse for a carpet? Or sell it for a good price? How about my bike? No, the bike wasn't for sale. I needed it. But I needed a harness and a buggy to carry out the plan I'd been formulating for when I arrived at Krefeld. And they had just the thing I needed. Yes, the bike plus some money would buy a buggy and a harness. I wondered if heaven had sent these Gypsies—or was it hell?

I'd saved some money selling the coffee beans and my half of the cherries and hash browns. I decided to try bartering. To see how I could make out. Back and forth it went. In the end I had a buggy with wooden wheels in back, worn rubber wheels in front, a gypsy-fixed-up harness too big for my Alex, and they had my bike and all my money.

After the first day's drive I realized they'd known how to trade me down. I was riding in a buggy so ugly it scared the dogs as I rode through the villages. But what the hell, the Gypsies were behind me and Greta was in front. I'd just make the best of it.

Riding up high in that buggy was a whole new world. I could tell what kind of surface I was driving over by the sounds made by the wooden wheels. Clatter meant cobblestones, announced already by Alex's horseshoes; creaking and squealing noises meant sandy ruts and gravel, and quiet hushing from the rubber wheels meant pavement. All that on one horsepower.

At midday I arrived at my first village. It was busy with a lot of people going about their business. They stopped and stared at us, their looks telling me how ridiculous we looked. I didn't blame them. What a sight we must have made, me looking down from the strange-looking Gypsy buggy hitched to a tiny white horse. But I have to admit, I relished the view, looking down on them. It gave me an exaggerated sense of being different from them, maybe better as I rode along…

On The Road To Krefeld
I passed them
and their barking dogs,
in the dog days of summer,
passed their crowded cottages
with picket fences,
and the stench coming from their barns,
oozing with manure
from bawling cows.

As I left a village,
a spire in the distance
located the next one.
Again and again,
past the up-and-down contours of the land,
I traveled from spire to spire
until lengthening shadows
in the trees and bushes
told me it was time
to find refuge for the night,
the time of day I enjoyed most—
when warm afternoon breezes
blew over the dry summer fields.

In one village,
there was a church,
embraced in both directions
by a row of crooked houses
that hung on to each other,

as if giving a last hug.
Just as I approached,
the bells peeled,
calling all souls from their tiny doors,
the low beams causing their heads
to bend down to get out.
They came out in dribbles,
like chickens coming out of the coop
in the morning light.
Old women in black
slipped outside
and headed toward the peeling spire.
Keeping their heads bent,
they took no notice of us
or the chickens
pecking in dusty soil,
or the swallows flashing about in the cow dung.
I did find bread and water for me there,
and stale hay for Alex.

Late the next morning we hit the road again, as we had every morning for many days now. We traveled through the gently rolling hills covered with green grass, fields in various colors and textures, nearly ready for harvest, and in between them, uncultivated flat brown fields. I enjoyed feeling the soft morning breeze against my skin. As I went along, both my dream to impress Greta's mother and what I could do with Alex and the buggy and myself in Krefeld, crystallized, mile after mile, into a concrete plan. I now knew what I could do.

As I neared Krefeld, I noticed more details around me, just little things, along the road that I hadn't noticed before. Again a village. Again the click-click-trap of Alex's hooves and the clattering cart wheels on the cobblestones. They had become music to me.

♣ CHAPTER 12 ♣

I knew Greta didn't expect me to show up again so soon. I'd just left weeks ago. I proudly parked my played-out pony in front of her house where it seemed only yesterday I'd said goodbye. I rang the bell, my heart pounding. What could I expect?

When she opened the door, it must have been a shock to see me standing there again, so soon, gazing at her. What a beauty! And her eyes! Under the spell of her stunning looks, I tried to act blasé, but reality set in—in the form of her mother's voice in the background asking sweetly who'd rung the bell. Being told who, her voice lowered an octave, like a curse, as she commanded that I come in. That told me she wished I hadn't come, but politeness required that I be invited in anyway.

Smiling from ear-to-ear, I entered the house and followed Greta along the dark hallway towards the living room, hoping to pass by her mother unscathed. As I passed by the kitchen door, I peeped out a hello. She answered by asking me where I was passing through to. That meant my stay was to be short for sure. I obliged her by telling her what she wanted to hear—that I was just passing through. Once inside, sitting down, however, I changed my mind. Instead of telling her what she wanted to hear, I gave my dream a chance by pointing at my pony outside the window while I blubbered out my hammered-out-on-the-road plan. Her face was blank. She looked stunned but said nothing.

I saw it as a chance to repeat all over again, as calmly as I could, that I hoped to start a porter service at the railroad station in Krefeld. I'd seen lots of people needing someone to transport them and their baggage. There wasn't any such service now. I should do well. I'd watched people with piles of boxes trying to get home, carrying each box from block to block, one at a time, keeping one eye on the box they'd left behind and the other on the box they'd taken up ahead, turning their heads to and fro, swiveling forward and back, running between their parked parcels. There was a real need for my service. I'd come all the way from Bremen to offer this unique service at the railway station in Krefeld so that I could be near Greta.

They looked at each other, then at me, then at my horse through the window. A long silence followed. The silence told me I'd become someone to distance themselves from. They shook their heads, both of them. I knew I couldn't change their minds because they came from an old world where only proven ideas were accepted. Their world couldn't solve a new problem with a new idea. Forget it! Certainly not any new idea of mine, especially one involving a pony and cart. Besides, it wouldn't be socially acceptable. What followed was exactly what I'd feared. Greta's mother, still standing at the window, looked at my Russian pony, then at Greta, and clapped her hands over her head, shrieking out her decision, "Greta, this boy of yours must go at once!"

I was being sent to the guillotine. I forced myself to smile at them and thanked them for having listened to my crazy plan. My extended smile was my last desperate attempt to convince them that I still wanted to make something of myself, to study, to do something honorable—something beyond my current plan—in order to hold onto my big dream, my dream of a life with Greta. I stood, totally devastated, but still smiling. I told them I would do what they expected of me, and that I'd better get started right way.

As I began to walk away, I hoped to be called back. Maybe they'd change their minds, telling me to stay and give it a try.

Silence. Nothing. I knew I had to find some other way to prepare myself for something I hadn't yet discovered. I knew I would do all right for myself in the end, somehow, but I also knew I would never be right for them—would never be accepted by them. Never. Even if I succeeded, I wouldn't fit into their world. I'd better concentrate on what was right for me alone. That's what I had to do. And that's how I left them, heavy-hearted, as I crossed the street to my horse, patted him, and never looked back.

* * *

Estelle pushed herself falteringly out of her giant-sized armchair, "Alexander, too bad it didn't work out for you then. What a boy you were! It's late, so I think we'd better turn in, but thank you for telling us your story."

We smiled at each other, got up slowly, wished each other a good night's sleep and as we headed for bed, John called out, "Don't let our *house-special* bedbugs bite."

Going up the too-steep steps to the slanted walls of our room, the peaceful night noises lured us out onto the balcony to listen.

"Greta, I just love listening to that stream. I can just barely see it out there where the lights from the cabin end. It's so beautiful out here. And I can just make out one birdhouse. Do you see it?"

"Yes."

"There are lots more in the trees. John planted them like a farmer plants potatoes."

"Not just planted, but made them too. Don't you think?"

"Yes, probably out of leftover scraps from building this cabin. He doesn't waste anything. You should see him puttering with the leftovers in his *playpen*, a shack filled with things he's found. He loves to putter. Smart people often prefer puttering to working, you know. But don't misunderstand; he can work hard too. He built a pond at the stream over there, making its walls out of thick slabs of shale he found near the streambed. That's heavy work, yes siree."

Early the next morning, I heard a sharp clink. John was building a fire, warming the cabin for breakfast.

We went down, feeling its warmth, the smell of frying ham in the air. We heard Estelle's morning work as she rattled around in the kitchen. We greeted her like guests usually do, early in the morning, overly friendly, a bit in the way.

She was comfortably nestled amongst the kitchen clutter, cutting grapefruit with a serrated knife, surrounded by the things she'd gotten out for breakfast—mugs and juice glasses, butter and jam for the toast. We exchanged pleasantries and sat down to enjoy breakfast beside John's cozy fire.

After breakfast John and I went outside to wander around. I couldn't resist peeling the curling paper-thin bark from some birches we passed. Their delicate twigs showed signs of spring, tiny dark spots ready to turn into buds. As we crossed a stone bridge, a cloud of black flies swarmed over us.

John chuckled, "This bridge doesn't belong to me anymore; it belongs to them. These clouds own it. They hang out under the bridge in damp rocky crevices, waiting for anything alive to pass by. I try to sneak past, but they get me every time."

"Those *no-see-ums* of yours carry knives and forks! I'm being eaten all over."

"Keep going; we'll get past them. I want to show you some of the pig iron the Yankees used for making cannonballs. The British came down from Canada, right through here, and chased the Yankees all the way to Washington where they burned the White House. There's still lots of their pig iron hidden around here, under the dirt and moss. To purify it, they probably made coke from the hardwood, got limestone from the nearby mountains, and carried the pig iron down from what is still called *Iron Mountain*, up that way. Here's some, see?"

"You know, John, I think this is just limonite, sometimes called meadow iron, oxidized mineral deposits brought down by the stream. Doesn't your stream still flood every spring?"

"Yes."

"Well, it's still making iron."

"You might be right."

"Now, don't show me any more hidden iron. Let me show you."

"How're you going to do that?"

"Get me a couple of wires, any wires, and I'll find some."

"Really? I don't see how. I have a hard enough time finding it, and I know every square foot of this place, but I'd like to see you try. Let's get some wire."

I trailed after John to his never-going-to-be-finished shack, his *playpen*, and stood in amazement at the clutter inside. Daylight coming through the cracks revealed slapped-up wooden shelves crammed full of boxes and boards and junk, all sorts of thrown-out stuff, seemingly useless, worn and rusty, packed clear to the ceiling.

"A mouse just ran past your boots."

"I probably scared the critter with my stirring around in here. There are a few living in here. They keep me company while I'm puttering around."

John came up with something that looked like a cable.

"Would this work?"

"It's fine, but you'll have to cut it. I need two pieces, each about two feet long. John, I meant to tell you something else about my pony. I sold him and the buggy to some guys on the black market for cash and canned meat."

John was sweating as he sawed on the rusty wire. The saw was dull with rust.

"Well, weeks after I'd sold them, I was still eating the canned meat when one day it dawned on me that it was horse meat. I'd sold my pony to butchers. I should have turned him loose in some pasture, somewhere to run free. But no, I was too busy with myself. After being rejected by Greta and her mother, I wanted to get rid of everything that reminded me of my failure with them, so I did it as fast as I could, not thinking."

"Don't you think someone else would have butchered your pony, sooner or later?"

"Well, I still shouldn't have sold him. He will never forgive me when I see him in heaven."

"Don't worry about that. You'll never go to heaven anyhow. You'll go to hell—just for that."

John was still sawing.

"Did you find that saw in the ditch too?"

"It's a little dull, but it's working."

In time he'd cut two wires, straightened them a little, and then handed them to me. I bent each into an *L* and took hold of the short ends, one in each hand, to allow the long ends to open outwards into a *V.* I began walking, slowly.

"Keeping the wires level and parallel is the trick. That's all there is to witching."

The wires opened to a wide *V*.

"There's pig iron right here, John. Did you see how the wires moved?"

"Yes. Boy, you must have sold your soul to the devil to be able to do that."

"No, you could do it."

"Really? Maybe I'll try it later, but right now I promised Estelle I'd run into Plattsburg for her."

"What for?"

"To buy a French newspaper, the *French Gazette*."

It was about an hour's drive into Plattsburg. The road was straight and the scenery flat, so we slid easily into talking.

"Alex. How does your mind react to girls?"

"What do you mean?"

"I mean, how does your mind react when you see a girl you find attractive?"

"When I see a gorgeous girl, one that gives my mind a *bang*, I immediately want to get to know her. But with the way life is, she usually disappears and I never see her again. She's gone and I'm left with an echo of the *bang*, with my mind seeing her again and again in an afterglow, until day-to-day events eventually push her picture into the background and she fades from my mind. That's the way it works with me. And it happens fairly often."

"You love Greta deeply, don't you?"

"Yes."

He probed, wanting to know how many girls I'd slept with. We talked about things that happened when we were young—when love is the devil—exchanging stories filled with bragging, bravado, excuses, and shame, the seduced and seducer, all rolled up together; somehow the visions of some got mixed up with others, none of them important today, and all the while the flat land kept rolling past us.

In Plattsburg we went to a newly opened grocery store where John showed me, waving his arms here and there, an electronic checkout system requiring no cashiers.

"The groceries are funneled along electronic conveyors that read the UPC codes, charge them to your credit card, and then release them into a cart for you to wheel out to your car. It's experimental, but it gives us an idea of how computers and robots will replace people."

"We should buy some shares in this company."

John walked off to ask for the *French Gazette*. He came back after learning the store didn't carry it until French tourists came later in the season. "The gas station across the way should have it."

John stopped for gas, and we headed back to the cabin.

"We forgot the paper for Estelle. What do we do now?"

"We keep going."

We were quiet, enjoying each other's company without a need to fill the silence. I was surprised at how quickly we got back. We saw Estelle on the porch, in her rocking chair, with her arms resting on its armrests, caressing the polished ends, as if holding back on some nervous thinking.

"Did you get the paper?"

"I'm sorry. I forgot."

"But that's why you went. Well—it's not the first time you forgot, is it? So, what did you do?"

"Looked around."

"Did you have lunch?"
"No, Choo."
"You're really something."
"But we had a good time, Choo. That's the main thing."

♣ CHAPTER 13 ♣

Estelle had spent time in her chair, with Greta sitting alongside her. They looked talked out. They asked me to stay and tell some more of my story, maybe getting closer to the end of it. John got some drinks to help us along.

"You'll remember that when I left Greta and her mother, I'd realized I needed to do things to please myself, not someone else. I had to make something of myself."

* * *

With that in mind I went to Berlin to find my mother, just to let her know I was alive and well. She wasn't hard to find. I knew who her friends were and soon found one who told me where she was. Once again I was amazed at how people knew these things by word of mouth. There was no telegraph, no telephone, no newspaper, and no postal service. There was nothing to buy, no running water, and no power. Most people lived behind drafty walls in the rubble, always cold, hiding, fearing the outside—but not my mother. She'd taken up quarters in a villa with some top-ranking Russian officers in Potsdam. After all, having lived in Moscow, she spoke Russian.

I eventually found the walled villa and rang the bell on the gate. Her head peered out of a tiny second floor window and she called down to ask who I was and what I wanted. I told her I

My Russian great-great uncle, Col. Meyer (*center*), with his co-physicians in the 1905 war with Japan.

My Russian grandmother, Aline Jordan, near Odessa, 1875.

Dad, a 1st Lieutenant in the WWI German Air Force, 1918.

Mom and Dad with me in Moscow, Russia, 1926.

Dad holding me at Novoslobodskaja No. 63.

Holding my *everything*, my scruffy Teddy.

First day of school in Berlin, dressed in my mother's hand knit clothing and a fine leather lunch bag with a banana inside.

My hoop and my scooter were my favorite toys when I lived with Dad in Kassel. Age 8.

My mother and stepfather in Berlin, 1941.

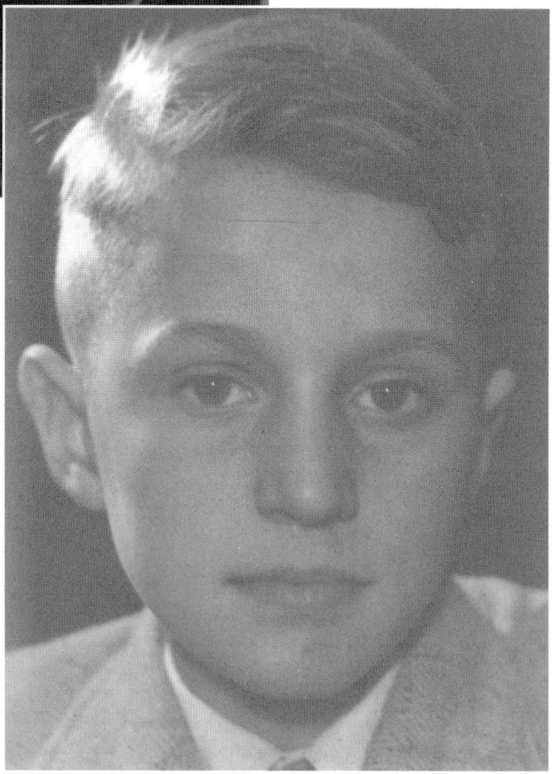

"My mother put bread on the table while my stepfather muddled through from one day to the next."

Age 14, when I was sent to Czechoslovakia.

Greta, age 3, finding colorful stones in the garden path that she kept as jewels in her tin bucket.

Sweet, innocent Greta in her garden in Krefeld.

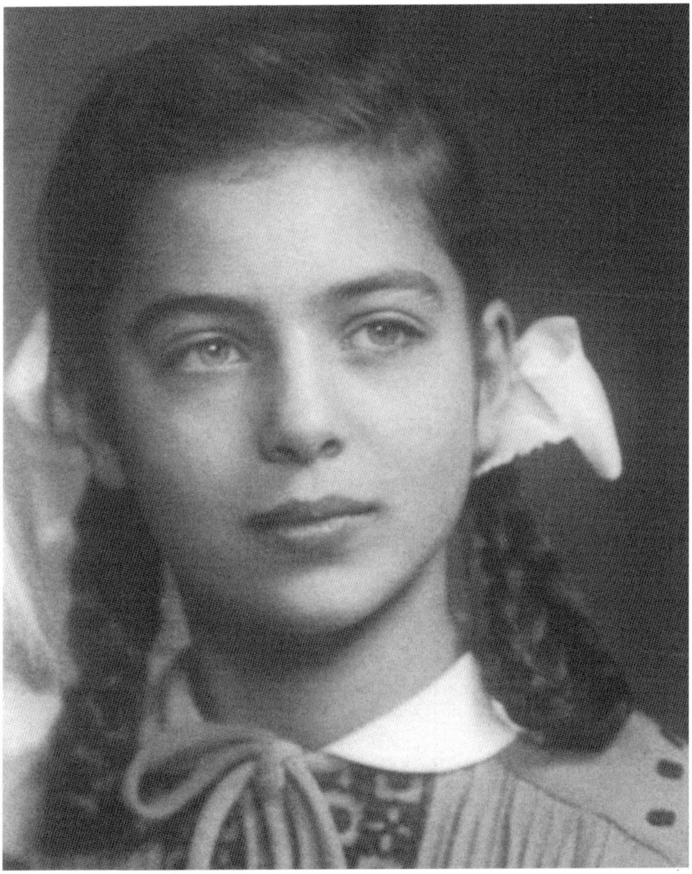

"I remember it still. She was like an angel fallen from heaven."

Greta, age 13, when I first met her.

Age 18, 1945, in the German Army uniform—quilted and down-filled—that I wore behind the Russian line, including a hood that we pulled over our faces for sleeping and hiding.

A portrait of Greta, wearing the dress she'd made from a bedroom drape—because no fabrics were available—to wear to her 17th birthday party in 1945.

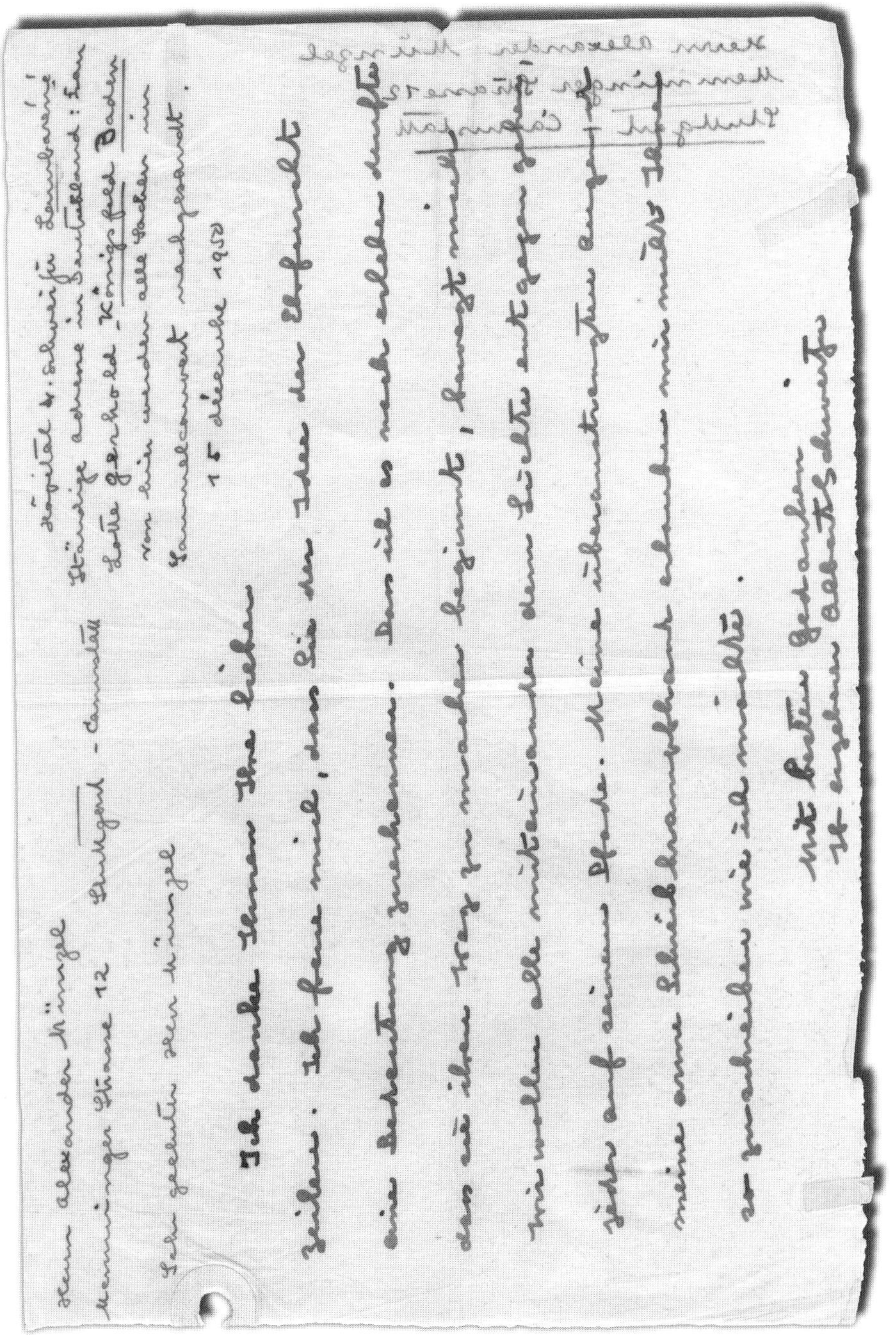
Herrn Alexander Hünzel
Memminger Strasse 12 Stuttgart - Cannstatt

Hôpital A. Schweitzer Lambaréné
Ständige Adresse in Switzerland: Frau Lotte Gerhold, Königsfeld Baden
von hier werden alle Sachen in Sammelcouvert nachgesandt.

Sehr geehrter Herr Hünzel

15 décembre 1950

Ich danke Ihnen Ihre lieben Zeilen. Ich freue mich, dass Sie der Idee der Ehrfurcht eine Bedeutung zuerkennen. Dass sie so rasch erleben durfte dass sie ihren Weg zu machen beginnt, bewegt mich. Wir wollen alle miteinander dem Lichte entgegen gehen, jeder auf seinem Pfade. Meine überanstrengten Augen und meine arme Schreibhand erlauben mir nicht zu schreiben wie ich möchte.

Mit besten Gedanken
Ihr ergebener Albert Schweitzer

My treasured letter from Dr. Albert Schweitzer, telling me he was delighted I'd found his "Reverence for Life" relevant. Signing it: *respectfully*. How humble are gods?

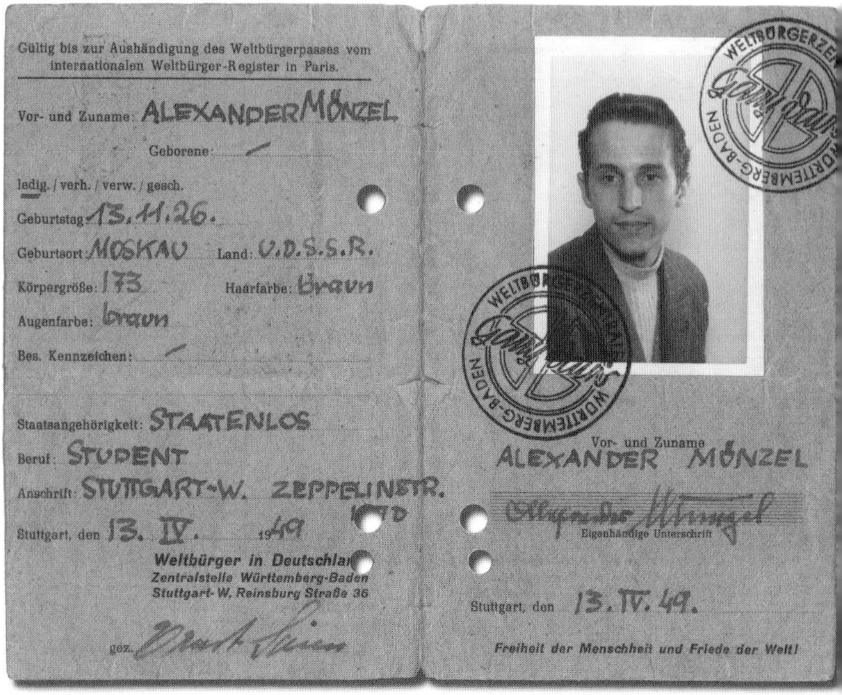

Gültig bis zur Aushändigung des Weltbürgerpasses vom internationalen Weltbürger-Register in Paris.

Vor- und Zuname: ALEXANDER MÜNZEL

Geborene: —

ledig. / verh. / verw. / gesch.

Geburtstag: 13.11.26.

Geburtsort: MOSKAU Land: U.D.S.S.R.

Körpergröße: 173 Haarfarbe: braun

Augenfarbe: braun

Bes. Kennzeichen: —

Staatsangehörigkeit: STAATENLOS

Beruf: STUDENT

Anschrift: STUTTGART-W. ZEPPELINSTR. 1?7D

Stuttgart, den 13. IV. 1949

Weltbürger in Deutschland
Zentralstelle Württemberg-Baden
Stuttgart-W, Reinsburg Straße 36

gez.

WELTBÜRGERZENTRALE WÜRTTEMBERG-BADEN

Vor- und Zuname
ALEXANDER MÜNZEL

Eigenhändige Unterschrift

Stuttgart, den 13. IV. 49.

Freiheit der Menschheit und Friede der Welt!

My World Citizen ID, issued in 1949 by the world citizenship movement founded by Gary Davis, an American GI living in Paris. It was an unofficial passport claiming that I was "*stateless.*" It was suppose to allow me to cross all borders freely, like every living thing except man. I was the first international traveler to challenge border guards with its validity.

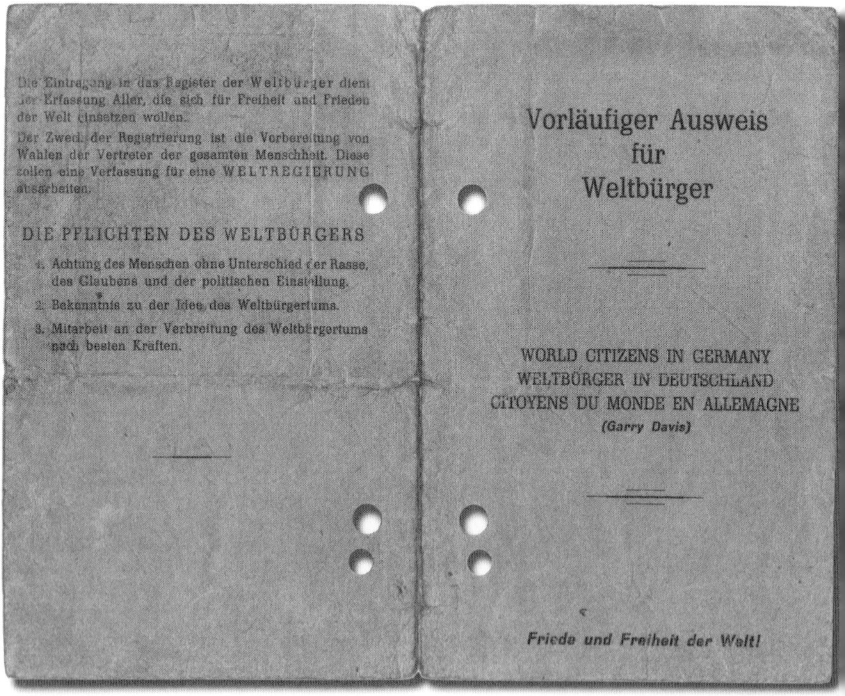

Die Eintragung in das Register der Weltbürger dient der Erfassung Aller, die sich für Freiheit und Frieden der Welt einsetzen wollen.
Der Zweck der Registrierung ist die Vorbereitung von Wahlen der Vertreter der gesamten Menschheit. Diese sollen eine Verfassung für eine WELTREGIERUNG ausarbeiten.

DIE PFLICHTEN DES WELTBÜRGERS

1. Achtung des Menschen ohne Unterschied der Rasse, des Glaubens und der politischen Einstellung.
2. Bekenntnis zu der Idee des Weltbürgertums.
3. Mitarbeit an der Verbreitung des Weltbürgertums nach besten Kräften.

Vorläufiger Ausweis für Weltbürger

WORLD CITIZENS IN GERMANY
WELTBÜRGER IN DEUTSCHLAND
CITOYENS DU MONDE EN ALLEMAGNE
(Garry Davis)

Friede und Freiheit der Welt!

Picture taken Aug. 15, 1949, on the deck of *La Canada* at "horse races" put on for the passengers, showing me melted into the crowd, a remarkable souvenir of my adventure as a stowaway.

Happy me, with my newly worked out plan to leave Germany.

Ticket stub of my streetcar ride in Marseille from the top of the hill to the ship in the harbor.

On board the *Kerguelen* I met a new friend, Francois Beslon, returning from South America.

Postcard of the *Kerguelen* on which I was sent back from Dakar, Africa, to Le Havre after being discovered as a stowaway.

STRASBOU

Un Français, J.-L. Rauzier a relev l'Egyptien Azzam au Pont de Ke

De l'autre coté du fleuve, un Allemand Citoyen du Monde, attend Garry Da

Un Français a pris, hier, la faction au pont du Rhin à la place de l'Egyp Azzam qui l'assura durant vingt-quatre heures.

Il s'agit d'un jeune étudiant de l'Ecole des Beaux-Arts de Paris, M. J. Louis Rauzier, 21 ans.

Aujourd'hui à midi, il serait remplacé par un Américain.

Par ailleurs, un Citoyen du Monde allemand s'est installé depuis mercredi soir à la gare-frontière qui sépare le territoire de Kehl du reste de l'Allemagne. Il s'agit d'un étudiant venu de Suttgart, Alexander Münzel, 23 ans. Il n'a pas de tente et a passé sa première nuit à la frontière à même le sol, enveloppé dans un simple sac de couchage.

Münzel déclare vouloir attendre Garry Davis qui doit passer par là pour se rendre en Allemagne au moment où il sera en possession du visa nécessaire.

Alexander Münzel n'est d'ailleurs pas un inconnu pour les autorités frontalières. En effet, nous relations au mois de septembre dernier, comment ce Citoyen du Monde, après avoir pris le train pour Marseille, s'était embarqué clandestinement à bord d'un navire qui l'emmena jusqu'à Casablanca, puis de là jusqu'à Dakar. On se souvient peut-être comment Münzel, arrêté par la police dans la capitale de l'Afrique Occidentale Française, fut ramené France par le bateau jusqu'au Ha puis refoulé en Allemagne après retour à Strasbourg entre deux darmes. Car en voyageant sans pa port, ce Citoyen du Monde vo prouver, comme le fait Garry D que les frontières ne sont que convention.

Par chance pour lui, Münzel fut pas poursuivi par la justice f çaise pour son voyage clandestin.

A la même frontière, des jou listes allemands attendent tou également la venue de Garry D en territoire allemand.

Ajoutons, par ailleurs, que le ting Garry Davis, fixé primitiven au Cinéma « Vox », aura lieu en finitive à la salle municipale de l bette, ce soir à 20 h. 30.

En effet, Garry Davis a es qu'il fallait permettre non seule aux spectateurs de cinéma, également à tous les sympathis de venir assister à ce meeting. plus ceci permettra d'avancer l'h de la manifestation (20 h. 30 au de 22 heures).

Au cours de cette soirée, G Davis exposera ses idées. D'au orateurs prendront la parole é ment, et le tout se terminera par séance artistique. Entrée gratuite

Newspaper article from the *Strasbourg Journal*, Dec. 12, 1949.

The story described my attempt to travel the world using my World Citizen ID and subsequent protest in *No-Man's-Land* on the Reine crossing of the German-French border where I'd set up camp to wait for Gary Davis, who was expected within a week.

was her son. She paused, looking more closely to see if I was for real, then turned into her old self, chastising me for looking uncombed. But as long as I was there, I'd better come in. As she closed the window, I wondered why I'd come and realized why my heart had sent me to find Greta first. I wouldn't be here long.

I was delighted to see my stepfather though, to see him happy, playing the piano as usual, night and day, for the Russians, and singing with them the sentimental songs that soothed the Russian persona. That ability and no more was reason enough for the high-ranking Russians to appoint him mayor of Potsdam, but under one condition. He had to add hot running water to the footbaths in the villa. Cold water wouldn't do. What they called footbaths, we called toilets.

After a couple days I left and went to Holzminden, where a school board offered courses to war veterans trying to get their senior matriculation. I tried it for a few months but couldn't settle down to study. And it wasn't because of Christie with the too-big boobies. I felt sorry for her because of that, and she felt sorry for me for being alone in the world, especially on my birthday, so she invited me to her home to have some place to celebrate. Her father managed a brewery so, for that alone, I took her up on the offer.

I remember that day as being a long walk in the dark, across flat fields in a cold winter wind, wearing my only suit, a light summer-weight one. There were no lights anywhere. The icy wind went in and out of my suit, remaining in my bones. In the distance the faint lights from the brewery kept me going, guiding me in the right direction. But it was a great party. The beer revived my spirits enough for me to stagger back home, braving the cold.

In a few months, spring arrived. Spring 1946. Time to move on. I didn't finish what I'd come for. I'd failed my courses. I decided to try something else somewhere else.

I went to Frankfurt, a big city, and a good place to start over—to try anything, even the black market, like others were doing. I dared to do it too. The black market was always busy. There were lots of American soldiers with cigarettes to sell. Soon I was part of the illegal underground. I became partners with a *mumser*, a Hebrew word for bastard, devil, redhead. My *mumser* was a redheaded Jew. We were busy, busy making money, mainly because he was trying to impress some blond girl with it.

We did all right for a few months until the American Military Police raided the black market where we traded. I was nearly arrested by the MP who stepped up to frisk me, but I was quick to give him everything I had—money and cigarettes—holding it out on my open palms. He pocketed it as quickly as I'd shown it to him, then had to let me go. My *mumser* didn't see things the same way I did. He figured what he had was his, and his belief landed him in jail for a few months where a Rabbi and I went to visit him. I figured he was bad luck, so I decided I'd better move on to a quieter place, some place away from there. I left Frankfurt.

I headed out into the country to try and sort out what to do next. I hiked through the land around Würzburg where farmers were now king of the land, untouched by the war. They'd had the basics and had kept them. I bummed through their villages, watching people at work, asking for bread and water and a place to sleep. It gave me some time to think.

After a few days, I felt renewed, freer, and began to enjoy following the curves of the land along the narrow dirt roads rutted by heavy cart wheels and the hooves of large farm oxen where…

The Fields Were Alive

with sounds of insects.
Everything smelled overripe,
ready for harvest.
I remember resting
beside a small stream,
lying in the tall grass

dotted with wild flowers,
finally beginning to feel like what I was seeing—
mist swathing the hills,
colors in the tree shadows,
a warm breeze closing my eyes.
Sometimes I closed my eyes,
and walked blindly,
slowly,
through the fields for a ways
then opened them
to see what new scene had appeared.
Swaying gold in the fields,
and the sun high overhead
became my new vision of happiness.
It was like a glimpse through
the window of heaven.

One day,
as I lay looking up into a tree,
I noticed that the leaves,
edged with brown,
were getting ready
to carpet the earth with soft colors.
It was time to find a place,
to put my body to work,
so I deserved to be in this wonderful land.

The church spire in the distance
rose over a village of houses,
huddled together.
Old women in black,
following the peeling of bells,
paused briefly to stare at me,
something I had long since gotten accustomed to.
I greeted them,
but they turned away,

soundless,
moving on to their church,
walking in a way that told me
I was evil not to follow them.
I sensed medieval sternness in this village.
I went on,
to another place with a spire.

There was no Rabbi to talk with, so I sought out the next kind man I could find—a priest. I begged him to get me a job on a farm, a place where I could stay and think for a while. I wanted to close the door on my past by doing hard work, to turn my mind away from the memories of war towards something new. As kind as he was, he did.

The farmer was a massive dark-eyed man with thick black brows. From the first moment I stepped through his door, he watched me closely, unaware that his daughter, who was my age, was watching me too, enticing me. What I saw was a plump young body, ripe for the picking. But *black-brow* knew what I was thinking.

I tried hard to please him, to put his mind at ease. I carried heavy sacks over my shoulder up long steep stairs to his airless attic, built a few hundred years ago. I stood waist-deep in his tall grass, cutting hay until the muscles in my arms burned from taking long sweeps with his scythe. And some days I spread manure over his fields, nauseated by the stench blowing in the wind.

Then, in the evening, I'd hurry to finish my last chore—forking dung out onto the manure pile—to get a seat at the table across from his voluptuous dark-eyed daughter, who eyed me and sent me flickering glances when her father wasn't looking. I thought someone was going to take advantage of his young daughter's curvaceous body, especially with the way she smiled and flirted with me. And I wondered how I could become that someone. Every evening of every day.

Sunday evenings I had off. I spent the easy evenings with the young men in the village, sitting around on a stone bench under the low-hanging leaves of a huge linden tree. Insinuating words flew laughingly back and forth about how voluptuous she was, what, how, and when I could do something to her. I explained that her father watched me constantly, with brooding eyes, knowing I was just passing through and eyeing his daughter any chance I got. He was suspicious of every gesture and word I uttered to her.

Once I confessed to the young men that she visited my mind often on the warm summer nights as I lay on the bunk in my room above the stable, but the daydreams never lasted long because the summer breeze brought the stench from the manure pile and with it, a return to the reality of my room where swatted flies stuck to walls from summers past. But the following Sunday, they'd make sure to ask what daydreams I'd had lately—just so that they'd have something to snicker about—and then asked more questions, wanting to know more than I had to tell.

Some days I got away from the farm, running errands with *black-brow's* favorite ox. I harnessed it early in the morning, anxious to get on the road to have some fun, flicking a thin stick at its back, imagining it was the farmer. It took half a day for the ox to plod along the dirt road to a mill where I'd get one sack of wheat ground into flour.

Some Sundays I had the whole day off. I explored the rolling countryside on a borrowed bicycle, riding towards the hills and an ever-present spire somewhere on the horizon. I enjoyed everything in between—sweeping soft gentle yellow and green fields. More often I walked, pushing the bike, feeling—after my long days of working in the fields—that I was now part of the land. One Sunday, I saw…

> ***Two Spires on a Church.***
> *Their peeling bells drew me closer.*
> *Alone on a hilltop*
> *towered an ancient monastery*

built for the glory of a religion
holding onto the past.
Its walls and roofs stood out
in sharp definition in the sun.
It was built on the hill
to impress the people in the valleys.
Muenster-Schwarzach
cloistered Benedictines in the spirit of Nursia.
It had stood for over twelve hundred years
to further their spirit in worship
and scholarly activities,
its monks shrouded in black robes and cowls.

I entered a stone courtyard,
magnificently constructed,
each stone perfectly fit to the next,
a haven of stones,
ingeniously interwoven,
somehow emanating a sense of love.
I became aware of a monotone,
prayers, barely audible.
Black statued rows of monks
faced each other,
stiff, hooded,
offering each other faceless faces
as they prayed in subdued tones,
lamentations.
I made out something like
"Incipit lamentatio Jerusalem convertere
ad Dominum Deum tuum."
I was spellbound.
This was their haven,
their heaven on earth.

They stood under a grand goddess-like Madonna.
One of the monks spotted me,

his beady eyes staring into mine,
countering my prying into their private doings.
Minutes later,
all went mute.
They left,
like a cloud fading away.
I heard their sandals hushing.

I peered along the columns to
where the black row now knelt,
heads bowed, hands folded.
Their whole heaven suddenly silent,
as silent as snow.
An eerie feeling overcame me,
an outsider,
in this strange silence
belonging only to them.
I wasn't curious anymore.
I needed to get out.

Unexpectedly,
from behind a large column,
a monk shuffled toward me,
the one who'd stared at me earlier.
He wanted to know why I'd come,
and where I was from.
His name was Theophil.
He was eager to show me his humble quarters.
There he held my hand for a moment.
As I glanced through his tiny window,
I saw roses blooming.
I became aware of his prayers
at the very instant he finished blessing me.
He still held my hand
while my eyes held the roses.
He begged me to stay

and share what he had.
I smiled and shook my head.
The roses somehow had reminded me of Greta.

I asked if he'd write some words blessing someone I cared for. He would—if I'd stay overnight. Then I understood. I left his room to write my own blessing, a poem about Greta, a rose.

By evening I'd returned to the farm where I'd worked the past few months. I looked over the fields and thought about the crop I'd cut from the land. I realized that fall would soon be gone. The earth was beginning to pale. I had planned to stay through the winter, but now I wanted to move on, to try myself in the world somewhere else, find my future some other way. I was done with this place. So I left the black-browed farmer and the voluptuous body I'd just dreamt about. I said good-bye to her unblinking eyes, mumbling a few words of farewell, while inside I complained at the fate that hadn't allowed me to do more than dream. I think they were glad to see me go, really. I was too strange to them, too different.

When I left, the sun took me in. As I walked into the rolling hills of leftover brown and yellow, the black-browed farmer soon became a blur in my memory. I wondered if my life would always be like this, coming and going from one empty place to another, meeting people always suspicious of my ways. One thing I knew, I'd never again imagine any ox I drove to be the *black-browed* one. I didn't know what would come next, but I did know what I was taking with me—the will to better my life.

I hopped a freight train to Mannheim. Standing erect, tie-fitted, I found lodging and work at an American army canteen as a busboy. I watched some American soldiers throwing a ball back and forth on the street, catching it with an oversized brown mitt, yelling at each other and laughing a lot. I didn't know what game they were playing. It was just something American, all new to me.

At the canteen I met a waitress named Marianne, a blond horse of a woman, with big breasts, as friendly as their size, and probably because of them, a favorite of an American colonel, a carpenter back home. I thought it strange that a carpenter could become a colonel, but I soon learned that was part of what America was all about. Opportunity to get ahead wasn't based on social status.

There wasn't much money or food there for me, so I moved on to a job as a messenger boy at another army base nearby. I delivered messages by bike within the base. That's where I met Paul, a kind and very, very strong German—no, the strongest man I've ever met. He was a cook at the canteen. He boasted that he could lift a tobacco bale weighing a thousand pounds, from the ground up onto a rail car. He had a funny build, as broad as he was tall.

He told me about three Polish refugees who tried to mug him one night. He laughed as he told how he grabbed one guy in one hand and sat him on a four-foot-high stone wall, then took the other two by their necks, bashed their heads together, and walked away as if nothing had happened. He was my hero at that place. I wished I was like him. And I made sure I was his friend.

Early morning at the canteen was the most important part of my day. The first morning I watched some soldiers eating cornflakes in milk with a huge chunk of butter and lots of sugar—butter and sugar had been scarce for a very long time—so right away I tried it and liked it so well that I had it for breakfast every morning after that. Eating like the Americans made me feel like I was more important than was good for me.

I met a girl who worked in a bakery. She was horse-faced, overweight, and blond. At the time I preferred brunettes. But she talked sweetly to me, from behind the counter where all the baked goods were to be had—on ration cards, that is. She wanted me and I wanted what was behind the counter. She wanted to give me anything, everything, herself and the baked goods—without ration coupons. Although she gave me the goodies, I never took her up on anything else. I did take her out once. We walked down to the river to count ships.

♣ CHAPTER 14 ♣

"Weeks passed and I realized I wasn't going to get ahead with a girl who wanted more out of me than counting ships. I'd heard there was money in buying and selling locally grown black tobacco, grown even during the war—those 1000-pound bales Paul had talked about—so I pulled up stakes and headed for Heidelberg where the Americans had a large army contingent.

I studied the goings-on at the railway station to learn how the black market worked there and how I could fit in. The dealers were mysterious-looking figures who dickered with their customers along the dark walls. I was scared of those dark walls, but knew I had to risk being part of it in order to make any money.

In the beginning I felt like I'd committed a crime just by walking into the station, or by standing and waiting around. I had to steel myself against it, my stomach in knots. I just had to learn what to do.

After a few days I knew how to find a buyer. I learned to look people in the eye and learned that in order to make a sale I had to keep looking around as if watching for other buyers, trying to give the illusion of being a hot seller. I had to be casual, moving and walking all the time, trying to blend in with the crowds coming and going at the station.

We sellers got to know each other. It was like belonging to some kind of club. We knew what was selling, where, and at what price. There were good sellers and bad sellers. The bad ones I learned to avoid. They always got caught by the American MP's who raided the black market frequently, in an effort to move it away from the station where people moved in and out in masses with the continuous trains coming and going. But the buyers were in those masses, so the sellers were back in the station within minutes after a raid.

We kept on the alert for the raids by watching for suspicious people or signs, mostly signs, as we bartered, our eyes shifting back and forth all the time. And we had to watch out for counterfeit money too. We tried to take advantage of the buyers. Sellers had the edge because buyers wanted the goods right away or a time and place to get them by the next day. It was all a game—standing, waiting, looking for a buyer who wanted to barter, then a quick haggle in a dark niche or corner.

One veteran hustler had a steel arm—a replacement for the one he'd lost in the war—that was always filled with dollar bills. He was the pro, stealth written in his movements. I tried to learn from him by watching him deal. His secret was how to convert the weaknesses and secrets of others into profit for himself. He searched for clues in the buyers' faces, figuring out how much to ask. He'd try to maneuver his customer's face into the light to read it better. And he could tell when trouble was coming. I kept one eye on him all the time just for that reason.

After a while it became easier to stand and wait for the right person to come along, the one who wanted whatever I was selling. I had one steady customer, a guy with a gap-toothed smile who was easy to deal with. In time it became fun to find a buyer. All I had to do was talk. In a few months I felt like a veteran myself, selling goods for at least double what I paid. Often buyers wanted something unavailable, and wanted it immediately. For that, they had to pay dearly. After a few months, I'd bartered a small fortune by selling cigarettes, cans of this and that, antique Meissen porcelain, cameras, etc.

One day I heard that the local authorities suspected me of being a spy for the Russian army, paving the way for the Russians to move into their town. I was shocked to hear this from a known communist, a wholesaler who dealt in two types of rationed commodities—potatoes and coal. He said that they were sure I was a Russian spy because I was born in Moscow. Being an avid communist he liked the idea that had been whispered in his ear and hoped I was on his side. He had asked me if it was true. I gave him no more than a smile, admitting nothing. Besides, what would he expect a real spy to confess to? Saying nothing was confirmation to him, so my landlady got plenty of potatoes and coal delivered for no money, no ration cards, and no questions asked.

That was enough for me, so I moved on and found less exciting lodging with a Jewish couple, near the station. The man was a *hiner-fresser*, an old man, but nice. Soon I didn't have to go to the station to make deals because I'd developed different contacts by then and dealt in large quantities with a partner. Things went smoothly until I lost most of my cigarettes in a break-in, worth thousands and thousands of marks. One day the old landlord pointed out the window at my partner walking by, whispering that he was the one he'd seen breaking into my place. That was one lesson about partners I never forgot.

A few days previously I'd given him a carton of cigarettes and a diamond ring for his birthday. And a week before that I'd sent him to Dresden to trade some of my cigarettes for silk stockings. When he returned, he told me Russians had busted him at the border. I now suspected what had happened to the silk stockings I was going to send Greta. She was still on my mind.

There were all sorts of places to make deals. On weekends I took the train into the country to trade cigarettes for bacon or meat, or a goose, whatever. On one trip back from the country, I met a Dr. Bremkamp and his friend. They'd dealt in the country too. Sitting across from me I could see that they'd gotten bacon and plenty more, enough for the party they invited me to after

I'd kept the doctor amused throughout the jiggling ride on the train's hard bench. He didn't fit in with the rest of us, average people like me, holding onto my backpack, and the farmer's wife beside me, holding her basket on her lap with strong working hands. The doctor looked overdressed, very much the bourgeois gentleman, with a hankie in his pocket and manners to match his elegant cuff links and somber tie. He looked like I'd like to look when I got to his age, which I guessed to be twice mine. The young man next to him appeared to be more like him than the rest of us.

So I went to their party. I was fascinated by the kind of people I'd never gotten to know after the war, upper class people with overly fine manners, almost feminine. The party lasted so late that I was invited to stay overnight and to sleep on a mattress on the floor of the doctor's room. After an hour's talk in the dark, he told me plainly that he couldn't sleep unless I came into bed with him. I told him, in no uncertain terms, that he had to sleep by himself, and I had to get some sleep, by myself. He didn't give up, threatening to kill himself if I wouldn't sleep with him. He threatened to bang his head against the rocks lining the garden path, something he'd done before, he confessed. I told him to go ahead. The moonlight would light his way. That shut him up.

The next morning, as I walked down the stairs, I passed him on his way up. He'd been waiting for me; he grabbed me, hugging and kissing me with the passion that must have built up throughout the night. Shocked, surprised, and confused, I reacted by punching him, hard, right and left. He just put up his hands, stared at me in disbelief and excused himself effeminately. Later, at breakfast, we talked normally, acting as though nothing had happened. He told me that he had just been visiting Heidelberg and was returning to Dusseldorf where he owned an insurance company.

Dusseldorf was near Krefeld, where Greta lived, so I put two and two together and asked if he'd be willing to go with me to visit her. Maybe I could impress her and her mother with his fine manners and gentlemanly looks, an appearance that commanded respect. He impressed me, so I figured he should impress Greta too. He quickly agreed, perhaps to make up for his behavior or maybe hoping for another chance with me. Ironically, he was willing to try anything to get on my good side and I was willing to try anything to get on Greta's. In the back of my mind I suspected both plans were doomed to fail. The truth was I think I'd just talked myself into an excuse to see Greta again.

We went to visit Greta, as planned, to impress her with Dr. Bremkamp's presence and elegant talk. She didn't know what to make of him, so I cut the visit short, the sooner the better, to protect whatever might be left between Greta and me. I'd blundered again, the third time, leaving my childhood love in shambles. Now Dr. Bremkamp wanted me as I wanted her, and since I wasn't interested in his wants, I left him the next day.

It was winter, Christmas 1946. I needed to find a place to make money, and in the afterglow of having seen her, I decided I would try to do it the way Greta wanted me to, to work my way up the honest way. I could think of no more honorable job than with the American army. The job agency had only one opening, one I couldn't possibly fill. They needed an organ player for the chapel. There were no other jobs, so I took it with a what-the-heck attitude.

I got past the guard and into the 7719th Army quarters. The chaplain was waiting for the organ player the agency had told him was on the way. I started by stuttering a bunch of excuses, to soften him up, and when I thought he looked mellow enough, I told him the truth, hoping he'd let me sweep the chapel or clean the organ I was supposed to play. He looked more than shocked. I stuttered more excuses and kept talking until he finally understood I was hungry and alone in the world, and besides, it was near Christmas. In the end, his chaplain's heart arranged for me to have a job as a cashier in the officers' mess, all done within minutes. It wasn't just his kind heart or my ability to persuade, but the spirit of Christmastime that really got me the job. I thanked heaven for Christmas.

The job was just what I needed. As a cashier I could get my hands on some American dollars from occasional tips. My luck continued in the form of the mess supervisor. She had a permanent wide-mouthed smile, a curvaceous figure and dyed-black hair, along with a kind heart and an interest, I suspected, in my ten-year-younger body. After the first night's work, she asked if I had a place to stay. Just like any girl asking that kind of question, she got a pat answer, so she invited me for a drink and I stayed at her place, sleeping on her couch in the same room she slept in. Nothing more. I had to keep my job, and I hadn't figured out yet how and where she fit into my job security.

After a few weeks, we began taking walks, playing in the snow with her dog, and enjoying our time off work together. More weeks passed of sleeping together in one room like sister and brother, until one day in the spring sunshine, while rolling around in the last snow of the winter, to our surprise, we fell in love. I was in love. But it wasn't a good idea for us to work at the same place, so I got an honorable discharge from the 7719th.

I went back to doing what I'd learned best, wheeling and dealing in the black market while making love with my now ex-supervisor. While most people around us barely scraped by, we enjoyed life with all it had to offer. It was now almost two years after the war. Most things and most people still didn't work and people had little more than hope.

The black market existed everywhere people normally gathered, like the railroad station and the park. One day as I was closing a deal in the park, an MP began watching my every move. He followed me wherever I went, for days, until finally I challenged him. Why was he following me? He hesitantly confessed that he liked me. If I didn't mind, he'd like to stick around; maybe I'd learn to like him too. I knew I had no choice. He was the law. I had to go along with him without letting him morally melt me down.

I played him along for months, but at a distance, with kind words and friendly gestures, because I could use protection from the law in my dealings. After a while word got around that he was my special bodyguard, perhaps in on the deals, so people streamed in to make deals with me. What a spin-off! The money rolled in, with him always a short distance away, like protection. It worked well until one day I took the train, leaving for good. He'd gotten too close for comfort. Promising to come back, I waved good-bye.

It was Greta's birthday. I was going to visit her, my pockets full of money. I had learned that she would be at Kulmbach, near Hof. Her uncle had arranged a birthday party for her at his carpet factory. He must have known what Greta's mother thought of me because he'd arranged for another suitor to be around Greta the whole time. I got one dance with her the entire evening. I knew it meant I'd better go back to where I'd come from. I sneaked away from the party, my fourth strike out, and returned to Heidelberg.

An elderly music instructor, who had an eye for me, persuaded me to take singing lessons from her, free of charge, of course. She claimed I had a natural voice to become a great singer. She taught me how to open my mouth and hold a note, often standing too close, blowing her breath into my mouth to show me how to breathe. I couldn't stand it for long. She never knew why I left so suddenly—her bad breath.

One day that winter I ran into my old supervisor from the officer's mess. She took the opportunity to tell me good-bye; she'd met someone else. She gave me a small wooden elephant, telling me to be strong like him, fear no one and always do right. Another good-bye in my life.

I decided to go to the Alps, remembering the snow and the sun and the sky in the mountains all those years ago near Zakopane. A different world awaited. The peaks were calling me to come closer. I climbed upwards on my skis, felts strapped underneath, taking thousands of steps, alone in the silence of the snow, until, at last, I reached the top where I stood gasping for breath. But now I knew why I'd taken all those steps—

The View
There was nothing but mountains,
as far as I could see,
with the sun shining down
and a carpet of clouds below.
My eyes flew with my soul
to the distant mountains,
paying my respects to them,
to the mountains who ruled this paradise,
this cool and sublime grandeur
made up of majestic mountains
who rule a paradise
just by being.

What a sight! I closed my eyes, capturing everything. My eyes stayed closed until cold breezes alerted me that the sun was leaving the snow-capped peaks. The clouds cleared.

It was time to ski down. I flew past the rocks and trees and down graceful trails reaching the bottom in only an hour, traveling the same distance that had taken me hours, from dawn to late afternoon, to climb. At the foot of the mountain I glanced back to take in one more incredible sight—the sun setting behind a rugged peak, edging the stone in sharp black. I stood for long seconds, my eyes and mind soaking up memories for later, much later. The mountain was inside me now. I turned and headed back towards the village, gliding along the icy road with extra-long skating strokes.

♣ CHAPTER 15 ♣

"I was off to Stuttgart to plot my future, to learn some respectable profession. I took an aptitude test for war veterans at the University. It resulted in my studying architecture, which required a prerequisite. I had to serve an apprenticeship—in plastering—to learn the trade by helping and watching them work. Before the plasterers even let me watch, they had fun with me, making me run—and I mean run—up a five-story building, carrying their supplies to them—water and sand and gypsum—on a wooden backpack. They never failed to laugh at my huffing and puffing. To me they soon started looking as mean as the black-browed farmer I'd tried to impress by carrying hundred-pound flour sacks up to his attic. It wasn't a voluptuous daughter now that kept me going, but their secret of how to plaster. The time I spent gasping for air at the top was long enough for me to watch them work and memorize details of how the goo was mixed, how it went onto walls differently than onto ceilings, and, most importantly, how to make a smooth finish. By the time I'd finished the apprenticeship, I figured I knew all about plastering.

Home was a room I shared with a gifted student named Hans, also studying architecture. He was kind and tall and lucky enough to be supported by his parents. I supported myself by staying in touch with the local black market, making a few *reichsmarks* there, and then riding the train into the country on weekends to trade anything I had with the farmers for food. Coming home from one pack rat excursion, Hans and I laughed ourselves into tears when I pulled a squealing piglet out of my backpack.

All in all, my days were hectic. Some days I studied, some days I found food and, in between, found time to do laundry and sew on lost buttons—too many jobs. Sometimes it was impossible to keep up with the day-to-day tasks necessary just to exist.

Occasionally Hans and I cooked noodles on a hot plate, but we had to be quick to keep from being caught by the landlord. Cooking in our room was forbidden. We'd sling down the food quickly fearing a surprise visit from him while the burner was still hot. Eventually we got caught. He took us to court, wanting us out that very day, just before Christmas, but the judge let us stay over Christmas, so until we moved, we ate dry uncooked oatmeal, chewing and chewing it. They were tough days but good ones.

Then lightning struck—national currency reform had replaced Hitler's old *reichsmarks* with *deutsche marks*. Everyone in the country was given twenty *deutsche marks*, no more. Overnight my only way to earn money was gone. The black market disappeared. Now everything and anything could be bought with the new currency. Stores were filled with everything anyone could want. Everyone wondered where all that stuff in the store windows had been the week before.

I got part-time jobs to try to earn enough to live on while going to school. One consisted of marking crosses and lines on tickets from the national soccer lottery. I made a little spending money, but it wasn't enough to live on. By the time I'd finished my first year at the university and summer had arrived I had a new companion—constant hunger. I lost so much weight that my teeth became loose, so loose that I was afraid they would fall out.

I needed a better job, so I went to the Student Union that

brokered job referrals between employers and students. The Swiss government was seeking farm help—about fifty students for the summer—to be given free room and board and to be paid 300 Swiss francs for three month's labor—hard labor I'd find out. But it was my ticket for the summer.

On the slope of a mountain near Lake Bodensee at Rorschach, I lived on a farm with a hook-nosed farmer, his family and an old helper, together with four horses, some cows, an ox, and lots of small critters.

I started at five in the morning, and within minutes, sweat was running down my face as I mucked out the stables and put in fresh straw. Around seven the helper and I ate a breakfast of white bread dunked in a mixture of oil and vinegar along with some cheese and milk. Then we hiked up to the mountain meadows where cut grass on the slopes had to be turned and turned, over and over, until it dried into hay while the muscles in my arms and back turned into a mass of pain. At noon we were rewarded with a substantial lunch, then chased back up the mountain to carry on for the rest of the day. In the evening I cleaned the stables again, then fed and watered the animals.

Part of cleaning the stables meant pushing a wheelbarrow—heaped so high that I couldn't see in front of me—along some planks running up onto the huge manure pile. Every night and every morning. At the top of the pile I'd rest, leaning on my pitchfork, my friend. I knew every inch of it, handle to prongs, after the one day when the old helper had jumped me and tried to push me down in the hay for sex. In the struggle I'd held the prongs of the pitchfork up to his face. That settled it for the time being.

When I complained to the farmer about the assault, his shrugging shoulders and blank face told me I'd have to look after myself, every hour of every day, and through the nights while we slept in the same room. The pitchfork was my best friend. I kept it close at hand day and night. He watched my every move. I don't know how I managed to stick it out.

Weekends were different. I borrowed a bike from the farmer

and went cycling along the Bodensee with some of the village kids. We bought chocolates and swam in the lake. Some Sundays I swam on my back for a mile out on the lake where the feeling of warmth from the sun on my face revived me.

In time, my chores got easier. For one thing I got into shape and got used to the hard work, so the old helper left me alone, realizing I'd now be too tough to take on. Then cherry season started. I enjoyed that, standing on a ladder high in a tree, filling both the basket hanging from my belt and myself with cherries. I watched the clouds moving through the leaves with the sun shining in my eyes. From up there everything seemed different. I had a giant's eye view of the world, with wafting sweet smells from the cherries and ongoing breezes ruffling the leaves. It was quite a world. I'd found a happy place on the farm.

The wholesome food put on the table by the good farmer, combined with the hard work, transformed my skinny body into a block of muscle, ready for new and bigger challenges. When the clouds moved north, so did I. Summer was over. Time to say good-bye. The farmer, who'd looked so tough the past three months, actually cried. I was glad I'd worked out so well that he'd actually miss me.

Back in Stuttgart, Hanna waited for my return. She was a good soul but had a peach-fuzz beard I couldn't stand the sight of. Poor thing. Hanna knew how I felt about it. She wanted me to meet her parents because I was kind to her. She appreciated my kindness, doing whatever she could for me, bringing me flowers and books by Heinrich Heine. But I had to say good-bye to her too. I was leaving school.

I couldn't keep going to school. I couldn't study and make enough money to survive on at the same time. I had to change my life. But how? What? Somehow I had to be free. After returning from the summer in Switzerland, living in a free country, I once again became aware of my inner longing to be free. I didn't belong in Germany. I never did. As far back as I could remember I'd been resisting being forced into a role I hated—over and over—the *Jungvolk*, the *Arbeitsdienst*, and the army—all those German ways that demanded I blindly obey.

I despised control, the very-German mentality of creating perfect order, of building reliable tools and machines. Man isn't a machine. I knew that at ten. Even that young I knew this land, where everything was controlled, was not my land. Without knowing it, I'd been biding my time, waiting for a chance to be a free man. Now was my chance.

It was time to find a place to be free, a free country somewhere, anywhere. At the end of the war, Germans, with very few exceptions, weren't allowed to leave Germany or have passports. The only legal ID I had left was my Russian birth certificate, which I decided to leave behind. Instead, I would take my World Citizen ID—an unofficial passport that said I was *stateless* and was permitted to cross borders anywhere, like every living thing with the exception of man. It had been issued by the World Citizenship movement that had been founded by Gary Davis, a former US soldier then living in Paris. I'd joined the movement at the University, and now dared to travel the world with it.

I knew I had to get as far away from Germany as I could. I poured over maps, choosing Africa. I don't remember why. I had no way to get there legally, so I needed to first get to a country with overseas harbors. France, I decided, so my first challenge was to get into France somehow. For that I needed a place where a German road ran alongside the French border. From there I could watch the French patrols to find a place to cross at night under a full moon, using the skills I'd learned prowling behind the Russian front. I found a place on the map where a German road ran alongside a French town, Lauterbourg, near Strasbourg. It was only a few days until full moon, so I got busy taking care of the rest of the details I'd thought out.

I had to travel light, so I had a tailor make me a durable corduroy suit that would look somewhat dressy even unironed. I got him to sew tiny pockets under each armpit and in the back seam of the pants to look like part of the lining. In them I hid rolled-up foreign currencies, and some gold and diamonds. I packed a plain zipper case with some shorts and socks, a toothbrush, soap, a shaving kit, and some chocolate. And I topped myself off with a straw hat, trendy at the time. I figured it would make me look kind of casual. Lastly, I took a raincoat I was sure to need.

I was ready to go, but first I had to say my good-byes to the people I cherished. Greta was at the top of my list. The good-byes were brief, and to the point, leaving a bit of my heart in each place.

I saw Greta for an hour or so. I traveled quite a distance to see her, to inhale her scent, to take a bit of her with me. She'd always been kind to me and considerate, too considerate. It was her nature to be that way with everyone. Thank heaven that included me.

I pleaded gently for the chance to be hers forever some day. I would do, I would achieve, something worthy of her. She listened and gazed, but was silent. That was the end. I knew. I had no place in her dreams, and I was devastated again. My last lingering hopes evaporated. My body grew heavy, my legs shaky. It was finally time for her to see me off—again—walking along the curved brick wall I knew only too well from previous good-byes. I leaned against the wall I'd cursed before, standing next to her, but looking ahead, past her, forcing myself to get used to not seeing her, perhaps forever. I wanted to talk, but couldn't. The streetcar arrived. I didn't know if Greta was standing where I'd seen her last, as I grabbed the handrail to pull myself up. I purposely didn't look at her when the car pulled away, with me its prisoner, compelling me to leave what was most precious to me. I stared through the rear window at the receding rows of houses that slowly became the horizon. I suspected she was glad to be rid of me, perhaps for good. And I now realized that she was the only reason I hadn't left Germany any sooner.

♣ CHAPTER 16 ♣

I said my good-byes to the others and was off. I took the train south towards Lauterbourg, France and got off on the German side. From there I studied the border crossing where a steeply bowed stone bridge led right into the town. French border patrols stood guard, paying no attention to me, talking casually, but observing everyone and everything crossing. I took my time and watched carefully, watched the lucky people crossing legally. I could see no way to cross there unseen by the guards, so I now knew that I was about to commit a crime. I had to cross the border illegally. I became tense, unsure of my plan, wavering, anxious about what might happen. Evening came quickly.

I walked along the German road I'd found on the map. It ran north, parallel to the French border, alongside a forest and opposite a stream that was the actual border. After half a mile, I slipped into the edge of the German forest and hid under a dark bush. From there I could look across the empty road and over the creek to the French side. In the moonlight, I tried to see what I could hear—dogs barking and guards yelling. I soon placed them, then determined the best place to cross unnoticed. It was time—take the gamble or forget it. I made myself go.

I rushed across the empty road and into the bush-lined creek, then froze. A large leaf-covered sign I hadn't seen from my hiding place: *Achtung Mienen*. "Warning: Minefield." I hesitated. What now? In front of me: France—hope. Behind: Germany—failure. I went for hope.

I moved slowly, step-by-step, well aware of the danger of hidden mines. Maybe some French guard was hiding in the dark shadows waiting to shoot me like the old man at the last minefield. Once past the sign I continued to inch ahead, checking the ground for mines in the moonlight. It was taking too long. I started to run, expecting the worst with every step. The next step could be it. I concentrated on what was in front of my feet, at the same time peering hard into the dark places where a French patrol could be hiding. Mentally ready to step on the unwanted, preferring to be shot, I ran and ran, hoping I'd passed beyond the minefield but still fearing the worst. I was exhausted but kept running, driven by fear, not realizing in the dark that I'd passed through a wet marsh several hundred yards wide and up a bank to an elevated rail bed. I threw myself down on the hard steel of the rail, relieved. I listened for dogs and voices, and watched for moving shadows in the flat fields up ahead. Nothing. Silence. Then, slowly, exhilaration, a strange joy grew inside me. I might be in France.

I crawled carefully across the railroad bed, down the bank and into the flat field, staying as close to the ground as I could. I was in a freshly plowed field. I wormed my way into a deep furrow and snuggled into a trough of dirt to wait for daylight, to see where I was. I covered myself with my raincoat, for camouflage and for protection against the swarms of mosquitoes. Exhausted, my mind blank, I slept.

A loud shout, *"Allez,"* startled me awake, still under the raincoat, soaked and covered with mosquito bites. I peeked out to see a farmer bawling at his oxen in the hot sunshine. He was near enough to see me. Panic. Blood pounded in my ears. Would he, did he, had he seen me? Should I lay still and hope and pretend invisibility? Or should I get up and run like hell? I looked again. Hadn't he seen me yet? I lay still, baking in the sun as the mosquitoes under my coat tortured my body, not daring to swat them. At noon, the occasional *allez's* were gone.

Imagination took over. He'd gone to report me to the border police. He must have seen me. No. He had seen me as I'd seen him. When I was sure he was out of sight, I jumped up and ran through a tall cornfield, across a paved road not on my map, and across a meadow to a big poplar tree where I sat down in the shade, leaning my back against its trunk. I tried to calm my feeling of panic by focusing on the rolling yellow fields and lazily moving clouds. Slowly, I began to think clearly, calmly.

In the distance some moving figures stopped and stood still—six to eight French gendarmes on bikes. They were looking for me, for sure. The farmer had told them about me. Yes. This was it. What now? They looked at me as they talked to each other. Sensing that this was a crucial moment—I waved at them—friendly-like. They kept looking and talking, then finally climbed back on their bikes and rode off. Maybe they'd decided I was a local, because of my wave, or maybe they were tired and wanted to get home and out of the heat, so couldn't be bothered to walk their bikes across the wide meadow to check me out. Whatever. I looked up at the quiet clouds and gave thanks.

I forced myself to wait a while even though I wanted to start running again. Finally the heat drove me to get up and get going along the road to search for the railway station in Lauterbourg. I was scared as I got up. Very. I had to move cautiously while working my way towards the station. I headed south where I knew it was, fearful of meeting anyone, especially border guards. Even a dog or a cat would have scared me at that point. I was overly aware of being on foreign soil, absorbed in a foreign atmosphere, alien and new and mysterious—but mostly dangerous.

I didn't meet anyone on the paved road, perhaps because it was noon on such an unbearably hot day. After a few miles I felt oppressed by the emptiness. The air was still. There was no sound and no movement. Just hot silent pavement.

When I thought I was far enough from the border, I rested

for a while on a white milestone. I had to chance a few minute's rest. I ate the sandwich my landlady had given me two days ago. The smell of the bread reminded me of her kitchen, and the comfort and safety I'd left there with her. But that was behind me. I was committed now. I had to go on.

Finally I passed a house, then another, by now hoping I wouldn't see anyone. I knew anyone I met would start talking, and sooner or later, would begin to ask questions. White elder blossoms hung motionless as I listened all the while for a voice ordering me to halt. I fantasized hurried footsteps, imagined someone watching me. I didn't dare look behind me in case someone saw me look back, making me look suspicious. The slight valley alongside the road began to close in. I looked for telephone poles to lead me to the railroad station but saw none.

At last huddled-together yellow and white stucco houses appeared. I entered a village. Red brick houses, close together, formed a wall of no escape. Then I saw a rusty, faded enamel shield boasting cool beer. I was thirsty. The door to the inside was askew. I slipped into the cool dark space, glad to get off the empty road.

The inside was empty too. I walked towards the counter. I didn't dare call out for service for fear of giving myself away by my accent. A large woman appeared suddenly from behind a ragged cloth curtain, checking me out. She waddled over to stand behind the counter. Not waiting for her question, I said, as casually as I could, in French, "A beer, please." I searched for the money to stay calm and look casual. I pulled out a thousand franc note and slipped it onto the counter. She watched both the note and me as she filled a dull glass, slid it across to me, grabbed the note, and disappeared behind the rags.

I swallowed the cold beer in one long draft. I felt uncomfortable in the quiet dim light. I listened for her. Nothing. Suspicious, I thought she should have been back with my change by now. I got nervous, worrying that maybe the thousand-franc note I'd gotten on the black market so long ago might have been counterfeit. Maybe she was calling the police.

Should I go? Slip out before the police could get here? Then I realized if she came back with the change and I was gone, she really would be suspicious. The curtain moved. I smiled at her as she put my change on the counter. I took it without a word and left, hoping no border guards waited outside.

The hot street was still deserted. I looked for signs to the railroad station, but didn't see any, so I continued along the road until I finally saw a row of telegraph poles, likely leading the way to the station. Just what I'd been looking for. I found the track and walked alongside it until I heard the familiar station sounds of squealing steel on steel. I came to some freight cars first, then finally the station where some country folk were waiting for a train. I felt human again.

The neglected brick station was the one I'd marked on my map. Now I needed to buy a ticket. I guessed that the wicket with the iron screen must be the place to buy tickets. There was no sign. As I stood in front of the wicket, a face appeared behind the screen, asking me where I wanted to go. I made my request in as few French words as possible, trying not to give myself away. "Strasbourg, please." He asked casually if I was German as he made out my ticket. I played dumb, not answering as he finished.

Ticket in hand, I had to figure out which was the right train. The nearest train in the station was empty. I took a chance that it was the one, so got on in case it was leaving right away. I waited, apparently alone in the empty train. I could tell by the silence—no voices, no doors slamming—that I was alone. I began to worry. Maybe the man behind the counter who'd recognized my German accent had called the police. He probably knew everybody in the village, including visitors. I listened intently for voices. The police would take a while, I thought, calming myself. They'd be slow today with this heat. Maybe it was too hot for them to bother checking out a suspicious stranger. Maybe I was lucky it was so hot.

I sat on the hard wooden bench for an hour. No one had gotten on the train, as far as I could tell. Just when I'd begun to worry that I was on the wrong train and should go check things out, risking being seen, I was surprised to hear chattering voices coming from a nearby compartment. Now I felt sure the train would leave soon, hopefully to Strasbourg. Slowly it began to move, south, where I wanted it to go. What a relief! I'd passed the second hurdle on my way to Africa.

The train moved through fields baking in the sun. Judging by how I was sweating, even with the breeze from the open window, it must have been extremely hot out. The train stopped to load and unload clattering milk cans at deserted-looking villages. Finally, the conductor came into the compartment from the running board outside, to check my ticket. A welcome breeze came in through the left-open door. He checked my ticket. Now I could relax. I swayed slightly from side to side, falling asleep on the wooden bench until I was woken up by the screeching of brakes on wheels, wheels on rails. The train had reached its destination under a monstrous glass-caged cathedral filled with trains and hundreds of people. I was in Strasbourg.

I opened the door, looking both ways for police. I saw two. I stepped out onto the platform. They chatted, hands folded behind their backs, eyeing the passing faces as they talked. I walked to, then past them, as casually as I could. Once past, I wondered why they'd let me pass. It looked as if my luck was still holding out.

I took in the people and their noises echoing throughout the station as I looked for a train to Bordeaux, the town I'd picked for its harbor. A gigantic blackboard of station names with flopping signs, coming and going, told me the places this station served. No Bordeaux. The only harbor listed was Marseilles, so Marseilles it was. A train left at ten that night. I had time to go into town.

From the station I could see the spire of the famous gothic Strasbourg Cathedral, so I went closer to get a better look. I wandered around casually, as if my only purpose in being there was to admire the cathedral, a wonder in stone. I was overwhelmed by its size and beauty. I walked around and around it, on ancient cobblestones, admiring the structural lightness. The spire rose well over three hundred feet into the sky, a tower of elegance, fitting well with its buttresses and stonewalls of light red and black. It was the first cathedral I'd seen that had been untouched by the war.

I entered solemnly. The interior was dimly lit by thirteenth century stained glass windows that transformed its vast space into a place of reverence. I gazed at the huge blocks of somber stone. They were dappled in a rainbow of colors, from muted to bright shafts of light that somehow mystified this place. I lost track of time, then finally slipped back to the world outside.

I was hungry. I found a table in the market that surrounded the cathedral, and got something to eat and a glass of wine, and then sat enjoying the view of the cathedral in a pensive mood. When it began to grow dark, I went back to the station to find the right train.

A whistle blew and we pulled out. My seat was in a compartment filled with French soldiers, kidding around, impressing each other with what they knew, and getting louder as the hours passed. I became tense, and focused solely on the dark passing landscape, while the soldiers tried, off and on, to coax me into their horseplay. They wanted a stranger to be part of their fun, but he needed to be French and a former soldier, of course, who could tell them of his time in the French army. That sure wasn't me. I distanced myself from their invitations, gesturing that I had a headache. I watched the soldiers covertly throughout the night, half dizzy from lack of sleep, then woke to an empty compartment. The train was in Marseilles.

The crystal-roofed station was filled with noisy people starting their day. I walked past the passenger cars, through the cloud of steam hissing from the locomotive. I spotted two police moving towards me in the crowd. I figured they were looking for me, alerted by the ticket seller in Strasbourg. I was face-to-face with them, ready to be arrested. They didn't even look at me. Surprised, I kept going, easing my way by. I didn't dare look back. Outside I looked up at a cloudless sky, thanking my good fortune. Now I could look around and take in Marseilles.

Outside the station, I discovered I was standing at the top of a monstrous hill. The harbor seemed miles down, down thousands of steps. I stood, took a deep breath, and tried to impress the view into my memory. I'd suddenly remembered reading that Napoleon had once walked this same passage down to the harbor. I wanted to remember every step.

Gravity pulled me lazily downward, past narrow lanes and strange people, past all kinds of small dingy shops where their shopkeepers stood out front hoping to lure a passer-by in. I saw hunger in their eyes. I walked down irregularly sized steps along the Arab quarters where strings of colorful glass beads hung in the openings, creating playful entrances. No door, just beads. And curious dark faces everywhere. Some looked unwashed, uncombed; some wore strange headgear.

I felt out of place walking through their exotic world. I didn't belong. I began to feel insecure. But I was young and naive and intrigued by the different sights and smells, so I disregarded my instinctive sense for safety in order to take it all in. I wanted to just sit and watch, but that was too risky. Occasionally I felt suspicious eyes taking me in. The eyes were everywhere.

The alleys sloped more steeply now, and a stench rose from the open gutters that flowed down to the harbor. It was fascinating, a colony from Africa. During the train ride, I'd anticipated Marseilles, but I'd never imagined this. Some alleys were so narrow I could almost touch the walls on both sides with my hands outstretched. Some of the unfamiliar smells coming from the tiny shops were so strong that I had to hold my breath until I got by. I wondered how people stood it. I was the only white man in the alley. I didn't have much with me: the zipper case under my arm, my raincoat slung over my shoulder and my straw hat tilted back on my head—just these and my ignorance and curiosity to see as much as possible wherever I went. It was a very long way down, and as I continued to pass more and more shops crowded with goods and exotic food smells and unwashed people, I became impatient to get to the harbor.

When I got nearer, the shops catering to sailors' *appetites* grew more frequent. From one alley, a leggy bleached-blond African beckoned to me. I passed on her offer, so she dismissed me as now unwanted. The air changed. I welcomed the smell of salt water.

At last I could see the harbor. It was enclosed by a ten-foot-tall black fence of spiked pipes that straddled a cobblestone supply road that ran along the water. The fence encircled the whole harbor, as far as I could see, holding the monstrous ships hostage, with the bows of these rusty giants hanging out over the busy supply road. People on board looked tiny as they gazed down onto the traffic below. One spit. It landed not far from where I stood.

I sat down at an outdoor table along the road and ordered a cold drink. I sat so that I could watch the men on the ships, wishing I was up there with them, going to Africa. Maybe they wished they could be where I was too. I sipped my drink and saw a guy on the bow watching me as I put my glass down. I studied the fence. Impossible to scale. I became depressed. I hadn't imagined a problem like this. How was I going to get on a ship? I had to find some way to get across.

When I'd finished, I set out to learn more about the fence by walking along the road to look at where it ended, out in the sea. Beyond were miles and miles of open shore-side piers filled with people promenading along, taking in the sights and sounds of the pleasure boats and yachts, bobbing up and down, their cables clanking against their masts as breezes blew in from the sea. I couldn't get enough of the sight. It made me forget about my problem of how to get over the fence. My fear of being discovered vanished. The playful, bobbing yachts in the bright sunshine seemed like a good omen.

I strolled along eating a bunch of red grapes out of a newspaper cone I'd bought from a street vendor. I listened to the people promenading, to the variety of languages flowing around me. Unbelievably, I made out the distinct sharp sounds of

German coming from two young guys up ahead. I followed their quick strides, almost too close, anxious to overhear what they were talking about, trying to figure out who they were, what they planned to do, where they were from and most importantly, if I dared to talk to them.

They were looking for a Catholic seaman's shelter, being Catholics themselves apparently. And they talked about finding a job on an Egyptian freighter, loading wheat. After I'd followed them for a reasonable time, listening, my heart told me to take a chance, to speak to them. I talked to them and eventually explained my problem. They listened, so I was encouraged to go on, to ask them for help getting on board a ship. I asked if any of the ships in port were going to Africa. Yes, there was one, *La Canada*, leaving the next evening for Duala, but I couldn't get on it because guards checked everyone entering the cordoned off harbor, including passengers going on board ship. I needed a harbor ID. Another problem I hadn't imagined. Then I realized that if they were looking for work on a freighter, they must have papers permitting them to go aboard to talk to the captain about a job. Did they? Yes, they each had a seaman's pass they'd gotten in Holland two years ago. I had to hook them. I was desperate. Somehow I had to have their help. I had nothing to barter, just a desperate need.

I pointed at one, hoping he would understand. "I could go on board with you, using your friend's ID, pretending to look for a job as a deckhand or something and stow away. That would work. Wouldn't it? I'm sure."

The one I had asked looked at his friend, asking silently what he thought of the idea. A pause, then his friend asked me straight out if I had any money. I nodded. In that instant, I knew I'd won them over. "In that case," his friend said, "we could get you on board, that is if you could spare us some money."

"Yes, certainly I could." I started to do a little dance on the sidewalk, then stopped, asking them if they really meant it. They assured me they did.

I couldn't believe my good luck: all the circumstances that

had fallen into place—the chance overhearing of German-speaking guys, that they were seamen with passes, and who, being young themselves, sympathized with my situation, and were therefore willing to help me get over the impassable fence by walking me straight through the gate—if not for sympathy, at least for some of my money.

I still wasn't totally sure they would help me. I figured I'd better sell myself to them a little more, so I invited them for a drink. I told them a bit about myself and gave them the rest of my grapes and some chocolate. Finally we all talked about times during the war and how they'd come to Marseilles.

They'd been German prisoners of war, held in France before they'd managed to escape by walking away from their camp at night. They had made their way to the Pyrenees and crossed over those mountains into Spain, along with other escaped prisoners they'd met along the mountain trails. That was in the summer of 1945. They explained how dangerous it had been for them to cross France, because they had to steal their food along the way, chickens and all.

Once they were into Spain, things were easier. People gave them food and shelter as they continued south where they reported to a Spanish army post. There they were interred, fed, and treated well. After six months, they were given a Spanish permit and told to leave the country immediately.

In Barcelona they were hired as deckhands on a Panamanian freighter, without pay, because they had no seamen's papers. They got food and lodging and backbreaking work. They figured the captain pocketed their pay. When they arrived in Holland, they jumped ship. They could speak a little Dutch, but more importantly they had the address of a priest who would be able to get them some seamen's papers and hide them while they waited. They waited a whole year. During that time they did odd jobs without pay, for the priest and his church. After they got their papers, they signed onto a Panamanian registered freighter, then twice onto English ships, and now were trying to sign on to a ship of Egyptian registry.

I was impressed with the story of what they'd endured, so I ordered another round and toasted all the thousands of homeless ones like us, wishing them good passage wherever they wanted to go.

We went over the details of getting me on board. It needed to be during the pre-dawn darkness when the guards disliked coming out of the guardhouse to compare faces to the ID's. The sailor, my escort, would hold both passes up to the window of the guardhouse and that should do it. He repeated that we'd meet at the rotunda fountain at four a.m. sharp—at Street Car Station 664. He warned me against staying in a hotel because the police routinely checked the ID's of all the guests.

After we went our separate ways, I felt like jumping up and down and hugging everybody in sight, but I restrained myself to keep from attracting attention. I feared any false move would lead to my being checked out by the police. Having gotten this far, I couldn't take any chances. I looked around, as casually as I could, enjoying everything I saw. An underlying feeling of excitement propelled me along with the rest on the promenade. I bought some more grapes from a vendor and strolled past the sleek yachts, rewarding myself for my good fortune. I was thinking about the sailor's advice not to stay in a hotel. I liked it. It told me they actually planned to help me. I was still convincing myself.

At the end of the promenade there was a long stretch of golden sand, and in the distance the sea splashed against a rocky outcrop, turning into white foam. I was drawn by this play of the sea. I quickly undressed and jumped into the water. I don't know why, but I think I was just so excited that I needed some way to work it off. I measured myself against the pounding waves that broke over my head, swimming towards the rocks with determined strokes, the hard exercise calming my excited state of mind. It was farther than it looked. By the time I got close to the rocks, the waves had worn me down to a state of exhaustion. The last few strokes I could only dog paddle until the waves finally pushed me up onto the rocks where I gasped for air.

Whatever fascination the foaming sight had held from back on the sand had dissipated. I wanted to be back on shore. I stood on the knife-sharp rocks, my lungs still gasping for air, and looked back at the beach. Dots were gathering where I'd left my belongings. I feared I'd lose what I'd left there. I jumped back in the water, eyes closed, and swam and swam, the waves now helping to push me towards shore. The dots turned into people staring at me. I felt sand under my feet. I'd landed a few hundred yards down the beach from where I'd started, carried off course by a current. I staggered back to my things, past the people staring at me, whispering *requin*. By the time I got there, I'd remembered what that French word meant—shark! All those people had been wondering how long I'd last in the shark-infested water. I was shaky and exhausted and needed to rest but had nowhere to go—no idea of even where to look for a place to get through the night.

By then it was twilight; the rocky hills were tinged with red. I was scared, and beginning to despair, not knowing how I would survive until my 4 a.m. rendezvous. I headed for the distant hilltop. It was dark by the time the streetcar dropped me off at the last stop, still quite a distance from the top. I began climbing up the steep rocks, past piles of rubble and garbage, but was suddenly startled by ghostly figures popping out of the ground, and then disappearing. More shadows came and went. People were living in tin-covered caves like rats in burrows, silhouettes of human despair, jumping in and out of sight. I hastened all the way up to the ridge where the evergreens grew.

From the top I was struck by the view of the city and the harbor with its millions of lights, some moving, some still. It was unbelievable. I sat down, trying to find the lights of the ship that would carry me from here out into the sea, now black. I was grateful just to have made it unmolested past those people who'd been degraded, reduced to living like animals. I was so tired. I crawled into a bushy thicket to sleep. I fought against creeping thoughts of loneliness and the memories of hiding from the Russians in the forest. I talked myself into thinking this was different. It was my choice to be here. It wasn't some senseless order I'd followed under threat of death. I felt safe in the brush. Rustling noises from the leaves and branches would warn me of anyone coming. I willed my mind to think of nothing.

The brushing of a twig against bark woke me up to an early mist. I shivered and wiggled out, lights still in the distance. I began thinking of the day ahead. Somewhere, among those ship lights in the harbor was the boat to take me to Africa.

I sneaked down the poverty-pocketed mountain slope that was home to so many. I met some of them as I waited for the streetcar back to the harbor. The tram filled with ragged hungry souls going to their jobs as longshoremen. The skinny conductor seemed to despise his poor passengers. He scoffed at them as he shoved his way through the car, laughing loudly when he signaled the driver to stop, then go, suddenly. We were controlled by his whims, stopping and going, all the way down the track to the harbor. He enjoyed making us sway en masse by stopping abruptly.

At one stop the bodies falling against me pushed me against a window hard enough to shatter it. He started shouting, yelling at me, as if he enjoyed it. I looked at the floor, playing deaf and dumb as he carried on. The people around me oozed a snarl back at him; it grew until they convinced him to back off. He signaled the driver to go on and forget it. I continued to stare at the floor, smiling inwardly, having avoided another close call, giving thanks.

I was glad to get out near the rendezvous point. I took a shortcut, avoiding the street, and hid behind some scruffy bushes. A policeman stood at the fountain, not the sailor, right where we planned to meet. The policeman paced around the fountain, looking as if he expected me. I felt lucky I hadn't taken the street. I waited behind the bushes. No sign of the sailor. I'd been double-crossed. But I stayed calm. What did I have to do but wait. I stayed down, then peered out again to see what was happening. Like the surprise of seeing new scenery when the curtain lifts on the new act of a play, the policeman was gone and the sailor stood in his place. But I was still suspicious. I stalled, watching to be certain things were on the up and up. Just as the sailor began to leave, I rushed down the hill to catch up to him and thanked him for coming.

When we got to the big gate, he held the passes against the window and the guard signaled for us to proceed. Another hurdle overcome. I looked back at the mountains, still the dark blue color of early dawn. The sailor knew where the ship was docked. We walked along, passing one quay after another. Then he pointed. There it was, mighty, sitting silently, a few puffs of smoke rising from its stacks, but showing no other signs of life. I read *La Canada* under a worn French flag.

He motioned for me to follow him up the gangway as if we were looking for work. I nodded, too scared to whisper anything. We walked casually up the gangway. At the edge of the main deck, the watch sat in a booth, checking all those who came and went. His head jerked up and down, snoring. We took advantage of our good luck and tiptoed by. I couldn't believe it. I was on board a ship going to Africa!

When we got to the upper deck, far enough from the snoring guard that I dared to speak, I asked the sailor where I should hide. Having no papers and not enough money for passage to Duala, I was about to become a stowaway. He suggested the machine room as being the safest.

We checked it out, sneaking down metal stairs, down and down, to the bottom of the ship, to the source of the rhythmic humming and vibration that affected everything on board. There was no one in sight. I looked at the steel walls and pipes and the mass of machines, some as big as houses, making ear-splitting sounds that pounded and echoed off the steel walls. I looked around and knew, safe or not, this was no place for me to hide. This was a place to die in. The piercing noise of steel-on-steel was intolerable. The air reeked of burned oil and grease; furthermore, he really meant for me to go down one more level, down to the bilge, the pit below this one, that was filled with grease and water and oil and years of machine-room leftovers, where the rats were at home. I begged for an alternative.

The lifeboats were his second choice, so up we went, up and up the stairs again, to where the air smelled of salt water. We got there without seeing a soul. I was impressed by the size of the lifeboats, but they had no covers. Any nosy passenger could stand on his toes to see inside. It had air, but no place to hide. I begged him to come up with one more idea. He shook his head, pointing first to the lifeboat and then to the bottom of the ship. He'd had enough of me by now. I could tell. He motioned that he had to go. Holding out his hand for good-bye and some payment, I gave him a large bill, thanked him quickly for everything and wished him and his pal good luck. Looking each other in the eye, we both knew we didn't belong where we were, but we had to do what we had to do. I waved good-bye once more from the railing and watched to see if he got off safely. Then he was gone.

♣ CHAPTER 17 ♣

I was alone with my wits, not knowing whether trouble or good luck would follow. I looked at the horizon as if it was my last view of the world. Faint light in the east behind the mountains had painted their rims red, their slopes already showing tiny bits of lavender. I inhaled the fresh air, stared at the high fence and couldn't help waving at it. What an unforgettable new day!

I climbed somewhat clumsily into the lifeboat, falling headfirst to the bottom. Once there, time passed slowly. In hiding I was cut off from the world, except for whatever sounds I could hear and a view of the sky. I listened for sounds coming from nearby, fearful someone would look inside, an unwanted face in my face. I listened for signs that the ship was ready to leave. The sunrise and a piece of chocolate settled me down a little. It was taking far too long. I concentrated on watching the clouds. I hoped that moving clouds meant the ship was moving but became discouraged when I realized the clouds had moved, not the ship. And so it went. The ship basked in the sun while I wondered if it would ever push away from the dock and head out to sea. Maybe it was a cruel joke, and the sailors had taken me in just for the money. No. They'd done too much for the amount of money I'd given them. Maybe the ship was going into dry dock for repairs, and it wasn't ready to go yet. Possibly. I had no way of knowing what was happening. All I had was sea air and boredom. Eventually I dozed off.

A ship's horn woke me up. Maybe we were going. No. Everything was still. Nothing happened. Nothing moved. Maybe the sound came from some other ship. I saw shadows move across me, but the ship couldn't be going. I felt no movement. The shadows must be from another ship going by. I saw another shadow, and another. Something was happening, but I couldn't tell what. Then I sensed a slight uplifting feeling in my stomach from the sway of the ship. We were going! The swaying increased as the ship began leaving the harbor. A never-to-be-forgotten feeling of joy fell over me, taking over my mind and body. The unbelievable had happened. The ship was pushing out to sea, leaving the harbor behind. I wanted to yell and shout and see everything, but I didn't dare. For a minute I'd forgotten what a mess I was in.

But I was on my way to Africa at last. The sun warmed me; the gentle up-and-down swaying increased, and as I closed my eyes, brushed by a slight breeze, I felt my body sway as if I was in the arms of a gigantic mother lulling me into a state of utter contentment and sleep—the restful home of the soul.

It was night. My first day of escape from Europe was over. The stars increased, the night was warm, and I was ready for more sleep. But first I had a job to do. I'd figured out that if I removed a buoy in the lifeboat, I could hide in its place. There were buoys lining the inside perimeter of the boat, buoys to keep it afloat if it should take on water at sea. Each buoy was held in place by a small wooden gate. They were big enough that I could take the place of one under the bench that ran along both sides. Late that night, after making sure the deck was clear, I climbed out of the boat with a buoy on my back, walked along the deck to the last lifeboat in the row and slipped it in. Back in my boat, I crawled into the empty space under the bench, which was on the side closest to the deck, and pulled the gate closed from the inside. Now I was invisible to anyone on the deck, so I felt safe and snug.

Near daybreak, muscle cramps and hunger drove me out onto the empty deck to stretch and to find something to eat. While I was standing on deck, an early bird arrived, a lively, wiry-looking French gentleman, dressed all in black, twirling a walking stick. He walked towards me, glad to find someone else out on deck, joyfully mocking, *"Ahh c'est dur, le regime du matin?"* "Ahh, you're stiff, your morning routine?"

I smiled, answering, *"Qui,"* and slipped away from him. Looking up and down the deck, I began to realize how vast the ship was. It was a labyrinth of steel. Bare steel was exposed to the sea in places where the thick paint had peeled away, paint just too tired to stick, weary of wind and salt.

I walked to the gangway to study a sign that said this ship could carry 800 passengers. Food smells came from a galley. I watched a few people all heading in the same direction. I could smell fresh coffee. I must be close to the food. I almost walked past it, a small dining area with a long table and wooden benches waiting for passengers. I looked down at my clothes. I seemed to fit in with the class of passengers there already. I slipped onto the bench to see what would happen. A black waiter watched everyone, overseeing his domain. Other waiters appeared and food began coming and kept coming, including French table wine. I ate all I could, and drank more than I should, not caring if I looked ill mannered.

Back on deck, strains of music floated out from small speakers, as *La Mere* advanced and receded across the deck on the whim of the breeze. I basked in the feeling of fullness, the fresh air, and the snatches of music mingling with the sounds of the sea. It seemed unreal—this overindulgence of food and wine so early in the morning. The French must be crazy drinking wine in the morning. I felt drowsy; I felt fa-a-a-bu-lous.

The calm blue sea shimmered in the sunlight, while on the desk a group of *beautiful* people moved around, filmed by a cameraman. Someone sat in the director's chair, and crowds of people stood around watching it all. A beautiful woman, wearing elegantly laced Roman sandals, stood at the focal point of the camera crew. That's what my life could be, what I wanted to be part of, but I had to get a grip on myself and deal with reality—I was a stowaway. My world was different from theirs. I walked to the railing and looked out at the endless sea. I gripped onto the railing, gripping it hard enough to feel how rough it was. It was very rough. I felt reality.

But for the moment I seemed to fit in, so I gave in to the urge to explore the ship: the gangways, galleries, and bulkheads. I climbed in and out of the hatches, feeling the vibrations in the steel sheets that came from the workings of the monstrous machines that drove this city of steel. I was amazed by what I saw. I went back to the deck to see if the movie star was still there. She was gone. I strolled along the deck, swaying with the ship, and lounged in a deck chair like some of the others. What a feeling. Ahead lay the whole world—just waiting for me. Yet I couldn't shake the feeling of insecurity.

At noon the idlers on deck wandered back to the dining area. I joined them, heading towards the same wooden bench. The same black waiter stood, arms crossed, at the doorway. I sat down to eat, enjoying more of the same dark red wine. I stuffed myself again. As before I walked along the deck, walking off my overindulgence. The African continent would be in view tonight. I felt confident about how things were going.

The midday heat made me restless, sending me to seek shelter in the galleries. The souvenir shop was a good place to waste some time, just looking around. Suddenly, a firm hand clamped down on my right shoulder. I looked around, seeing more mouth than face. A stranger, quietly but firmly, asked for the number of my cabin. Just the number. He now demanded an answer, more forcefully. My heart sank. I felt in my pockets, as if feeling for a lost cabin key, stalling for time to think. A few more seconds. My time was up. He was sure I had no key. He grew taller, his face more stern, now filled with authority. He changed into a different man right before my eyes. With the unmistakable sign of command, his right arm pointing, he ordered me to follow him.

He stopped at a door with a brass sign, *Commissaire*, pointed that I was to enter, and then shoved me into a stately cabin. A tall uniformed officer, dark-faced, paced up and down, as if he'd known I was coming with the crewman. He looked me over, from top to bottom. I looked at his face, my heart sinking. Suddenly he started yelling at me in French, with what I assumed were curses, lots of them. Then asked in broken English, "Was I or was I not a stowaway?" I nodded that I was.

My nod released his pent-up fury. His huge fist plowed down. I grimaced in pain. He hit me again and again, the weight of his body behind each punch. My head snapped back and forth, taking my body with it. He kept swinging. All I could do was to take it. I forced myself to stay standing upright. When he had exhausted himself, he stopped. He stood, panting, red-faced, hair disheveled, staring at me with wild eyes filled with rage. I could see the crewman who'd delivered me, standing near the door, smirking as if he'd enjoyed it.

The commissaire stood glaring, thinking for long minutes, then finally broke the silence. Did I have any money? Yes, I had some. Enough to buy a ticket to the first port, Algiers? I'd be a paying passenger. I nodded agreeably. He went to his desk, and I reached into my pocket, shaking all over, searching for the rolled-up twenty-dollar bill I'd retrieved from my stash to spend at the souvenir shop. He unrolled the bill, studied it, and then put it into his pocket. He motioned to the crewman at the door, giving him a command I didn't understand. The crewman grabbed my arm, pulling me along like a dog. I saw the commissaire behind me, waving his arms, as if to tell me to get the hell out of his sight.

I was scared, fearing the worst. I kept my head down and followed dog-like, seeing only the steel floor as I walked along. I was at his mercy. My legs were still shaking so hard they hardly supported me. We went through inside passages, gallery after gallery. The thought of escape came and went, but I couldn't see how. Besides, by now I didn't know where I was. We were walking through areas I hadn't seen before. A voice inside me whispered, "The worst is yet to come." I was sure of it. I figured this guy and some others were going to throw me overboard, out of sight of the passengers. That must be what the commissaire had said.

We'd gone down a number of stairways and were now in the unlit galleries that had no electricity, deep inside the ship. I followed his flashlight down another set of stairs, finally reaching the very bottom of the ship. The air was filled with the stench of garbage and people. I had let myself be pulled along as though I had no will of my own. At that point he could have done whatever he wanted, and I would have had no way out. He told me to stay put. I did. His flashlight left my eyes.

I was two stories under water, near the hull, close to the rhythmic pounding of the sea, and in darkness, except for some flickering candlelight in the distance. A soft sound began, people murmuring, slowly coming towards me, and becoming mute as they drew closer.

I made out dark faces with huge white eyes staring at me, curious, like animals sniffing out prey, taking a closer look at the white man that had been tossed down here with them. My eyes adjusted to the dark. I saw very dark Africans standing uncomfortably close to me, and many more behind them, enough for a village, some lying on bunks, others on the floor. The cavernous space was filled with rows and rows of bunks. Some were busy. Busy feet moved the treadle of an ancient sewing machine, while hands fed a white sheet into the needle by candlelight. Some were making fishing nets. All seemed to be men, but men different than any I'd seen before. Their leathery-looking faces were deeply scarred, perhaps by some native ritual. Most held sticks smelling of eucalyptus that they rubbed up and down their teeth, continuously.

Seemingly friendly faces came closer, mumbling, giggling in the dark, talking a strange language—filled with long *aa* and *uu* sounds. They began laughing loudly, some pointing at me, as if teasing. From the back a deep male voice began singing something stirring, silencing the laughter. I couldn't understand it, but it sounded significant, a slow, methodical religious song, perhaps tied to some ritual. I stood still, listening for a long time.

In the distance, at the top of the dark gangways, I could see a faint light. I moved towards it. It was a long stair that ran clear up to the deck. I had to get back up to the light! I began to climb, rung after rung, all the way back up to the sunshine and fresh air, to people like me, and to loudspeakers with songs from a different world.

Now I had to be careful. Eventually I got hungry, and I knew I had to return to the black hole where I'd been told to stay. The crewman who'd delivered me would come back expecting to find me there. I climbed back down into the darkness, past the banging steel and humming engines, hoping for something to eat. In the dim light the black men were patiently standing in a line, talking and giggling. Those at the front were getting something to eat. I got in line and eventually moved along to a place where I picked up what looked like a dented dog dish and a bent spoon. Then a hairy arm reached out through an opening in the wall and filled my dish with some unidentifiable brown slop. And I ate it. All of it. Sitting on an empty bunk just like all the others. No wine, no bread, no fancy tableware—just slop on a dog dish with a dipper of warm water.

I looked around and realized that even this was better than being thrown to the sharks. And I now knew the helplessness of having no papers and of being aboard a foreign ship illegally. There was no record I existed. I could have been thrown to the sharks easily. No one would ever have known what had happened to me.

After my *dog food*, I sneaked back up on deck. I couldn't stand to stay in the dark hole overnight. Somehow I'd get back into the lifeboat where I'd stashed my stuff. I wasn't going to get off at Algiers where the commissaire had told me to get off, even under threat of being thrown to the sharks. I was on this ship, and I planned to stay on it. Besides they'd never find me in my hideaway. I wanted to get further south into Africa, trusting that since *Lady Luck* had gotten me this far, she'd get me farther. From the deck I watched for my first glimpse of the African coast. I imagined lighthouses blinking faintly where the coast would soon appear. Dawn was near and so was Algiers.

I climbed back into the lifeboat making sure nobody saw me. It wasn't long before my muscles cramped up from being boxed in. But I was safe. All I had to do now was wait. I fell asleep waiting. Running footsteps vibrated the wooden planks above my head, knocking against my skull. They were looking for me! I heard voices shouting from an arm's length away. I was afraid they'd find me. I waited for someone to jump into the boat, find me, and order me out. More footsteps, a bunch of them now—for sure looking for me—jumping from lifeboat to lifeboat. Then they stopped, just like that. My muscles ached. I felt like I was being turned into a hunchback. It grew quiet outside. I wanted out but didn't dare.

I wanted to see Algiers badly. Hours later I decided I would risk taking just one look when the ship pulled anchor. In the faint dawn light I heard heavy chains being pulled. Peering carefully over the edge of my lifeboat to make sure there was no one on deck, I climbed out, taking my stuff with me, and ran over to the railing to see what I could of Algiers.

I saw flickering lights on the curve of a hill where rows of white buildings alternated with brown shacks—no signs of life anywhere. Slumbering tranquility. I listened for sounds, anything, eager to hear something from Africa. There was nothing. It was too early in the morning. But at least I was seeing an African city, the first in my life. The buildings became whiter against the silhouette of the mountain as the dawn created graceful shadows moving over the hillsides. The ship and I swayed slowly out to sea until, too quickly, just a small glimmer remained of Algiers.

My first glimpse of Africa left me excited. I hid back in the lifeboat. A day and a night passed. Then thirst more than hunger drove me back down the dark gangways to the stench of garbage and human filth, down to the bowels of the ship, enduring it all for another plate of dog food and tepid water. But as soon as I'd had my fill, I was impatient to get back up on deck and lose myself amongst the passengers.

I was just in time to see a massive mountain and hear someone say, "Gibraltar." The shape was distinct. It was August 15th. There was a crowd gathered around some activity on the deck. I melted in and maneuvered until I could see what was at the center. It was a horse race of sorts. Wooden horses were being advanced by the throw of dice. An enterprising black bookie called the race in his native African language, waving his hands and arms, making it exciting and entertaining, relieving the boredom on deck. No one could understand exactly what he was doing, so no one made any money on the bets, but it didn't really matter. We had a few laughs and enjoyed his antics.

Another entrepreneur took pictures of the crowd and developed them within the day to sell as souvenirs to the people. When I saw one print, there I was grinning at the back of the crowd, so I bought it to remember the day.

Later, as I strolled along the deck watching the people, I divided them into two groups. One group strutted along, whispering, while they watched the ones lounging in deck chairs. Meanwhile, the ones in the lounge chairs, who had either stripped down to reveal everything or were covered up to their chins, enjoyed watching the strollers passing by. I was one of those strolling by, passing the same lounge chairs again and again until they stopped noticing me as I went by. All looked bored.

I was eager to disembark. I wondered where we were. Here and there the coastline of Africa appeared, then disappeared. In a day or so, I expected to see Casablanca.

I must have grown careless. That evening on the way back to my lifeboat, a hand clamped down onto my shoulder, as before, while my arm was painfully twisted behind me. Three tough-looking crewmen motioned for me to follow them down into the ship. At the end of a narrow passageway, a crowd of smug sailors was waiting. They locked me in a padded rubber cell and looked through the steel bars, laughing at me, now caged in their loony bin. It was hot and stuffy everywhere on the ship, but it was worse in the cell because of the smell of the stale rubber. It was a place where a sane man could become insane. I told myself to keep calm.

Perspiration ran down my body in rivulets. The guard told me it was 40 degrees Celsius outside. It was even hotter where I was. Just talking with the guard made me sweat. He felt sorry for me and insisted on sharing his wine. The wine seemed to rush through my body and pour out of my skin. It was a long night.

In the late morning the sailors unlocked the cell and gestured for me to follow them. They took me up on deck to a gangway. We were in Casablanca. I was surprised to see it spread out in front of me. The ship must have docked during the night. I was told to wait for the harbor police.

I looked around, taking in the situation. I could see the harbor activities from where I waited. The people moving around on shore wore long white robes, faceless white figures. One gestured, trying to get others to move, to do things. In vain. He ended up just talking at them. A few wore traditional red fezzes. A noisy newspaper boy darted around trying to sell papers. He pulled on people's clothes when the prospective buyers didn't care to take notice of him. Everything in the port made of steel was rusted—ships, cranes, corrugated roofs, everything. Even the people lying lazily on the roofs and in the shade looked kind of rusted. It seemed that if it wasn't rusted, it didn't belong. Even the palms were scruffy and brown from neglect. Things just seemed to be used up and generally unpainted. The wooden harbor pilings were covered with barnacles. The whole scene formed a picture of rot and deadly quiet. Junk drifted alongside and between some small dingy boats and the rusting hull of our ship. It was almost high noon—the time when everything stood still—dead.

Then I became aware of what was happening nearby on deck. Curious passengers had been taking my picture. They looked at me closely—examining me from head to foot. Word had spread that I was a stowaway, waiting to be picked up by the police. I made out the French word for stowaway. My guards translated for me that the onlookers figured if they waited long enough, they could watch me being taken off the ship in handcuffs. Some figured I was a Nazi. Others said I was a criminal wanted in France that had made the ship unsafe to walk around on. I couldn't be a smuggler one said—I looked too poor.

Most passengers murmured and whispered as they passed by or stood around, but a few talked loud enough so that I could hear more than I wanted to of what they thought about me. Some tried to look at me inconspicuously; others were direct, asking, "Who are you? Where are you from?" One lady offered to help. She'd take me with her and help me get a job. A heavy-set man wanted me to go across Africa with him selling machine parts. He needed somebody to help carry parts and sleep in a tent with him. I figured he was gay.

The harbor police arrived on deck—the moment of great suspense, for everyone standing around, had arrived. The passengers watched the police examine my only document, my World Citizen ID. They compared me to the ID picture, shook their heads, and left the ship to check with authorities to see if I was wanted. All eyes followed the police as they left the ship. The waiting crowd grew.

After hours of waiting, in the early evening the police came back. The passengers crowded close to hear what they said. The police told the passengers first, then my guards, that the new Moroccan government in Rabat—unexpectedly to everyone—had refused permission for me to be set ashore in their newly acquired land of Morocco. The new state had decided that the French ship was to leave at once and me with it. By chance I'd fallen into a political squabble between France and the now independent Morocco. I was in the right place at the right time. Overcome with joy, I danced a short jig for the crowd—both for those who'd hoped to see me off in handcuffs and for the others who shared my relief and now clapped along with my footwork. My patient jailers gestured that I was free to go back down to hell to my black brethren. I knew the way.

More days in darkness eating from tinny dog dishes, and time on deck watching the stunning coastline of Africa sail past. Dakar was next. I was buoyed up by my good luck in Casablanca, and expected the same at the next harbor—authorities that wouldn't want to have anything to do with me.

Days passed—all the same—with occasional trips to the deck where the coast of Africa passed by in the breezy sunshine to offset life in the stale stink below deck in the dark, where monstrous machines competed with pounding waves to shake the hell out of the steel plates deep in the hull—my hope rising and falling. Reality waited.

Three roughnecks came down to the hold, woke me, handcuffed me, and put me back in the rubber cell. Unknown to me, the ship had docked at Dakar during the night. Later they took me up on deck. Passengers came by on their way to breakfast and said hello. I stood on deck and looked at the ropes that had been thrown down from the ship, ropes with metal collars attached to prevent African rats from becoming stowaways like me. At that point I realized I should have climbed down the ropes to get off the ship during the night. But I'd lost my chance. Now I stood near the gangway again, waiting for the harbor police. The sailors watched me carefully.

I stood at the same spot on the deck where I'd studied Casablanca. This time there were so many passengers standing around with me that I couldn't see the harbor. More came, most quickly looking away if I looked at them. They waited to see what would happen next.

"The police will be here any minute," my roughnecks said. Things happened quickly. Suddenly five French police officers stood at the bottom of the gangway. I knew then that I was going to jail in Dakar. They boarded quickly, no hesitation. They knew what to do. The ship's crew was tired of me and wanted to make sure they got rid of me. The police motioned for me to stand in the midst of them, with two ahead and three behind me, and off we went, down the gangway. I and, I suspect, all those waiting around to watch were surprised at how quickly it all happened.

Now standing on the strange hard ground of Africa, I looked up at the monstrous hulk of steel and at the crowd at the railing looking down, watching. Some waved, some shouted *bon voyage* as if I was a celebrity going off to do something of consequence. I waved back, thanking them for the moment. We walked only a short distance to a smaller boat nearby, the *Kerguelen*.

Once aboard, the police led me to the ship's bar and, to my astonishment, invited me to have a beer with them. I thanked them and raised a toast to them and to the inventor of cool beer. It was a different world. The policemen smiled and patted me on the back, toasting me as if to tell me I was okay, then told me—now that we were drinking buddies—what they shouldn't be telling: I was to be shipped back to where I'd come from and, according to French law, *La Canada* would be obliged to pay my passage back to France, in addition to a penalty payment of one thousand dollars to the Republic for harboring a stowaway, so I should relax and enjoy the prepaid royal service back. I grinned in disbelief, then sympathized with the commissaire who'd ranted and raved at me. Anyone else might have thrown me to the sharks to save the expense of sending me back and of getting a black mark on the ship's record. Out on deck I looked up and thanked heaven for sending me that commissaire. God, life is complicated!

I thought back over everything that had happened on *La Canada*, trying to figure out where I'd gone wrong. It was obvious. My mistake was returning to the dining room for the second meal. The black waiter, standing with his arms crossed and always looking around, had been waiting for me. Surely, he'd reported me. That's how I'd been caught at the souvenir shop. But, all in all, I'd been lucky and was now on board the *Kerguelen*, with a real bed and white linen.

I was impressed by the luxurious surroundings—a private cabin. The purser surprised me further by showing me around the ship as though I was a paying passenger, even inviting me to use the lounge and other facilities on board. Meals were served on bone china, with linen napkins and silver. The size and layout of the ship was more that of a luxurious freighter carrying about fifty passengers. It wasn't a city on water; instead, it was more intimate, like a floating village, more relaxed.

I was delighted to meet another young man, Francois, a tall smiling Frenchman. He came into the lounge with his arms outstretched to welcome me on board. He'd heard there was young man sitting in the lounge who'd just been put on board by the Dakar police.

Francois had boarded in Rio de Janeiro. He'd left France years before to seek his fortune in Brazil, trying his luck at a job with an iron ore company at a smelter near Belo Horizonte, where he kept records of the pit iron production. After two years, when he could speak Portuguese fluently, he got a job in the office of a textile factory near Sao Paulo. In the end, the call of his old love to come back to her and to France won out over his dream of making a fortune in cruzeiros. He told me all that and more. He was interesting, and I enjoyed hearing about what he'd seen and done.

There was another young man returning to France who had blown the trumpet at a nightclub in Rio for years. He now blew a lot of hot air on the *Kerguelen*, telling everybody I ought to be locked up. Being from Germany, I must be a Nazi and up to no good. I would make the ship unsafe.

I ignored his talk and spent my time with Francois. We talked for many long hours on deck in the balmy breezes blowing off the African coast, two young men who'd set out to conquer the world, and were now trying to understand it. We agreed it was most important to absorb the beauty of the surroundings wherever we went. Every new place offered its own beauty. On one of the first nights on board, I spotted the Southern Cross with its distinct glittering pattern of stars in the

African sky. Whenever I'm in the southern hemisphere, I look for it still, as a reminder recalling those days. Those nights spent under the Southern Cross were when we became lifelong friends. I confessed that I'd had so much good luck for such a long time, it almost scared me. It moved me to sing a song I'd made up, a tribute to *Lady Luck*, light-hearted words of owning up to my good fortune. Years later we'd both quote the last line whenever we met, laughing about it, as a way to touch our common past, an important time in our lives: *Und vergiss nicht ein Laecheln in Dein Haar zu flechten, innen und aussen.* "Don't forget to braid a smile in your hair, for your inner self and your outer self."

And Don't Forget to Braid A Smile In Your Hair
Who knows where her winds will blow you.
Dare Lady Luck!
And smile at her!
Go on!
Go and roam at your free will,
rove on all the lands you will.
Go on and see, see the lands you will.

Once there, your strides will gather dust,
the dust of your new land.
Inhale the dust and clouds,
and all those stars you see way up there.
Only then will you know the land,
and only then Lady Luck may
blow her winds for you again,
and fan your robes to go on,
to roam in some other land.
And should she, boy, should she,
look down,
to where your strides have gathered dust,
where only flowers bloom,
It's time for you to braid a smile into your hair

For you are one she favors.

And don't forget to braid a smile in your hair,
for your inner self and your outer self.
Braid it deep. Yeah!

The twelve-knot *Kerguelen* took her time going north. Francois told me it was going to Le Havre. Le Havre weighed on my mind like a dark cloud as I watched Africa go by. The Canary Islands, rugged, barely green, and desolate, were no more than three hundred feet away. That last glimpse of African land called to me, telling me to jump in and swim for shore. Or should I listen to a black fellow named Frank standing beside me? He was the friendly type, quiet. Where he'd come from, I've forgotten, maybe from the States. He told me outright this would be my last chance to jump ship. But there were sharks in the water, lots and lots. I got the point. He had a folksy, kind way of giving me advice, telling me it would be foolish to jump, but if I felt I had to, I'd better do it now. I didn't. It saddened me to watch the last of Africa slip by.

The days began to fly by. I enjoyed watching the kaleidoscopic colors in the water spraying up where the hull cut into the sea. On one of those days the cook provided some entertainment. He was sore at the captain and tired of the captain's cat tasting the food in his kitchen, so he tied a string trailing tin cans to the cat's tail, then chased it off. The poor cat streaked off, meowing, chased on and on by the clattering behind it. The crew joined in, laughing as the cat ran around and around the open deck of the ship, past the hissing, yelling cruel cook and them. It seemed as though the crew was getting back at the hated captain by tormenting his cat, wishing it was him.

The passengers amused themselves differently, by dancing through the balmy nights, seeking love, finding it. The food was good, and the wine and beer flowed freely. What a time! And I hadn't paid a cent for it.

By then it was August 28th. I remember the date because of

a gorgeous Egyptian girl, in her twenties, with a Rueben's-like figure that should have been painted in the nude. But oh, fate. She had a huge nose like a potato. One evening as I walked down the mahogany-paneled corridor of the guest quarters, where all the cabin doors stood open because of the heat, her strong arm reached out from behind a door and caught my shirt, trying to pull me into her darkened cabin, like a waiting spider. She shared the cabin with her mother who seemingly understood her daughter's desires. Holding tightly onto my shirt, she softly whispered promising words, first in English and then in French. I kissed her to lull her into relaxing, persuading her I would be hers, until she loosened her grip enough for me to slip away, to then laugh and sing her name down the length of the corridor.

Later I regretted slipping away. The next morning she whispered she would get me yet, slipping me a note that said,

> *To Alex on the 28th of August on the* Kerguelen*:*
> *God made the world and rested.*
> *God made man and rested.*
> *Then God made woman and since then,*
> *neither God nor man has ever rested.*
> *Jackie.*

The *Kerguelen* plowed through rougher water, blacker, colder. The mornings were now cloaked in gray haze. We sailed along Spain, then up the Portuguese coast. Along with the colder, stormier weather, the sighting of land signaled that I would soon reach the end of my dream of escape, of all I'd been longing for.

♣ CHAPTER 18 ♣

We dropped anchor in Le Havre on August 30th. I said good-bye to Africa and my new friend Francois. I gave him a rough hug and a note with the song I'd made up. Francois and the others busied themselves filling out the green customs form needed to get ashore. He filled one out for me, giving me a chance to test my World Citizen ID with customs. I casually joined the line on the deck, form in hand. When it was checked, I was told to stand aside for processing some other way. I said good-bye to the others as they passed by. The line disappeared. I was alone with the customs officer. He glanced at me, instructing the captain to hold me until my status was cleared with the higher-ups—and gave me a last somber look.

I was locked in a cell like the one on *La Canada*, rubber pads and all. I almost felt at home, wondering if French ships had standardized them for people like me. Rumors floated in through the bars of my cell that I was to be sent back to Africa. It seemed *Lady Luck* was still with me. Late the next afternoon two French police officers appeared, handcuffed me, pushed me down the gangplank, out onto the street, and into a streetcar. Once inside, people stared at my handcuffs then at me, more and more people. Some questioned the officers.

They took me to the Prefecture Maritime. I sat on a chair, surrounded by one civilian and numerous fast-talking officers who cross-examined me, inundating me with questions. They checked through my few belongings. They started off by speaking slowly and gently but were soon yelling and gesturing. Not getting anywhere with that approach, they became stern and quiet, then determined, hard, and smart-mouthed. I let the verbal dirt bounce off. I felt no guilt. It must have shown and eventually got across to them. The civilian spoke for the first time, motioning that two of the police officers should take me somewhere else—the Prefecture de Police a Le Havre. Handcuffed again, I passed the questioning eyes of the people on the streetcars and the streets, giving them something to talk about. I saw in their eyes how they judged me to be a criminal. I smiled at the ones who stared at me, which generally resulted in one last hard stare before they turned their heads to look away, telling me I was nothing but dirt, not worth looking at.

I took it one step at a time on my journey "home" having failed to find a free country. I followed the officers wherever they led me, telling myself that after a certain number of steps it would all be over, somehow, sometime.

At the police station a group of officers stood waiting behind a counter, as if safer behind it, protected against whoever walked in. They looked me over, frisked me, still handcuffed, emptied my pockets, and shoved me towards a small hole in the floor to pee, the stench of urine making me gag. Then I was put into a large concrete cell with a steel barred window and a tiny peephole in the solid steel door.

I sat alone all night on one of the two wooden benches. I did have one thing to be pleased about, and that was how well the tailor had hidden the pockets in my linings. My money and jewelry hadn't been detected by their frisking.

In early morning—I think it was a Sunday—a shifty-eyed, wiry Frenchman was thrown in with me. Sloppily dressed, he sat on the other bench, silent, trying to find his bearings as I had. I kept a close eye on him. He looked back and forth between the bench and the bars on the small window. He went to the steel door to peer through the peephole to see if anyone was watching. Soon he began to loosen up, smiling as he asked what I was in for, whispering that he'd just murdered an old man with an antique revolver. He showed no remorse. He knew we'd eventually be sent further inland to an old castle-like prison up in the Seine Valley.

After talking some more, he demanded that I stand watch at the door, to peek through the peephole to warn him of anyone coming while he tried to pry the bars off the window with a plank from the wooden bench. I was afraid not to. I didn't know what he'd do if I refused. The bars didn't give. Exhausted, he gave up and fell asleep. But I still kept my eye on him. A guard slipped in some water and bread spread thinly with jam. Another walk to the urinal and back. Before noon my cellmate was taken away.

The following noon two officers came to pick me up, carrying small suitcases. They gave me back my World Citizen ID, my raincoat and zipper case, and plunked my proudly worn straw hat back on my head. They handcuffed me again to parade me safely through the nosy streetcar people on the way to the railroad station. By now I was used to being herded around in public, and at people looking at me and asking questions in French I knew by heart. I began watching the people who questioned the officers, studying their faces as they listened to the answers, and saw that, inevitably, they studied me before walking away.

I was loaded into a railroad compartment with the blinds pulled. My hands were uncuffed, and I was informed that we were going to Paris. During the trip the two guards talked to each other and ate homemade lunches from their briefcases. When they saw me watching them, they occasionally threw me a bite.

Holding my head high, we pushed through the masses at the Paris train station, the crowds making room for us to get through. The guards hailed a taxi to take me through the grand city, proudly pointing out famous landmarks, both talking at once, with me nodding, seeing too much. The excursion ended at the Gare du Nord, where I was told I was being shipped back to Germany.

One man at the huge station entrance asked the guards a lot of questions about me, question after question. After each he looked at me, then at my cuffed hands. After an hour of that, I burned to tell him my cuffs and I weren't for sale. He must have had too much time on his hands waiting for his train

The train took us to Kehl, on the German border, where they handed me over to two waiting Suretee officers of the French Secret Service. I was sad to see the guards leave; it was almost like losing two friends. I thanked them for their kindness and shook hands with both of them, my hands still in the cuffs. They saluted, as if to say I was all right.

The officers at the Suretee Kehl were something else, impressing upon me what they and the Suretee stood for and, most of all, what authority they had, what they could do to me if they wished, and that I had committed a serious crime by entering France without a passport. In the end they made me sign a formal Suretee document stating that I would never again enter France, ever. I was unfazed. Neither of us knew how soon I'd be back. Three guards took me to the border and turned me loose on German soil. I was totally devastated.

Rubbing my bruised wrists, defeated, I studied the Suretee document barring me entry into France. It was all I had to show for my trip. The Suretee document was now my only official ID. Wait until the thorough Germans studied that! I figured they would be totally perplexed, checking first to see if it was authentic, likely not having seen one before.

Stepping onto German soil, I slowly walked the direction my heart had said no to, back to the country I'd tried so hard to leave.

I walked for hours and hours, grateful when I came to a Catholic cloister of welcoming nuns. I explained myself, who I was, and where I'd come from. The nuns took me in, in a motherly way, and quietly served me an oversized plate heaped with noodles, put some German marks in my pocket, and pointed me in the direction I needed to go. I thanked them. They crossed themselves. They knew I needed their blessings. I looked up at the sky to do my talking to the clouds.

And then I was back in Stuttgart, the city I'd started from many weeks before, returning to my few former friends and to all those others that weren't, the ones I'd tried to get away from. I was angry to be back—forced to face my failed dream, but I had to endure it if I was going to get another chance to leave. So I made the best of it, biding my time, rebuilding my courage.

I re-registered at the university as a student-on-leave, in case I found a way to go on with the studies I'd abandoned. I found a room, hard to come by, and usually with some hitch attached like garden work to do or an ugly daughter to court. I found a job as a movie house attendant where I could see all the new movies free of charge. That was a start at least.

Somehow, from the university, a magazine found out that I was the student who'd recently made it to Africa on a World Citizen ID. They interviewed me and printed a story about my trip, stating I'd challenged the world in a corduroy suit, carrying a briefcase stuffed with underwear, to test whether the World Citizen ID was legal tender with foreign authorities. They wanted to use my story to gain recognition for the movement, so they posed me sitting on an army cot in *no-man's-land* between the French and German border at Kehl, wearing my old raincoat and holding an umbrella and a sign that said: *I am waiting for Gary Davis*. He was stationed in Paris, barred by the Allies from entering Germany. Passing tourists gave me food to eat and drink. One fat American even spared a box of Cuban cigars. The magazine report made it sound like a lark, an adventure, a far cry from the truth—my utter desperation to get out of Germany, like the flight of a caged bird who suddenly finds the door open. I couldn't have endured the tough parts of the trip if I'd only done it as some sort of escapade.

A partner in a nightclub, who'd read the article, was quite taken by my crazy story, taken enough to get in touch with me and offer me a job working in his nightclub in the night life of the rich. I was turned into a cigarette boy in a stunning tight-fitting red uniform with lots of gold buttons. I helped ladies and gentlemen in and out of their coats, got some of the men ladies to sit with, watched over the locked-up liquor stocks and generally kept an eye on things. Some ladies kept more than an eye on me.

The owner was in love with one of the entertainers, a graceful, elegant Swiss singer. At the end of her club engagement she gave me an autographed picture with good wishes, referring to the German humorist Ringelnatz, "Greet every cigarette boy you meet in a friendly way. You never know. One day he could become your boss." And she'd added, "To tell the truth, I have a hunch it fits you to a *T* Monsieur Alex. Good luck. Your Susa."

A lady named Ilse took a liking to my tight-fitting red uniform. She had a doll face that brought her dozens of suitors. My mind feared, but my heart hoped, that she would knock at my door one day to visit me. And she did. She'd let herself in and was lying naked on my couch, as if posing for a picture, waiting for me when I came out of the shower. Shocked, I wondered how she'd gotten in unseen by my landlady who'd decided I was hers. Ilse scared the hell out of me. She was endangering the balance of my small universe—my room and the landlady who watched my every move. I eased her out, doing the right thing for the wrong reason. Later, thinking about it, I wanted to kick myself for not having taken her up on her naked offer.

It was time for a new job. It was the summer of 1950. I got a job with a textile wholesaler I had met at the nightclub. I learned about textiles and fibers, about long-fibered Egyptian cotton, rough cotton from Brazil, material from the States, silk from China—which sold well—and that rayon was no good. My job was to sort and ship textiles and to be a general handyman. When the time came that I couldn't learn much more, I left to find a new job.

A paint wholesaler hired me on as a traveling salesman—no,

really, his wife did—promising I'd make lots of money. I sold his paint out in the country. I rented a 1935 jalopy with a hand-cranked motor, a square-shaped monster that looked like a hearse. But it was the only vehicle available for rent. Cars were scarce. I was ashamed to park it anywhere my customers would see it, so I parked on the outskirts of the small towns and walked door-to-door. I made good money with that hearse.

One day, when I delivered my orders to the boss, his wife persuaded him that I was the man they'd been looking for to plaster their new house. She'd inquired about my background and had found out that I'd once worked for some plasterers. She asked if I wanted to plaster her new house. Did I? Well, I did want the pile of money I'd make doing it. I was tired of being on the road, so I dared to be the plasterer I wasn't. To my dismay, when I was finished, it was a terrible job. But the boss's wife was satisfied with the crooked walls and ceilings that I'd tried so hard to make straight and plumb. The truth is she probably didn't notice how poor a job I'd done. They were happy with the money they'd saved using me to do a tradesman's job, and I was happy with the money in my pocket.

Then I met Wilma. I was watching a movie when I noticed a girl pass by in the dark, attracted by her perfume. She looked pretty good from what I could see in the dark. I decided to take a better look after the show.

I followed her. As I trailed along behind, I was distracted by her shapely legs in high heels, as I tried to figure out how to approach her—what to say. I knew it had to be just right to get her to respond. Apparently I did it right. Soon we were talking as we walked along towards her home, along the winding streets in the upper part of town. She said I could call on her the next morning, a Sunday.

I arrived on shaking legs, flowers in hand, in front of the house. It belonged to an American district judge. She was his court interpreter. *Lady Luck* had sent the judge off that day and the next. It was sunny. She made breakfast with all the trimmings, putting both flowers and her charm on the table.

Later we walked through the woods, and I caught an occasional glimpse of her sexy legs in her high heels again. With food and wine and a radio, we lay on the grass in the sunshine. She listened to the music and me. I told her I wanted to redesign the world one day. I threw all my wisdom and charm in her lap. She let me stay the night. She was lonely for love and affection. I promised to stay dressed, sleeping beside her, but love was the devil, just as we'd both hoped.

A few days later she moved out of the judge's place and in with me. The judge must have wondered what persuasion a young, good-for-nothing kid could have used in just the two days he'd been away. I enjoyed living with Wilma. She had trapped me with her scent—for good, it seemed at the time. Just being in the room with her was enough. I was…

In Love With Wilma
It's raining, it's almost raining.
It drizzles silent droplets.
I have fallen in love with her.
Time stands still with open arms,
and I smile at each droplet falling on my face
with my mouth open to catch,
then dizzy myself with,
while hoping for more to come my way.

Wilma and I went to the Alps to bask in the sun, to climb the cloudy peaks, to ski, and to tumble, both in the soft snow and in bed. I rented an Alpine hut from a farmer, a small shack sparsely furnished with a wood stove, two army bunks, some crude benches, a three-legged milking stool, and a rough table. Above the table was a Madonna adorned with dried summer leaves, placed there by the herdsman who lived there in the summer while his cows grazed on the green grass of the mountainsides. Wilma and I loved the place.

Early each morning while it was still dark, as soon as the farmer down below finished milking his cows, he started up a tinny motor that ran a cable up to our shack. The cable clattered and jerked against a deep gouge in the wall, waking me. Shortly after, a loud bang on the wall announced that the cradle box had arrived, filled with fresh milk, homemade cheese, and bread. That was my signal to stamp out of the snowbound hut to the wood piled under the snow and to bring in a few armloads to warm the shack. Happy mornings. What came later was work—Wilma's insatiable longings to make love, all day, all night.

A week in the shack and I'd had enough—the lovemaking, the cramped quarters, the wind-blown snow drifting continuously, even the wholesome food. Then Hans appeared, giving the situation a new twist.

Hans and I talked all night. He sat on the well-used three-legged milking stool, tipped back on two legs, while we laughed and talked and gossiped about mutual friends from the university.

One morning I was shooting off my mouth—telling Hans how Wilma never tired of making love on our wide-enough-for-only-one bunk—with Hans waiting to hear more, when suddenly Wilma spoke up. I was amazed at her topic—religion. She started off soft-voiced and shiny-eyed, staring at the statue of the Madonna above my head, explaining herself as a believer, revealing her passion with a glow and deep-burning faith that I hadn't seen in her before, even in all our lovemaking. She talked about promises in another life—eternity and eternal rewards—occasionally caressing her hair with her fingers. As I gazed at her, watching her young, pious face, she became seductive to me, making me want to make love to her.

One day soon after, Hans jumped up and announced that he wanted to go to the top of the ridge where the snow blew off its face. We all needed to go he said. Wilma didn't care for his idea, so she stayed put in the hut with the Madonna while Hans and I took on the blowing snow.

Once outside we didn't talk. We needed all our breath to climb, step by step with our felts under our skis, to the top of the ridge. It took hours to get to it, the border between Germany and Austria. There we discovered a green-uniformed figure, round as a snowball, watching us from about a mile away. We figured he was an Austrian border guard. He stopped our plans right there. The guy just stood there, almost as if he knew what we wanted: to ski down into Austria. We watched him. He didn't move, so we took off.

He came after us, gaining on us. We raced downhill, occasionally looking back to see how close he was, seeing how well he skied in spite of his shape. We skied like the wind, down, down. My eyes watered so much that I could barely see the trees. Rushing between increasingly larger trees, we came to a snow-covered trench used by loggers to shoot logs down the mountain. We jumped into the narrow flume, holding our poles between our legs to brake the downwards schussing—going as fast as any logs—to the bottom of the valley where we came out at an old hut. Out of breath, we sat down and rested with our backs against a sun-warmed wall, watching the place between the trees where we'd come out, waiting for the Austrian. By the time we got our wind back, we realized *Lady Luck* had shone on us by letting us find that flume in the nick of time and in sending an overweight guard after us, perhaps one too wide to fit into the narrow chute.

Carrying our skis, we walked down a snow-covered road to a village, hoping to buy some hard-to-get tobacco, and leaving Wilma to worry overnight. In the village folks enjoyed watching passers-by; it gave them something new to talk about while their dogs sniffed at us. When a St. Bernard sniffed at Hans's behind, I told him to ignore it. When it was time to take my own advice, the bastard bit me hard enough to cause bleeding. Though the bed sheet was stained red by morning, we got a good night's sleep, our tobacco, and skied back to Wilma.

For hours we climbed towards the ridge, anticipating the moment at the top, hoping the guard would be nowhere in sight. We were exhausted by the time we got to the top, and then as we began our long downward glide, we sank in up to our knees in soft snow. Warm winds had turned the snow into slush. We had to lift our legs and skis, slowly, step after step, mile after mile, day into night. We laughed and cursed our way down in the moonlight. The planned supper arrival had turned into breakfast.

All that day, Wilma wanted me to make love to her, but by the next morning I'd decided I wanted freedom from my desire for her and from her beliefs. I saw peace in her face but figured she had to go home. A tearful Wilma got ready to leave the next day. Hans and I took her to the bus. We stayed a few days longer, enjoying some wonderful times between men and snow. By the time we returned, I was glad to see her again and to be back in her arms.

It was time to concentrate on how to make money. I wrote letters full of hot air, trying to make deals out of nothing, and eventually started my first company, IHG West, a wholesale business distributing various goods. I sold textiles, scissors, candles, and drugstore items, stuff nobody really wanted to bother selling. I didn't sell much of the small stuff either, but the textile business went okay. To get it rolling, I rented a room on the second floor of a plush European coffee house. Then I put an ad in the paper telling people how much money they could make selling textiles out of their own homes. And people came—lots of them—so many that I was overwhelmed. How could I convince such a large crowd? But they were hungry and I had the dream of how they could make lots of money selling for me. Put together, it worked. I was now in the textile business.

About that time the papers were filled with stories about a remarkable man, one of those half-gods who walk on earth once in a while—Albert Schweitzer. He was making news with his quiet philosophy that he called *reverence for life*, which was about experiencing a new consciousness as an emanation of the creative impulse that seeks a new world.

His ideas moved me. I read books about him and then wrote him, telling him how his humble way of life had touched me. Unexpectedly, he replied—on a type of India paper that I still treasure—from his hospital in Lambaréné, French Equatorial Africa, now called Gabon.

Hospital A. Schweitzer,
December 15, 1950

Alexander Munzel
Stuttgart

I thank you for your kind lines. I am glad that you have given the idea of reverence for life some value. It moves me to see this idea finding its path now even during my lifetime. Let us all move together toward the light of its path, everyone in his own way. My overburdened eyes and my gnarled hand do not permit me to write to you as I wished.

With good thoughts
Your devoted Albert Schweitzer

He was in Africa, the place of my faded dream, and I was in Stuttgart, where I didn't want to be, carrying on with my textile business and the daily struggle of finding food and making enough money so that I could hopefully leave again. While I kept his *reverence for life* in the back of my mind, he was living his philosophy. "What of him today?" I ask myself. "Was he a noble fool lost in the jungle? Was he enough of a realist for this ignoble world?"

Lady Luck stepped in again by helping me spot a tiny article at the bottom of the page in the daily newspaper. It said Canada urgently needed plasterers. That would be my ticket. In my mind I was already in Canada, showing Canadians how to plaster things.

I took the train to Karlsruhe to the Canadian embassy with a letter of reference from the lady with the crooked walls. The Canadians liked her letter praising my work. They accepted my application, gave me written authority to apply for a passport and, what's more, gave me a voucher for passage plus $150 dollars for miscellaneous expenses. They explained that it wasn't free. I'd have to pay it back, including interest. There was one hitch. I needed a German passport.

For that I had to have German citizenship. My World ID said I was stateless. I needed to sweet-talk a lady with the necessary authority. I found one and got my passport. It was easy to get documents in those days because German authorities were wishy-washy, lacking specific references as to how much authority they'd been given by the Allies. Their main task was to keep watch, to ensure that Nazism wasn't creeping back.

With my passport in hand, everything else fell into place quickly. I said good-bye again, to Greta first, of course. I didn't tell her about the failed trip to Africa. Even when I'd told her I was going, she thought I was making it all up anyway—to impress her. She didn't take me seriously—probably never would. Then the day came for the last few good-byes—my mother and dad and a few others.

I didn't see Wilma again. I don't know why. Maybe I was too busy leaving Germany and everyone in it. Or maybe because my mother, after meeting her, filled my ear with, "I hope you're not going to marry her." Fate repaid my shoddy behavior a few years later.

I did see my old flame from Heidelberg before I left, standing at the other end of a streetcar. She looked old and alone. I pitied her as I watched her stare at the floor of the car, as if listening to the squeaking wheels. I got out before she saw me.

The last day Hans delivered me to the railroad station. When the train whistled, I hung out the window with my arms thrown out, and yelled cheerfully, "Tallyho, here I go." We smiled at each other and wished each other good fortune in our lives to come. When the train had eased halfway out of the station, I continued waving even though I was no longer able to see him.

I wondered what would become of us both. Little did I know then that he would become a gifted architect, and that we'd meet again as old men when one day I would recognize his back on the street and call out one word, "Hans." And without having to face me, he'd reply, "You are Alexander." Nor did I know that he'd lose most of his eyesight, and that between the two of us, I would be the one to put my hand on his gravestone.

Finally I was on my way, leaving this land and its people. The station gave way to tracks rolling across the countryside, and the train clattered along towards France.

♣ CHAPTER 19 ♣

I crossed the border into France with a real passport, complete with a French visa stamp, just two years after I'd signed the French Secret Service document barring me from ever again entering France—a false promise as it turned out. This time I rode through France and into Paris on a train, instead of running through a creek and a French mine field. This was definitely preferable.

I was eager to see Paris again, uncuffed. I couldn't believe I was walking its streets as a free man. I went back to the gate of the Gare du Nord, as a tourist—to the very spot where I'd been forced to stand in handcuffs and wait for an hour—but gave the gate no more than a minute this time. That was enough time for the past; I wanted to see the people of Paris. I walked for hours. I found the people charming and the girls beautiful—so many girls. There was too much to see. Worn out, in a small hotel room, I fell on its bed and woke the next morning—like so many young men before me—in love with Paris.

That day I caught the train to Le Havre, where more memories waited. I booked in at the marine office of the *SS Washington*, which was sailing the next morning. With the ticket in my hands, I felt closer to Canada already.

I remembered that Le Havre was the homeport for the old *Kerguelen*, so I searched for its agency and, once there, got a postcard of the ship under steam. I studied every inch of that picture, reliving the places on board. With time on my hands, I even visited the police station where I'd shared a cell with a murderer and the streetcar station where people had gawked at me in handcuffs. When it got dark I went to a movie to help pass the time, anxious for morning to come. The old-fashioned intermission screen was dark red and brown, painted in an art nouveau style, and advertised local services. I don't remember the movie though.

The next day was May 10th, 1951. Just getting on board ship legally was a thrill for me, as well as seeing the crowds of people with the longing for the New World written on their faces. What an event that was in my life. From the rail up on deck, I watched everything—the mass of people with their belongings, the chaotic activity in the harbor, cranes moving this way and that, goods being loaded and unloaded. I listened to the sounds of steel and people, clangs and horns, and warning whistles in the early dawn light. Then gently the sights and sounds of the harbor receded as the *SS Washington* slipped soundlessly out to sea, along with my silent farewell—going to a new beginning.

We stopped in Southampton and Cork to pick up some Scots and Irish en masse. They brought their light-hearted ways on board our city on water, a city with glittering lights and happy sounds that rang like hope for a new and better life. The ship was luxurious with a crew to match—eleven hundred passengers with a crew of five hundred. Too much to eat and drink was delivered by white-uniformed stewards in the blink of an eye. I was wide-eyed the whole week it took to cross.

We docked in Halifax. My first view of Canada was dismal, a vacant harbor with empty brick buildings. In one of them, on Pier 21, I was checked through, one amongst the hundreds debarking from the ship, sifted through the same pier as thousands of immigrants who had preceded us.

I hadn't brought much with me: a suitcase, the rubber raincoat and straw hat that had gone with me to Africa—the latter for good luck. My two freight items had been checked through to Toronto—a huge army tent plus an old typewriter that I'd packed in a used ammunition crate.

I hoisted the suitcase onto my shoulder and set off, eager to see something of Canada immediately. I had to see it. The train didn't leave for hours, so I headed for the city that spread out along the shore.

The harbor was mostly abandoned, rusty, and barnacled, as if waiting to die. A feeling of panic swept over me when I realized I was totally alone on the other side of the world in a place that had given up. I knew this place had been a busy hub during the war, but it now seemed almost dead. But I also knew Canada was big enough to carry a deserted harbor. Its time would come; people would make it new again. I was sure of it.

With enough spoken English to buy a piece of bread and get directions to the train station, I went on looking, shifting my suitcase to the other shoulder. I came to a black neighborhood, the first I'd seen. People sat in rocking chairs doing nothing, just watching those who went by, which happened to be me at that point. Tired from the heavy suitcase, I sat down to rest, becoming like them, watching others passing by, and observed their curiosity, which mirrored my own…

First View of Canada
In the distant harbor,
the sky and the ocean were the only things alive.
The rolling countryside seemed wild and desolate.
I couldn't believe I was actually in Canada,
and my life would finally begin here.
I could sense how big this new land was,
and felt it was a place
I could grow up in.
It would be all up to me.
No more bubbling along anymore.

I could barely make out the train.

It looked a mile long,
waiting for the mass of immigrants
it would take to Toronto.
Wanting to see it from closer up,
I picked up my suitcase
and started towards it.

It was made of thick steel plates,
solid and rugged,
built to last forever.
Just what I'd expected
in this new country of mine,
everything built solid and rugged,
to last forever.

On board,
the inside looked the same,
solid and rugged,
with rows of wooden benches,
and an old cast-iron stove
to keep us warm.
There were tables between the benches
and wooden bunks that pulled down from the ceiling.
When the train had taken in all the immigrants,
Scots and Irish and the others and me,
Someone fired up the stove,
bunks were pulled down and taken,
and the tables filled with men,
happily shuffling cards.
They came from different lands
but with the same hunger: Canada.
We were ready!

Our car filled with talk and laughter,
sudden outbursts from jokes,
and songs remembered from each one's past.

I watched and listened,
enjoying the shared feeling of excitement
in a totally new world.
The clatter and rattle of the cars
moving along the rails
was occasionally drowned out
by a deafening high-pitched whistle,
as we sped through empty crossings,
no one in sight.
The whistle got to me
the very first time I heard it,
right down to my spine,
as if making promises
of what lay ahead for me.

The clatter and rattle and whistles
cut through the barren land.
Swamps and beaver ponds
gradually gave way
to waving green fields dotted with farms.
It took two whole exciting days
to get to Toronto.

* * *

"Alexander, we have to eat now. I'm hungry from listening to you. When does Greta reappear in your story? Soon I hope. Although those other things are interesting, they're not what I really want to hear. Greta, would you like to help me in the kitchen?"

I heard a snap and *psst*, as John opened two bottles of Labatt's beer. "Don't mind Estelle asking about Greta all the time."

"What date is it today?"

"May 2nd. Why? When do you have to leave? You can't go until you finish your story."

"Really?"

"Sure. There's some saying about finishing what you've started. Besides, Estelle would be very disappointed if she didn't hear you tell about how you met Greta again."

"We don't have to leave for a few more days if you're sure we haven't worn out our welcome."

"Not at all. It's been a long time since we've been able to spend this much time together. Who knows when the next time will be?"

After dinner, Estelle was back in her personal chair waiting for me to go on, hoping I'd soon tell her about Greta and me.

* * *

Toronto was the complete opposite of what I'd seen in Halifax. It was a bustling metropolis of stone and steel and streetcars—lots of streetcars—and cars and crowds of people, all gathered into one huge moving mass. I wasn't there long before I was sent on to Guelph, along with some of the card-playing, singing Scots and Irish, and a few Englishmen.

We arrived at a cute Victorian railroad station and got off. I watched the train disappear down the track, and when it had become a mere point on the tracks, it said good-bye with its whistle knifing the air one last time. I stood at attention, stiff, as the familiar shiver ran down my spine. It had become a symbol of my personal freedom. But I didn't know why.

The station was silent. A newspaper flew past, blown about by the wind. I realized I was alone; my new friends had already gone. And I had somewhere I was supposed to be, somewhere my future boss was waiting for me to show up. I wondered how I'd make out as a plasterer, wondered if they'd tolerate crooked walls in this country. Hoisting my suitcase up once again, I set out to find the address I'd been given in Toronto.

I was immediately taken in by the family who had gathered in the living room—the boss, his wife, the grandmother, and the kids—even some friends who'd come especially to meet me. They looked me over. Eventually I began to feel their approval by the way they talked, so I began to relax. Mostly, they wanted to see if I was healthy and smart enough to do what they expected of me. They asked where I was from—not the first time I'd been asked that since I had arrived in Canada. It touched me. It was as if people here took an interest in me, not like back home where no one cared. After dinner—a huge steak—we continued to talk until quite late, and I ended up sleeping in an oversized crib. It was all they had. Tomorrow they'd said they'd take me to a rooming house they'd found.

At breakfast we all laughed about how I'd climbed into the crib. I ate bacon and eggs and potatoes, learning what a Canadian workingman ate for breakfast. My boss had plans for me early that first day. I caught him looking at my slightly built hand, free of calluses, and wondered what he was thinking.

We drove back to the station to load up the tent and wooden crate containing the typewriter, and then went to meet my new landlady at the rooming house and to drop off my stuff. My room was on the second floor, over a restaurant, a handy location for a new guy in town.

My boss was especially cheerful on the way to my first job. He seemed delighted to finally have a hard-to-get, but urgently needed, plasterer. He put me to work, on the public sidewalk of a busy street, of all places, to plaster a wall around a store window. He left all the tools and materials and told me he'd be back after lunch.

While I got everything ready, the sand and water and so on, I saw him talking to the store owner, promising the job would be finished this morning. Both watched for a while. I heard my boss boast that he'd hit the jackpot getting me from Germany where all the good tradesmen were from. I even heard them talk about how strong and healthy I looked. They were kind of jolly with each other. I shuffled my things around to gain time while I figured out how to best tackle the job. Finally, they both left.

Alone now, except for strangers stopping to watch, I couldn't delay any longer. I had to get started. I mixed the goo carefully and slowly, watered the old wall, and hit it with my mix, almost closing my eyes, not wanting to see what I inwardly feared. Sure enough, the goo wouldn't stick. It ran down the wall and onto the sidewalk. Up I pushed it and down it went, faster down than up. The wall and the goo were too wet to stick to each other. There was no way to keep going. I had to scrape it off and start over with a drier mix.

By then a crowd had gathered, watching, staring, trying to figure out what I was doing. Unseen by me—but as fate had arranged it—my boss had joined the crowd. Suddenly he stepped forward and stood in front of me—bewildered—gesturing, pointing here and there at the wall and at my goo. I gave him excuses: materials and tools I wasn't used to. He didn't listen. He didn't even look at me. He just wheeled around and walked away.

A short time later he returned with a small manila envelope and gave it to me without a word, swinging his arms around, gesturing. I mumbled more excuses he couldn't hear because he was already on his way to find the storeowner he'd boasted to earlier. I knew what it meant. I would do no more of what I had come to this wonderful country to do.

I looked into the little envelope and saw a few dollars, my first. I felt rich. I was young, and while I didn't know much, I knew I could work and was willing to work at any job I could find.

The employment office sent me to a construction site as a laborer. It was tough. I used a pickax, chopping at ground still frozen from the long Canadian winter, to dig holes for a foundation. As soon as I'd finished one, I started the next. Soon my head was pounding painfully and my hands were bleeding. When I finally finished the holes, they gave me a wheelbarrow to push, a heavy two-wheeler that held a whole yard of concrete. I shoved it up and down plank runways, using everything I had in me to get it up the inclines until, finally, something inside me broke. I'd reached my limit. I fell apart.

I rushed over to an old brick wall where no one could see me, pressed my nose against its dirty bricks, and cried like a baby. I felt forsaken in some kind of hell. I looked at my bleeding hands and cried some more. I cried until I began to remember what I'd endured in the war. I'd survived all that. What was wrong with me? I snapped back, wiped my nose on my sleeve, and grabbed the damn wheelbarrow.

As I pushed it along, I thought back, trying to remember the last time I'd cried. I worked back through my memories to the night I'd slept with my clothes on and woke up to the policeman and how I'd cried my way to Berlin. I'd cried for a whole day then, but I was a just a little kid. I never again sank down far enough to cry or whine about my situation, never for myself. I did cry for the loss of others, and later in life, much later, when something moved me, something so beautiful that it didn't seem real—like a champion skater or a beautiful melody.

In time I began laughing more, the way I saw others doing, learning to laugh at things that got me down, but mostly at my own stupidity. Life had been so serious up to now, such a struggle to survive. Now Canada was teaching me how to laugh.

The smells of freshly poured concrete, new lumber, and constant dust combined with the sounds of banging, hacking, jack hammering, and hollering created a continuous activity that was exciting to be part of. We were building a new wire factory.

That First Summer Was Very Special For Me
Wonderful days,
morning walks to work,
filled with exciting discoveries:
quiet residential streets lined with huge trees,
their monstrous branches
crossing from one side of the street to the other.
I walked under their dark green canopy
where light played in the morning sun.
I strode along in the dappled sunlight,
happy to be going to work.
Every day of that summer was like that.

At the end of the day,

walking a little slower
in the hot humid evenings,
I was grateful for the shade
from those majestic trees,
their still leaves
filtering late afternoon sunlight
down to the sidewalk.

People sat in rocking chairs
and on worn-out couches
on their porches,
hoping a breeze might stir the still air,
as they watched people like me passing by,
following my every step.
I was fascinated
to see old folks rocking,
all the time rocking,
some as if trying to rock
a hole in the floor,
not really watching
who went by at all.

I tried to imagine
what they'd done in their lives,
what they thought of me.
Did I look like an immigrant?
Did they sense what I did
and who I was
just by watching me
day after day?
Everyone smiled and was friendly.
Everywhere.

I learned that this was Canada,
these people,
and their easy-going ways,

not pushing and shoving
as if their lives depended on
getting something done.
Nice folks.
Few stern faces.
Faces that looked as if
they wanted to help you,
if only asked.
People here knew how
to have fun,
how to look for enjoyment
in little moments
that came along,
in the small things
that made life funnier
and made for happiness.
I loved it.

Everything was so different
from Germany.
Germans didn't know
how to look for funny things
that happened each day.
Their fun was in drinking too much beer
while big drums and loud horns
blasted their ears.
They knew how to do things well,
how to take things apart
and put them together,
to make them better,
always concerned with
the "doing and being better" aspect of life.
Their way to be happy
was to strive for perfection
with a thoroughness which can't be tolerant,
which makes for harshness in the end.

Here people didn't idolize perfection.
They did things as well as they could
while having some fun.

Guelph was a nice little town, almost too nice, too good to be true. Everything was big. When some new friends came by to pick me up, I couldn't believe their big old boat of a car—big enough to walk around in. I felt privileged just being allowed to sit in its bigness. We drove for two hours to some cafe to have a five-cent cup of coffee. It was a little crazy, and I loved it.

Life was good and cheap, but tough. My room, for two-dollars-something a week, had creaking old floors and walls and was impossible to sleep in during the stifling, hot summer nights. The wrought-iron bed had a sagging mattress, and the night table held an old radio that blared Sunday morning sermons that I used to learn English from. I hung my things on nails. An old fridge, shared by the borders, sat in the hallway where, like the others, I stored milk and butter. At night, a glaring strip of light came in under the door and lit up my room, while greasy food smells wafted up from the cafe below. I didn't mind.

It was easy to live on a few dollars a week. Five dollars bought all the groceries I needed for a week. The cafe served a good meal with all the trimmings for forty-five cents, and a ride on the streetcar was one big three-cent copper coin.

I wrote to Greta, telling her I was all right and hoped she would write and that I missed her, and I sent a poem to tell her…

You Are My Breeze
I feel a breeze on my lips
that makes me smile.
I stand still, very still.
I very much miss you kissing me,
you, the smile on my face.
I very much miss me kissing you,

you making me feel this breeze,
you, the breeze on my lips.
I stand alone.
Hush.
A breeze.
It's gone.

The letter and poem came back ripped to pieces, no note, nothing. I would have been glad to have her tell me to go to hell and leave her alone. But nothing? She probably figured I was in hell already and she didn't want any part of it. In time I got over the ripped-up letter and threw it away. By then I'd begun to feel a part of Canada. I felt I fit in. My savings account at the Imperial Bank was my proof.

It wasn't long before I bought a car for fifty bucks, a '36 Chevy convertible that had no top, just a ragged, rusty knife-sharp edge to indicate where its roof had been. The seats and trunk were stuffed with straw that smelled of a pigsty. The right rear wheel had only two bolts holding it onto the rear axle, and one of those I had to tighten every few miles. The steering wheel had half a foot of play before it steered this way or that, and it had no second gear. But I thought it was a beauty.

In the mornings, though I started work at seven, I got up early enough to spend some time polishing the few bits of rusty chrome the Chevy had left, rubbing and rubbing, totally content.

When I went to take my driver's test in it, everything went well as I happily drove the inspector around—until he told me to drive up a hill. When I started revving the motor high enough to gear down into first, he said to take it easy, just to put it into second. That's when I had to admit I didn't have a second, and that's when he told me to stop right there—on the hill. I figured that was the end of getting my license, but I asked him anyway, as he got out to walk up the hill, if I'd flunked the test. He shook his head and laughed, telling me I'd passed. I knew then that anything was possible in Canada. Anything.

♣ CHAPTER 20 ♣

"I was lucky, wouldn't you say?"

"Yes, very. Today they wouldn't let you drive a car like that, especially to take a driver's test in. They'd haul it to a junkyard and you'd pay for the tow."

"I was proud of it anyway and started saving to get it fixed up. I was young in the head. Having a goal helped me accept the sweat of the job and the stuffy summer nights. My body ached day and night from pushing the heavy loads of concrete in the two-wheeler. Do you have any idea how much one load weighed, John?"

"Over a thousand pounds, I'd guess."

"That's what I'd figured, but I didn't believe it. There were two huge wheels on it."

"A standard wheelbarrow carries no more than a couple hundred pounds. I haven't seen one of those two-wheelers in years."

"Neither have I. People don't have to work that hard now. They'd refuse to lift a load that heavy. Workers' Compensation wouldn't even allow it. Hell, UPS drivers went on strike so that they wouldn't have to lift packages over a few measly pounds."

* * *

I was pretty green about a lot of things, especially women. I misjudged things badly with the attractive wife of an immigrant co-worker I'd been introduced to while sunning in the park. One day she knocked at the door to my room in the boarding house, to knock me up—literally. She stood at the door, overdressed, with her right hand resting on a colorful parasol, and asked if she could come inside to talk.

Once inside she explained her presence: she wanted me to make a baby with her. I let her talk, and she talked sweetly, but it bothered me something awful. I put on an imbecilic expression. I knew it wasn't her *true self* standing there, but some carried-away emotion. She went on explaining that her husband was impotent and more. I'd heard that story before. I looked at her with a quick glare of rage, then retreated behind the imbecilic look and hid myself in silence.

She begged and motioned—not listening to what I'd said—undressing in front of me, denuding herself of self-respect. I explained the recklessness of her idea, especially of her coming to my room, where mice came and went in the dark, and my neighbors heard everything that went on. I spoke quietly. Between my extra-slow words of reason, I was tormented by what I felt and saw with my eyes—wanting to grab her to let her have what she wanted. Unaware I was doing it, and to the dismay of my feelings, reason swung open the door and I begged her to leave, thinking that she knew full well why she should. And she did.

I visited her a short time later. She was alone. I could feel her wondering, hoping I'd changed my mind. I just smiled, neither of us mentioning her strange visit. We were carefully polite. I inquired about her husband and how they were getting along in Canada, then explained the reason for my visit: to ask if she could store my U.S. army tent, which unfolded to the size of a house, and my *Model-T* Remington typewriter, so important when I'd left Germany but useless now that I'd arrived. I'd lugged them all the way from Germany to France on the train, on the ship across the Atlantic, and from Halifax to Guelph. I no longer knew why. They were *dead on arrival*, together with all the ideas I'd had for them in Germany. I never saw her or my tent or my typewriter again. I'd visited her to get rid of my things and to clear my mind of her in preparation for my adventure with Jack.

At work an old guy named George had asked me to help him tie steel bars together with wire and pliers, to form the skeletons used to reinforce the concrete. I did so well at it that the company asked me to stay on and become a foreman, just when I'd decided to leave. I wasn't interested in becoming a foreman. I just wanted to make a few dollars and get on with other things I was sure were waiting for me.

Over a couple of beers, my friend Jack sold me on a new moneymaking idea. He was an Englishman I'd met on board the *SS Washington*, and he was fun. He had persuaded me to quit my job to make some real money—picking tobacco. He was persuasive; that was his strength. Convinced I could make big money, we drove the Chevy to Simcoe, hoping to get hired.

Jack's last name was Peabody—easy to remember from the first time I heard it. I pictured him *peeing* in front of a body. The picture was overdone, like Jack. He was slim, single, and a hot talker with the girls. I noticed purpose behind the looks he gave the girls he entertained with his stories, stories with a lot of hooey, overplayed for laughs. Although he wasn't much to look at, people warmed up to him quickly once he started talking. And he could tell jokes fit to kill. His jokes and stories made his listeners feel good. When he sensed they were with him, he'd really get going, smile wider, and emphasize the telling with body movements that embellished the stories even more. He told lies too and got away with it. People wanted to believe the lies because they loved hearing him tell them.

As we wheeled along the pavement in the bright sunshine, I enjoyed listening to Jack's stories as a warm breeze blew around my face in the topless convertible. The Chevy was moving surprisingly well in the heavy traffic, holding its own among the newer, sleeker cars showing off on the highway. Then it gave notice, through specific noises from its ailing parts, that I should get off the highway to a quiet back road where it would be safer to pull over and tighten things up, so I turned onto a rutted dirt road that wound along past the farms.

After I'd gone in and out of the ruts for a ways, I realized the brakes were badly worn which, along with the loose steering, made it harder for me to stay in the grooves and avoid the potholes, and I had to listen hard to hear those certain clicks from the good-for-five-miles chronically unwinding lug nut. All in all, the Chevy took pretty well to the hard ruts. It puttered along, as if it knew I cared and worried about its well being, and left a cloud of dry summer dust billowing up behind us. It was safer for us on the dirt road.

Girl-hot Jack spotted two girls as distant dots on the road up ahead. I stopped and Jack talked sweetly to the girls, offering them a ride—he knew I had a two-by-twelve board for a makeshift rumble seat in the back. He was in luck. They were hitchhiking to Simcoe—also planning to make big money in the tobacco fields—so they happily climbed in.

As we drove off, Jack filled me in on the girls' jobs. Most *worked* the pickers, which I saw later—pickers standing in line, eager to shove their hard-earned money under the skirts of willing girls. That job was the easy one. The hard one was tying green tobacco leaves all day so that they could be hung up for drying. These girls had broad shoulders. They looked like the tobacco-tying type.

Jack watched them in the rearview mirror. Typical. After a while, between glancing at the road and studying the rearview mirror, he started smiling, letting me know he'd thought of something. He jabbed me with his elbow, indicating that I should steer towards a big pothole coming up, the ones I'd been trying to avoid. The minute I hit it, he looked in the mirror to see how high the back wheel had made the girls jump, and then—the best part—how hard they'd landed back down on the board. He studied their faces for a reaction. After that he zeroed me in on the big potholes, again and again, nudging me with his elbow to go this way or that, with a wide grin on his face.

We were taken in by our own game: Jack watching the girls

and whispering how high the last rut had made them jump—sometimes showing it with his hands—and me listening and aiming, my eyes gleaming. And so it went, mile after mile, right and left, in and out, with me getting sore ribs from Jack's jabbing—but as happy as I could be—with him joyfully directing, and with the girls and their hair flying up and down, but with all of us getting to Simcoe in the end.

* * *

"Alex, I don't get it. You said your Chevy was a pile of parts. Why did you hit all those potholes? You couldn't have figured on getting to Simcoe that way. Or were you crazy enough to think you would?"

"I was crazy enough all right, getting a kick out of it all, not worrying about my old car, just enjoying the fun on the way. We knew that once we arrived our jobs wouldn't leave us any time for fun."

"And I'm surprised. I would have expected him to get out and pad the board with some straw from his seat to soften the blows."

"No, hell no. Jack was English but no English gentleman."

* * *

Simcoe was a hick town. Main Street had a row of grimy once-white-washed shacks that looked as if they were built directly on the ground without foundations. There was no sign of life behind the curtainless windows. It was as if the inhabitants had skipped town to escape the chaos happening in front of their houses.

There were scruffy-looking men—loud, boisterous, repulsive-looking, seemingly misfits—sprawled along the curb and on both sides of the street. Bums, prostitutes, and confidence men had drifted into town along with the legitimate workers—students and seasonal laborers—all lured by high tobacco-picking wages. They blocked the streets and filled the parks. In the evenings, those who hadn't been hired plunked themselves down on private lawns and begged for food door-to-door.

Farmers drove up and down in their old jalopies looking for eager pickers, good workers amongst the sprawling mass that hoped to be hired and fed and paid well by some *dumb*—or so they thought—farmer. The knowing eyes of the farmers looked for experienced pickers they recognized from previous years, not the sprawlers, no-pickers, liars. They needed workers who could pick the leaves properly and quickly so that they could get their crops in fast and earn enough money to repay what they owed on their land to the bank in nearby Delhi, as well as pay off the debts they'd run up at the grocery store. Everything hinged on this time of year. They would get deeper in debt paying sprawlers who caused trouble with drunken brawls in the bunkhouses. Most men were drunk, hiding empty beer bottles behind them, wanting no more than the money to buy more.

The Whole Scene Was Unreal
Like a circus—
shouting from crap games,
drinking when the farmers weren't nearby,
boasting with loud voices,
trying to show others they knew it all.
Adding to the din,
rumbles and rattles
from the farmers' haywired-together jalopies,
badly needing repairs
as soon as the crop was in.

They stopped and started,
looking for the best
from the good-for-nothing-looking men,
men who didn't fit in
with the hard-working farmers
worrying about ripe tobacco in their fields—
now safe from the frost,

missed by hail and mold,
but still vulnerable to drought and insects—
and hoping that the price of tobacco would hold,
all the while being chased
by their load of responsibilities and debts.

I studied the mass of bodies. They looked like they'd stick it to anybody, and be hard to get along with. I suspected some had been in jail for who knows what. It was going to be hell working with them, but even harder to be cooped up with them at night. They grinned, their eyes glazed from the beer, lying to the farmers that they'd picked before, trying to promote themselves. I watched the farmers' eyes. They listened with a certain measuring look that I later recognized as the same one they used at cow auctions.

Thanks to Jack, we stood out. He looked spry, had a good smile, and knew how and when to say the right thing. He knew hundreds of jokes. One farmer who'd leaned over to Jack to smell his breath ended up laughing. When I saw that, I knew we had ourselves a farmer. His arms told us the direction of his place. He mumbled to hang a left at the end of the road he'd just pointed out; it would be easy to find. It had a bunch of kilns, two big red barns, and a white farmhouse with an enclosed porch.

We told him obligingly that he could count on us, and that we'd head out there right away. He gave me a doubtful look when he heard my accent, but Jack yelled, "Let's go! Some of these guys might have heard his directions, and they'll try to beat us out there. Hurry!"

I did, almost driving over some guys on the curb.

Jack yelled again, "Don't put too much spin on it. We'll be killed before we even get a chance to get rich."

We found the farm easily with Picotin handwritten on the mailbox where we turned in. We were the first pickers to meet the farmer's wife, Madame Picotin, who explained that the name was Belgian. I filed her name away, combining picking tobacco with nicotine. She showed us our places at the table and our bunks close to the door in the bunkhouse, taking pains to lay out all the do's-and-don'ts along the way. She was kind of nice.

The next morning, after breakfast at six, about twenty of us would-be-pickers were herded out to the fields and into the rows between the wet tobacco plants. I was soaked to my skin within minutes from brushing up against the wet leaves as I bent down to twist off the lower leaf of each plant with my right forefinger and thumb—one or two leaves at a time from each plant—which I then placed flat between my left arm and body while I took two steps forward to the next bush, row after row, endless rows.

My left arm had to be pressed hard against my body to keep the picked leaves from slipping down. When I couldn't hold any more, I put the stack in a *boat*, a narrow box as high as my armpits that fit snugly between the rows of plants and was pulled by a horse.

After the first few hours of bending down to pick leaves, I couldn't stand up. My back ached from keeping my eyes at knee-height, searching for the lowest leaves while the wet leaves slapped my face as I worked my way along the rows. By noon the hot sun was beating down, drilling into my bent back. After an hour for lunch, we picked until dark, and then had supper at a loud table. But the day's work still wasn't finished.

All through the day the horse-drawn *boats* had been delivering the stacks of tobacco leaves to the barn, where the girls had tied the leaves in pairs and hung them on six-foot-long wooden laths. After supper we had to load those laths into a kiln, where they were left to cure for a couple days until the leaves were just the right color of brown.

Every other day, at five in the morning, we emptied the cured leaves from the kilns and hung them in the big barn, where they'd stay until Christmas when the buyers would arrive. Then we washed up at a faucet and hustled over to the loud table where we wolfed down pancakes and bacon and eggs with lots of milk. And back into the fields. That's how it went, day after day.

By the end of the day, I was exhausted, worn out from the thousand twisting motions and the body-bent steps in the beating sun, but it was hard to get any rest. I had to put up with the stench of flatulence in an over-crowded bunkhouse that was already filled with stale air from the hot still day. Some of the men were always hollering and brawling, stirring things up that often ended with bloodied, broken beer bottles in the fists of the toughest. Nights were hell, worse than the days. Tobacco picking seemed like the toughest job I'd had yet.

But I stuck it out, earning just enough to buy a new top for my Chevy. I spent it all—the whole five hundred bucks—on my fifty-dollar car, what I treasured most, my all-I-had Chevy. Handing over the big wad of cash to some guys, who were supposed to be experts at making convertible tops, gave me a feeling of being more important than I was—like I could afford to be such a big spender. They claimed they made tops all the time for the local farmers, but all the while they were thinking that I was an idiot to spend that kind of money on my old heap. I could see it in their faces as I explained how I wanted the top made. But they were getting my money, so they played along, obligingly making me a top as well as they could with the know-how and hands of those who have always worked on a farm. I was very disheartened when I saw the new top. It didn't look like it belonged. It looked out of place, like a girl's bonnet on a farmhand.

I headed for Toronto, driving against a mean wind—the new top fluttering—as I fought the now-scary play in the steering wheel, zigzagging back and forth. I could hear the rear wheel bolt beginning to loosen. And I was still getting occasional pungent whiffs from the straw-stuffed seats, impregnated forever from some pigsty. Which was the *last straw*. Time to get rid of my all-I-had-Chevy. I cursed myself for having thrown away my hard-earned money on it. I'd trade it in as soon as I got settled. I shook my head from side to side, smiling at my own stupidity, but not being able to do anything about it now. I realized the smart deal I'd made for the new top had been stupid. Maybe I should avoid making smart deals. Not this kind anyway.

♣ CHAPTER 21 ♣

I was living at the "Y" in Toronto. Wanting to fit in, I joined the in-crowd and slicked my hair back with Brylcreem while the "*little dab'll do ya*" jingle blared repeatedly from the radio. It was winter. I'd been putting up with the Chevy's problems, trying to get a few bucks in my pocket, when I discovered a new problem with it, one with the heater. The water-filled heating coils running from the radiator back under the floorboards were supposed to warm my feet, but the coils were leaking so badly that they soaked my shoes and left my feet freezing. I literally squished when I stepped outside into the snow. I'd had enough.

I went to a used-car lot filled with shined-up cars and a dealer standing in the midst of it. He pretended he liked the looks of my Chevy, knowing full well I wanted to trade it in. He promised me a good deal on the Cadillac he'd seen me eyeing. He opened the door so that I could look at and smell the interior. Its soft perfumed scent sure smelled better than my Chevy. He must have seen me sniffing. He swore that it had belonged to a nice little old lady. I stared at him, asking myself why used-car dealers always said that. By that statement I knew he was lying, so I left, with him following, hollering for me to come back, making promises, and telling more lies.

At the next lot I saw a big guy scanning the cars, his head swiveling left and right like radar, as if looking for a nice car for himself. Then I realized he was looking for anything alive that had come onto his lot. That would be me. He oozed across the gravel in my direction, past the freshly washed cars, and was standing in front of me before I even had a chance to look at one car or kick one tire. He stuck out his hand for a shake. He was overweight, big, and friendly, and he'd trapped me. He stood, chewing on a toothpick, with one hand in his pocket, the other waving and gesturing, then started off, "Looking for a car, mister?"

I gave him my not-too-interested response, "Maybe."

"We've got 'em all. What would you like? You name it, we've got it."

And he made me listen to what he wanted me to hear. He blathered on and on. I began feeling guilty for taking up his time, so I felt obliged to listen longer. I soon got the message that he expected me to take his advice on cars. He probably figured that once he'd hooked me by spending his time on me that I'd go along with what he said. His idea was to make me like him so that I wouldn't move on to another lot. As far as he was concerned I was his. I played along, killing time. I had no job to go to and enjoyed seeing if I could outguess him.

He went on talking—about the weather, what was happening in town—and told me all sorts of things I forgot within seconds. I began to feel uncomfortable. He must have picked up on it. He smiled more frequently, almost as if begging me to stay. He began touching me on the shoulder as he talked, trying to give me the impression that I was his buddy. That was my cue that he was ready to make his pitch.

He listed the good points of the car he said I should have. It would fit like a glove; moreover, it was a special that he only showed to nice people like myself—a 1947 Buick. It looked good from the outside. That was important to me. He must have seen my eyes start to shine as he talked on about the car, trying to cinch the deal.

"You're crazy if you don't buy this car right now before somebody else finds out about it. I'll work out a special price, lower than the $899 the boss wants."

He promised. But I really didn't want his promise. I wanted to look at cars. Just look at them. Leaning close, he said, "Tell you what I'll do. You look like a nice guy who really wants this gorgeous car that's only been driven by a nice little old lady."

I thought, "Here we go again with that nice-little-old-lady stuff." I was ready to leave.

He put his hand on my shoulder. "I've taken a liking to you, so I'll tell the boss he should sell it to you for $550. You've got $550, don't you?"

He didn't wait for me to tell him I didn't.

He explained, "I'll tell the boss we'll never get $899. But the $550 has to be cash, and today. Okay, I think we have a deal."

I still hadn't had a chance to tell him I didn't have that much money. He went off to talk to his boss. I saw them through the window of a shack, under a big sign: *Jack Saves You Dollars*. I watched the boss leaning back in his chair, with his arms behind his head and his feet on the desk. He put his feet down when he saw me watching. With an unlit cigar in the corner of his mouth, he stared at my face while apparently listening to his salesman. Then he banged his fist on the desk, knowing I could see it. His reaction said he didn't give a hoot if he sold me the car or not. On his lot it had to be his way. I figured that meant $899, nothing less.

The salesman started back while the boss watched through the window. I was curious about what would happen next. He almost danced back, smiling broadly. It was like a movie scene. He acted as if he had good news. He played with the toothpick as he assured me that he'd tried hard to work on his boss for me, but his boss was a real bastard. He'd take $750, nothing less. I saw them watching me, reading my expressions and body language, trying to figure out what to try next.

I shook my head and left. Within seconds I could hear his boss cursing, hollering at his salesman, telling him to let me have it for $550, but it had to be cash, and right now. I kept walking, as if I'd heard nothing. Then I heard footsteps on the

The border patrol had no idea what was happening when I put my cot up, put my umbrella down, and got out some rolls of paper to state on posters why I had come: to wait for Gary Davis.

A French patrol officer and a Secret Service man at the Customs building debated whether I would be allowed to stay since I had previously broken the law by entering France illegally. In the end they let me set up my cot with instructions to check in with them should I want to leave because I was now in *No-Man's-Land* between France and Germany.

Pictures that accompanied the story show the French border guards smiling while the Germans were more skeptical. I had drawn a poster to hang on my cot, "I am waiting for Gary Davis!"

In the meantime I explained to the French, German and Americans passing by my camp that I couldn't understand why my World Citizen ID wouldn't permit me to travel anywhere I wished and, in particular, why Gary Davis wasn't permitted to come to Germany. At any rate I would remain where I was until Davis was permitted to enter Germany.

At age 24 I started a textile business in Stuttgart by convincing others they could sell textiles out of their own homes for me. It was my first business venture.

My friend and roommate, Hans and I—just before he saw me off to Canada, still wearing the straw hat I'd taken to Africa.

The two girls, who hitched a ride to the tobacco fields, sitting on the hard 2x12 makeshift seat in the back of my then topless '36 Chevy.

Englishman Jack entertaining Farmer Picotin in the midst of a tobacco field while the rest of us worked.

My first car, a topless '36 Chevy convertible that I bought for $50, its seats stuffed with smelly pigsty straw, now sporting its new $500 *bonnet*.

Camp in northern Quebec, 1952 for the Q.N.S. & L. Railway showing the tents with plywood sidewalls and canvas roofs where we lived in temperatures that fell to more than 50°F below zero.

Eleanor, my first friend in Canada. My Buick *(below)* now took second place.

Working as a transitman on the railroad survey crew in northern Quebec in 1952.

The "new" '47 Buick I bought because of its ivory-looking steering wheel.

Q.N.S.& L. Railway Project

(above) Bulldozers first roughed out the route of the railbed through the forests and swamps.

(left) The railbed of rocks and dirt was shaped and compacted by scrapers and graders in preparation for the ties.

(below) A row of ties has been laid in preparation for the rails. Ties were dumped along the road by mule trucks. The crane engine that laid the rails can be seen in the distance.

(above) Men working the spike machine to fasten rails to the ties.

(right) Remaining crew quarters at the end of the train and disassembled rail-carrying cars left along the roadbed would be reassembled and returned down the track for another mile-long load of rails.

(below) I remember my 25th birthday only because we spent the day digging holes in five feet of snow looking for a survey stake. We shoveled all day and never found it.

Skins Lake in Northern B.C.

Alcan earthen dam project in Skins Lake, one of the watershed dams for the hydro power station in Kemano, B.C.

Monstrous TD21's made the project possible.

The camps were rough—twenty men to a tent, similar to those I'd just left in Quebec, filled with noise and carrying on. From here it was 500 feet to my movie house.

John Braams and I playing chess in an open field in camp in 1953 where we first became friends.

My first Canadian business venture was a movie house I set up in a big rented tent and jokingly called *The Paladium.*

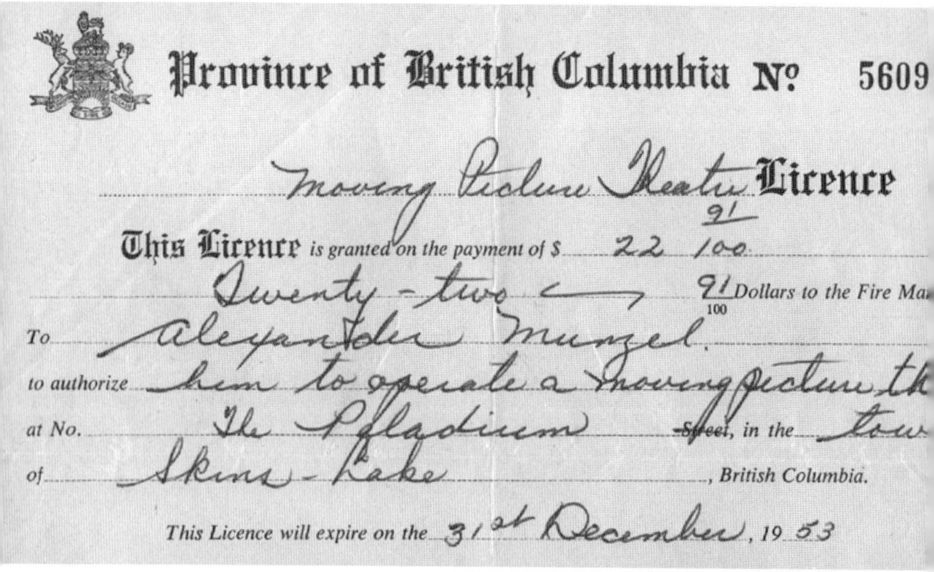

Province of British Columbia No. 5609

Moving Picture Theatre **Licence**

This Licence is granted on the payment of $ 22 91/100

Twenty-two —— 91/100 Dollars to the Fire Ma[rshal]

To Alexander Munzel.

to authorize him to operate a moving picture th[eatre]

at No. The Palladium ~~Street~~, in the tow[n]

of Skins-Lake, British Columbia.

This Licence will expire on the 31st December, 1953

The men and kids didn't care what movie they saw as long as it had plenty of action.

gravel as the salesman rushed up behind me, shouting, "You're lucky, but you're a tough cookie. If everybody was like you, we'd be broke before Christmas. You can have it for $550."

* * *

"So I took it. They took my Chevy as a $150 trade-in and the $50 in my pocket as a down payment. The deal was done within an hour. I thought I had a good deal. They likely knew different.

"Frankly, John, it was the big ivory-looking steering wheel that made me want that Buick, just the steering wheel."

"You are nuts, Alex. A few days earlier you were laughing at yourself for making a dumb deal and here you go again, not learning from the last one. I don't get it."

"He was young, John. Don't be so hard on him."

"John's right, Estelle. If stupidity was painful, I'd have been in agony by then."

"Go on, Alexander. Let's keep going."

* * *

I paid thirty-some dollars a month for a year to pay off the balance. I felt so proud sitting behind that ivory-looking steering wheel as I drove it off the lot.

It was the end of November, and I was job-hunting again. I found one as a surveyor's chainman on a huge project in northern Quebec, so I had to find a place to park my new Buick over the winter. I took it to the good people at the YMCA. Then I packed my things and headed up north to work for Morrison & Knudson, to build a railroad 500 miles into the wilderness of northern Canada to haul iron ore. *"Iron ore by fifty-four"* was their slogan; the rail line was to be finished by 1954. It was the link to a 400 square mile sixty-nine percent pure iron-ore deposit lying 300 feet or so below the surface. Hungry American steel mills at the Great Lakes needed the ore for their booming postwar economy.

It was a mammoth project, the size and scope of which was only possible in North America. Huge smelters were needed to purify the ore-sand near its point of discovery, turning it into pellets to be hauled by rail. A hydro power plant had to be built, a town, Schefferville, created in the ice and permafrost, and railroad stations put up along the line. Ten thousand men would accomplish it all, taking over six years. American money and know-how did most of it.

The first men needed were the surveyors and crews with rods and chains, levels, and transits, followed by the earthwork contractors who brought tough men and monstrous machines: bulldozers, earth scrapers, graders, trucks, cranes, and much more. The remoteness of the project in a harsh northern climate where it was cold most of the year, coupled with the swarms of black flies and mosquitoes in the few months of summer, made it tough for everybody who worked on it.

To get there I took a train to Mont-Joli on St. Lawrence Bay and from there boarded a plane to Sept-Îles, the future harbor that would receive the railcars of iron pellets from Schefferville. The pellets then would be loaded onto ships that sailed back down to the Great Lakes and finally dumped into the ovens at the mills to make steel for automobiles.

From Sept-Îles I was driven to the first of dozens of survey camps—*Mile 12*. The survey crews mapped and staked out the route for the future rail line, and told the contractors who followed just how much dirt and rock needed to be cut away or filled in to build a level roadbed through the mountains and swamps. I was a chainman on the first survey crew on the project. Camp *Mile 12* was located twelve miles north of Sept-Îles. My job was to pull a metal chain at a ten-pound pull to measure distances—child's play.

The survey crew slept and ate in tents, about a dozen men to each tent and a dozen tents in each camp, spaced at twenty-mile intervals along the entire length of the line, starting at the Moisie River, then going five hundred miles further north. DC3's delivered men and supplies to the isolated camps.

The tents were made of double layers of white canvas, with air between the two layers to act as insulation against the cold. I was surprised at how much light the white canvas let into the tents. The floor and eight-foot high walls were made with two-by-four studs, insulated, and then covered with plywood. A converted 40-barrel oil drum served as a stove. That was it.

The most important places in camp were the cook's tent and the latrine. In that order. The latrine was usually cantilevered over the river with a peeled log to sit on.

The cook's tent, where we ate as much as we wanted at mealtime, had rough wooden benches at long tables covered with plastic. The center held the food and an assortment of dispensers filled with sugar, salt, ketchup, seasonings, and more. Sugar or milk was passed down the table when someone hollered for *the gravel* or *the cow*.

The cook's tent was also the social center for the latest news and gossip and the place where each man earned his spot in the social pecking order, which determined where he sat at the table. How close he got to sit to the center of the table—where the food was—depended upon how well he could amuse the current guys at the top while they sat around eating. Telling good jokes and stuff like that all helped. I didn't care where I sat.

I had no problem getting along with the men or with the cold and wind when I was working, but living with them was another matter. They were wild creatures without manners—they hollered, they stunk, they farted, and most never washed. Their ways fit in with the harsh nature of the land but were hard for me to take. I was determined to keep their ways from influencing me or slipping even slightly into mine. I didn't want to become even a little bit like them. It's no wonder I was lonely. Living with them was the hardest part of being there. There was constant noise: talking, laughing, and music playing all night long. They were unruly, boorish and crude—not a half-decent guy in the bunch.

I watched their naive behavior and crude habits, and listened to what they said. I figured what most of them had in common was wanting to stick it out for the money. Most had no families or girlfriends and no ambitions beyond good food, booze, and money. A few were husbands who had a home and family but didn't like what they had well enough to stick around.

To get away from them, I spent a lot of time outside trying out my snowshoes and doing target shooting with the rifle I carried to scare off wolverines that are especially fierce, smart, and scared of nothing. Most guys carried a rifle away from camp. I'd bought a 40-40 Winchester for ten dollars. For that price I got a gun that veered right.

There was a special silence in the cold at 40 below. Snowshoeing made me breathe heavily which produced a cloud that turned my eyebrows white with frost. There was a magic in the endless white where the snow and sky met and nothing moved. The snow glittered in the white light, and the only sound was the dry snow crunching under my snowshoes. I loved it out there. I went out, not caring which direction. I just went.

I tramped out from camp until I was far enough away to no longer see or hear anything of it, then lay down in the dry sparkling snow, arms outstretched, listening for some sign of life. Nothing. It was wonderful. It was as if the world had stopped. Life and death seemed to be one, and the air and sky a part of the sun. It seemed almost holy.

One day I found a valley full of skinny tree trunks wearing long green beards. Beyond them I spotted something shining on a knoll, and the closer I got, the more it glittered. My mind grew hot; I sped up. I couldn't get to it fast enough. What I saw when I got there was a vein glittering with gold and silver and all sorts of metal, more than three feet wide. It ran all the way up to the top of the knoll. I felt the sharpness of the metals—like tiny knives bunched together. I looked around to make sure no one else was in sight, wanting to keep it a secret. There was no one. I gouged out a fist-sized chunk; it was heavy. My mind began singing and dancing. The air cooled, so I had to start back to camp before it got too dark. Once the sun starts down, the temperature drops rapidly. I returned quickly, propelled by excitement.

I hid the sample under my blanket and slept with it that

night, feeling it in secret. The next day I sent a piece off to be assayed, wondering how much gold it contained. It was hard to keep my mouth shut for the next few weeks while I waited for the assay report which finally came—pyrite, worthless, totally worthless.

We had a series of accidents just before Christmas. The first happened where a bridge was being built over the Moisie River. An Italian worker slipped and fell into a house-sized box of freshly poured concrete, a future abutment for the bridge. It was forty below. He fell into a thirty-foot-deep box filled with soupy concrete, in and under, gone. Nothing. There was no way to get him out. The abutment became his tombstone. It gave me the shivers just thinking about it.

Then one morning an Italian, in a tent filled with a dozen of his own kind, poured a tobacco can full of diesel into the potbelly stove to get it red hot so that it would warm the tent quickly. He'd done it before. This time the intense heat caused the open 40-gallon diesel drum, set too near the stove for convenience, to catch fire. The explosion that followed killed them all. There was little left.

There were lots of dumb men among the ten thousand or so workers. One crane operator, as a lark, dumped oversized rocks into the mule buckets. Mules were loaders with huge buckets that dumped things into the river by racing towards the river bank, then stopping suddenly at its edge so that the inertia would make their loads fly out and over the bank. This time the oversized rock had gotten stuck in the bucket so the inertia carried the whole mule over the edge, and the driver with it. The deaths had a sobering effect on me.

By then it was Christmas. Most guys went home for the holidays, but my first Christmas in Canada was spent there in camp. On Christmas Eve I was heading for the cook tent in the dark wearing my soft-soled moccasins when, just outside the door, I stepped on an 8-inch spike sticking out of a two-by-four left behind by the carpenters who'd built the camp. The spike came all the way up through my foot with its tip sticking up through the top. I couldn't believe what I was feeling with my hand. I put my other foot on the board to hold it down while I pulled the impaled one free, and then continued on into the tent for my coffee, as if nothing had happened.

I told the fellows inside that I'd noticed that the carpenters had left a lot of studs lying around. They agreed but when I told them what had happened, they howled with laughter. The bastards laughed. I hobbled back to my tent to put some iodine into the hole, stung by their reaction, still hearing their laughter. To get my mind off the pain, I started doing mathematical equations, calculating how much rock needed to be taken out of a nearby mountain to build the rail bed at that point.

I'd forgotten it was Christmas Eve until a big moth flew into my kerosene lamp. I don't know why it reminded me of Christmas, but suddenly feeling nostalgic, I pulled out a recent letter from Hans and re-read the part where he said he hoped I wouldn't be alone at Christmas; in fact, he prayed I wouldn't be. I was moved by his kindness, which made me think I should rescue the moth, but when I looked, it wasn't there, not even a spot on the glass. I hoped it had gotten out somehow, although I doubted it.

Christmas morning was sunny and the air was crisp, so I went for a walk to look at the newly finished tunnel that ended at the riverbank where we were building a bridge. Water seeping down its inside walls ran out of the end of the tunnel and over the bank, over a hundred feet down to the frozen river. The access ladder went down alongside the seeping water. I decided to go down to the river.

I started slowly, carefully, rung by rung. Ice had formed on some of the rungs, getting progressively thicker as I made my way down. Fearing I might slip, I slowed, being extra cautious at each rung. A few rungs later, what I feared most happened. I slipped off a rung, sliding down the ladder, faster and faster, until fortunately my arm hooked on a two-by-four stake jutting out from the rock. I jerked to a stop, wrenching my arm and shoulder, tearing the muscles. Hanging from the stake I managed to slowly swing my legs back onto the ladder, carefully wrapping my whole arm around the ice-covered rung. The thick ice coating, more than fist-sized, made it impossible now for me to climb back up. I had no choice but to continue downwards.

When I got to the bottom, I began shaking. I couldn't stop. I sat down on a rock to recover, ignoring the icy wind that constantly blew down the river from the north. As I stared up river into the wind, I saw the battered mule truck and realized that I'd almost ended up like him. I don't know why I went down the ladder in the first place. It was a foolish thing to do. I was freezing by then, so I made my way back to camp by another route.

Inside the cook tent it was breakfast time. I stood near the stove to warm up, looking around slowly. The French cook's radio was blaring his favorite music, a French fiddle tune. Two guys were up, clapping in time, one moving his feet faster than my eyes could follow. Some hollered at his feet in French, others with Scottish accents. Most were eating steak, heaps of this and that, and throwing around slang I couldn't understand. It seemed that they sought respect from each other through their loud ways. They were the rugged survivors of the brutal life up north, doing a tough job others didn't want to do. To them, challenging death in these conditions gave them a kind of pride, a feeling that it was a job only they could do.

It got harder for me to get along with them as the months passed. I was still trying hard to avoid their coarse ways and bumping them with my European manners. Eventually the day came when I couldn't take any more. I felt sick just looking at them, disgusted. I found it degrading to have to put up with their loud ways, their bull, and their smiles at the dumb things they said and did. It was time for me to quit. Maybe when I was older I'd be more tolerant. I had to learn patience. That much I knew. My impatience had brought me a lot of unhappiness so far.

♣ CHAPTER 22 ♣

When I got to Toronto, the first thing I did was to go see my Buick. I was surprised to find it where I'd left it and happy that it was still okay. It was all I had. I moved in to live with the Buick, at the YMCA.

The good-hearted YMCA manager found me a job at a paper box factory. The factory looked run-down. It appeared that the owner was squeezing money out of the building, doing no repairs, just keeping the steam going to run the equipment that made him pretty paper boxes and plenty of money. A work crew of girls made the boxes, turning them 'round and 'round on machines to glue on the cover paper that prettied them up. I was a cutter. I fed hundred-pound colored, slick paper rolls onto a steel rod, rolling and cutting the paper to length for gluing on the boxes. I made just enough money to get by and keep up the payments on the Buick.

Each morning I carried a black lunch bucket to work that was shaped like a coffin and filled with sardine sandwiches on rubbery bread. Every other workman on the street had one just like it. It told the people we passed that we had a job, sort of a badge of honor that announced we were making an honest living and didn't have to steal to survive.

On weekends I went to my favorite Hungarian restaurant, run by two fellows who'd escaped from Hungary in the fifties.

Not surprisingly, Hungarian goulash was always at the top of their handwritten menu. For fifty cents they served huge portions. Two years later their price jumped to fifty-five cents. They weren't money grabbers; they just served decent food. Their place was always crowded with people like me, workmen. I never once saw a couple eat there.

In the evenings I listened to sermons on my radio. I listened to what they had to say to learn how to pronounce words more correctly, and at times learning new ones. I had done it for two years, but my accent was still bad. I soon understood what they were talking about because they talked about the same darn thing all the time. They helped me a lot with my English. I doubt that any of those preachers had any idea that there was a guy, hanging his ears onto the speaker to learn how to pronounce English like them, but didn't care about their promises of heaven.

Once in a while I'd treat myself to a movie. That's where I met Eleanor. I thought she was the prettiest cashier in town. I should know; I'd been to quite a few theaters by then. And on top of that, she was a lady. The only problem was that she was twenty-two years older. It didn't matter to me, but it mattered to her. To me it was tit for tat. She was older, but I was a nobody, an immigrant. I had a better chance with her than with the younger ones who eyed me, and then turned their heads away after I'd said a few words to them in my broken accent.

Soon Eleanor and I became friends. I finally had a friend in Canada. The Buick slipped into second place. To have a real friend meant a lot to me—someone to talk to, and maybe some day to love. I'd learned that life without love was hell.

Eleanor was something special. She had a sixth sense about things I never quite understood. Once she told me that something awful had happened to me—that I'd almost been killed falling off a ladder. She went on to tell me all sorts of details, the exact time when it had happened and how. I confirmed that it was all true. I told her about an accident at the box factory where I'd slipped off a ladder and fell with my back against the end of the steel rod in the cutter. Luckily, I wasn't really hurt and had recovered in minutes.

She took me with her to religious gatherings, which took place on the second floor of a dilapidated building on Yonge Street. The floors creaked as we walked along the hallway, so I tiptoed into the meeting, which was taking place in a room that didn't look anything like a church. We sat quietly on chairs as we listened to a mysterious voice that came from speakers sitting behind a flowing multi-colored silk curtain. It fluttered in the subdued lighting as a humming mantra sound emanated from far away. Was it supposed to be from heaven?

The religion seemed to be some sort of a private movement, led by a mysterious lady no one ever saw. Over and over she exhorted everyone to prepare to follow her to heaven—soon—or even better, right away. Literature lying around described her powers of healing and how she was watching over all her disciples. I didn't believe any of it but figured there was no harm in being there with Eleanor. It was just something new I was learning about Canada.

I drove the Buick to Guelph to visit an old friend I'd met my first few days there, Jack Harcourt, the son of an Irish family. Jack had been the timekeeper at the wire factory where I'd dug holes. He'd just gotten engaged to a smart girl, and I wanted to meet her. As I cruised along Queen Elizabeth Highway, I pushed the Buick to its limit, surprised it could go a hundred miles an hour. Suddenly there was a loud bang, an awful bang, followed by a huge cloud of black smoke that blocked my view. I stopped and opened the hood. When I looked at the engine, nothing looked different; all the parts were in place. Maybe it had just gotten too hot. I started the motor. It made a hell of a racket—clattering noises—as if everything inside had come loose. But it ran, which was a wonder, so I drove on to Guelph, still thinking what a great car it was.

People passed me with a look that told me to get my car off the road. When I finally reached Jack's, he held his hands over his ears and shouted for me to turn it off. He said I'd blown a piston and would never make it back home. I should leave it in Guelph and take the bus. And there I was—trying to impress him with my great Buick and show him what a success I was. I just nodded and smiled, remembering all the times my plans to impress somebody had backfired.

It was good being with his family again and meeting his bride-to-be. We talked about old times: a visit to their cabin on Lake Huron and places we'd gone for coffee, carrying on and having fun. He'd just gotten a commercial pilot's license and was looking forward to getting married soon, not soon enough to suit him.

Against his advice, I risked driving the Buick back in the dark. I made it, with the loud noises getting more catcalls on the freeway, and when I got back to town, I kept right on going, past my place, and clinkety-clanked all the way back to where I'd bought it, to the sweet-talking toothpick-chewing salesman, standing beneath their bright neon sign—*Jack Saves You Dollars*.

I parked it at the curb in a manner that said I didn't want to have anything more to do with it. With his mouth holding what seemed to be the same toothpick, he looked at the car, then at me, and for once was out of words, knowing this wasn't the time to try to talk me into buying something else.

I left with my head down and slipped out from under the glare of the lot lights and away from his following eyes, having lost all I had: my Chevy with its testy steering wheel and the shiny Buick with its ivory one. I didn't bother to see if the boss was watching from the window beneath his oversized sign I now read as: *Jack Saves YOUR Dollars*.

I needed more money than I could make at the box factory to be able to buy another car, so I asked the railroad company if they would take me back. They would. I said good-bye to Eleanor, who was heartbroken and promised to follow me somehow, and went back north, back to Mont-Joli and Sept-Îles, back on the DC3 supply plane to an isolated camp. And my friend Jack from Guelph, with his new license, was its pilot. It's amazing what fate can arrange. In the unpressurized cockpit he showed me how to blow the air out of my ears as wc landed at *Mile 40*. "Hold your nose and blow. Easy." I never saw him again.

Another camp, another job, new faces just like the old ones. I wondered how I'd make out this time.

The rails had already been laid forty miles from Sept-Îles. They were now laying between a few hundred feet to a mile of track a day—depending on the terrain. In a few weeks I was promoted to a levelman and worked with two others to record elevations with a leveling instrument that marked cross sections every fifty feet to determine the amount of dirt to be cut or filled at that point. We had to survey for a rail bed that was almost level to make it possible for even several engines to pull the mile-long trains filled with heavy iron pellets.

I Held Out For a Few Months
against all the ones who by their nature
degraded me each day,
and just when I found two decent young boys
to be friends with,
neat and clean,
they decided they couldn't stand
the men around them any more.
They had to leave,
right away.
It was sad for me
to see them go,
to see them catch the train
to return down the track,
alongside the flow of the stream.

They'd had their belly full
and looked happy to be leaving.
It hurt to see them packing,
their things on their bunks.

When I felt the sideboard of my bunk
shake under my hand,
I knew the train was coming for them.
The boys felt it too,
and smiled,
waving good-bye to us all,
making us smile.

The screen door banged shut.
They were gone.
"Fine boys," someone said.
The train left.
My bunk stopped shaking.
I heard the stream again,
rushing down,
following the boys.

My boss was a loud, obscene man with crude habits, one of them being to pee from his bunk into an insulated plastic pipe to the outside. His hostility kept everybody on edge. One problem was his drinking. Drinking on the job was a *no-no*. If you were caught, you were fired. But we didn't mind his drinking because he was more likable and had a little warmth then. He was still obscene, but in a funny way, kind of entertaining. With his mean edges gone, he'd talk as if he could handle the world with ease, so people looked the other way when he was drunk because he was such a mean bastard when he wasn't. Sober, he pushed me around, calling me nothing but a fucking Nazi. He'd yell, "Fucking Nazi, come over here. Fucking Nazi, do this." On and on. One day he'd said it once too often, so I put in my notice at head office in Sept-Îles.

When they asked why I was leaving, I told them. It went all the way up to the top, to the vice-president, who called me in and asked for more details. I explained that I couldn't understand why he called me a Nazi when I wasn't one and that heaven knew I'd fought their system with my kid ways. I figured if everybody in Germany had done as I had, the Nazis wouldn't have gotten people to do their bidding. The vice-president listened, apologized for the company, fired the guy and transferred me to another camp, 260 miles north of Sept-Îles, to work for Jack Lewis, a fine Frenchman.

He was Jack number three for me in Canada, all good Jack's. This Jack told dirty jokes—just like the other two—and taught me how to calculate more complicated systems for figuring out optimal road bed construction, how to run a transit, and how to read stars and calculate a given position on the ground from their bearings. I learned to run spiral curves on the transit for the tracks and references for the curves of the roadbed—all the things that go into surveying a rail line. I soon became his assistant and helped him oversee two other survey crews, in order to keep ahead of the track-laying crews.

I saw the railroad making some headway. For the first time I saw rails laid. After the roadbed was shaped and compacted, we staked out the centerline for the rails. Mule trucks dumped piles of wooden ties neatly along the prepared dirt bed where men sorted out the ties and lined them up miles ahead of the rails that were eventually laid by a mile-long train carrying nothing but rails. It was pushed from the rear by a huge diesel engine with a crane attached to the front of the train. The crane picked up a rail from the first freight car behind it and swung it out front, laying it down on the row of wooden ties where it was then fastened down by a spike machine. When the freight car behind the crane was empty, that car was disassembled—all of it: rolling stock, guards, axles, and wheels—and set alongside the tracks so that the next car loaded with rails could be coupled to the crane-engine.

The crane and men could lay a mile of track a day on a good day, leaving a hundred or so freight cars disassembled along the way. When it was time to return for more rails, the cars were reassembled behind the engine and pulled back to be reloaded at a spur line down the way. This was how it went, over and over, day after day, for the next 300 miles.

In winter ties and rails could be laid directly on the frozen swamps. During the spring thaw that followed, the swampy sections had to be filled beneath the rails to keep them level. This was done by a monster of a machine that lifted thirty-foot sections of track just high enough so that ballast could be thrown under them from the ballast cars being pulled behind. It was one of the most advanced engineering methods known at the time.

Eleanor wrote that she was now working in Sept-Îles. She'd meant it when she said she would follow me. Time went quickly. Two hundred and sixty miles of track had been completed, the tunnel had been finished, and the Moisie Bridge was done. We could now come and go by train. I enjoyed the…

Red Evening Sunsets

In this wilderness at Mile 260
the rocks in the creek had turned red
from oxidized iron in the water.
It was as if we were somehow closer
to the big iron ore deposit
the railroad would haul south.
The wind blew
the red dust of iron ore
onto the landscape
turning everything red.

Outside the tent window
the whole world had turned red
from the evening sun—
a big red fireball on the horizon—
pressing its hue
onto everything in front of it:
the rocks in the creek,
the brush,
our camp.

Then—like a knife—
this sound came from the sky,
as if from heaven,
a piercing whistle cutting the air,
making me stand at attention,
making goose bumps run down my spine,
reminding me of its promise
of personal freedom in this land,
a promise kept
when I came to this big rough part of it,
to help build a railroad.

The train arrived, loaded with people and supplies. It was always a shock to see the trains coming and going in what had been untouched wilderness just days earlier. The train brought a letter from Hans reminding me that we'd promised to stay friends forever. It was nice to be reminded like that, such a long time after we'd last talked and laughed together.

On my birthday in November the cook arranged a party for me, but I don't remember much about it. What I do remember was that we spent the clear cold day looking for a survey stake under five feet of snow. We shoveled all day and never found it.

I still escaped on snowshoes occasionally, heading out across the flat, endless white landscape. On this particular day the weather was nice with no wind and lots of sunshine. I was miles from camp when I saw a white cloud racing towards me, startling me. It came straight at me and landed where I was standing—a flock of white ptarmigans. It seemed unreal. I stood still. The birds fluttered and chattered, walking on feather-covered feet around my legs, and pecked at my snowshoes. I watched for a while until I'd had enough of their pitter-patter and pecking. Then slowly and carefully, I snowshoed backwards, periodically stopping to watch, then stepped back further, looking again, until I couldn't distinguish them in the snow. That kind of special experience fed my soul enough to keep me going on the job.

When I got back, there was big news. One of the men had gone stir-crazy from our monotonous routine and had set off to kill himself by freezing to death in the night. He'd had enough of us and himself. A bunch of guys went searching, and when they found his tracks, they realized that he was going in a circle. Some of them knew that people lost on endless flat terrains usually walk in a seven-mile circle, clockwise, so they were able to find him before nightfall. The next day he was back to normal and nobody mentioned it again.

I think we all realized it could have happened to any of us. The days were tough. We worked in bitter cold and howling winds, fighting to drive stakes into the frozen ground and standing on ice with transits at 65° below Fahrenheit, afraid the sweat under our clothes might turn to ice and cause hypothermia. It wasn't hard to understand why someone might suddenly go out of his mind.

A few days before Christmas I went to see Eleanor at Sept-Îles. Most people had gone south for Christmas, leaving the town quite empty. It was my second Christmas in Canada, and this time I wasn't alone. We had private parties where sweet Eleanor held me tight while we shared pleasant words, laughter, good food, and each other's company. The days went by quickly; too soon it was time to go back to *Mile 260*. Eleanor made one of her eerie prophecies before I left, telling me that this would be our last Christmas together. Was her prophecy born out of fear that it would be our last? Or was it a question she hoped to hear me deny with a laugh? As always though—she was right.

Back at camp Old Jim, the Indian trapper, had returned after two months of hunting caribou and setting traplines. He was tiny in stature and over seventy years old. He'd pulled a sled loaded with furs and meat for a hundred miles or more. We were impressed, knowing we couldn't do it now, let alone when we turned seventy. On his own time he still did some trapping, catching ermines with rotten sardines, but he worked with us most of the time on the survey crew, blazing site lines in the bush so that we could get readings with our equipment.

He taught me how to sharpen an ax razor-sharp and how to easily zip a trail with it. He used to fill his back pockets with the pitch that he chopped from the trees as he went by, and then at lunchtime he used it to light a campfire, usually near a huge boulder. Within minutes, even at 40° below, he had good coffee made from melted snow in a two-quart tobacco can. As a lark, he'd build up the fire, hoping to split the boulder. Often he did. With a loud bang! Then he'd laugh and dance in the snow, showing us his wide toothless grin.

Near camp there was a beautiful lake. The wind blew over it fiercely most of the time, but I remember one particular day in late spring when it was incredibly beautiful, nothing moved, and it was covered in…

Stillness
The air is crisp, nothing moves.
Reflecting the surrounding hills
is a waveless lake in sky-blue,
sheltered by a cloudless roof.
There is no wind, no sound here.
I stand alone and listen to silence,
all that there is.
My eyes take one deep breath
to inhale all there is.
I sit down in awe,
slowly,
quietly,
like one would sit in some holy place.
I fold my hands.
I wonder.
I just wonder
about the hues in the woods,
about the sprinkles in the waves.
I gaze around,
filling myself,

Like one does sitting in some holy place.

In the stillness
I suddenly feared it could all fade.
It made me call on all that I had
to burn each image in my mind—
the surrounding hills,
the woods,
this waveless lake in sprinkling lights,
and the sky-blue over all—
for my golden days,
before the wind returned,
with the clouds and the snow
to take it away from me.

It was time to move on. I wanted to head out West where Wilma had immigrated, where she had said she would be if I wanted to find her. At night I cranked up my old gramophone and played records that reminded me of her. The same day I had finally decided to leave, I was offered a permanent job with the company, that of a section foreman. I'd be in charge of a sixty-mile stretch and get a putt-putt to drive up and down the rails, checking the track for cracks. But I already knew the stretches I'd be travelling—having been over them too many times already. There was nothing new in it. I passed on the offer, said my good-byes to the camp, and went to tell Eleanor.

As I held her hands during our good-bye, she handed me a letter that she asked me to read in front of her.

> *I remember the nights we stood in the hall and you held me close in your arms and I held you too. I made love to you, hoping you'd fall victim to my charms. Did you?*
>
> *I had a dream, darling, that I want to share with you now:*
>
> *After marrying a stranger, I looked from my island*

across the water and saw a man rowing towards me, waving, but never getting any closer. I walked into the water towards him. Waist-deep in the water, I saw his boat blown upside-down in a terrible storm. Back on the island I saw him rowing again, but away from me. I called and called, unheard, then cried, unheard. I was scared and cold. I hated him for not helping me.

I walked inland on the island and became lost. Then I met a very old man kneeling in prayer. I asked him to help me. I did not see his face. I told him about my marriage.

In a soft voice he said, "You're not married, my child; it's but a dream. Take your boat and go away from here. Do not be frightened. You will get to the other side."

With that he stood up and took my hands in his, and I looked at his face. It was your face, and you were smiling and walking with me to the boat. I didn't want to leave you, but you didn't seem to know me. To you I was a stranger. You said in parting, "Have no fear, my child, of anything. We will meet again."

You disappeared, the sea was calm, and a beautiful rainbow appeared in the sky.

Know, Alexander, in you I have all I desire for my heart and soul. I feel in my heart that if you and I had met years ago, we'd still have been attracted to one another. Always my memories of you will be happy ones.

Forever, Your Eleanor.

It shook me. I hated leaving someone as attached to me as she was. I'd made a friend for life. While trying to decide what to do, I wandered through Sept-Îles. The melting spring offered puddles of slush filled with garbage that had been collecting for months as the whistling winds played in the snow with flying papers. The town had had a long winter. Eight months of snow had turned into mud and water everywhere, untended, while the people now hid behind their dingy curtains and plastic-covered windows, stagnating, ignoring the garbage. I decided to go. After that everything happened quickly.

♣ CHAPTER 23 ♣

In hours, not days, a plane put me down on the *green* of a new land—Vancouver. The contrast between the land left behind and that before me was startling. From the plane window I saw sunny mountains and green valleys huddled along the Pacific; everything was green. Tall buildings surrounded a bay near a long suspension bridge, and water from the Pacific curved around land that rose steeply out of the harbor to become sun-capped mountains. What a world! When I got on the ground, I had to feel the grass before I could believe it was real.

I tracked Wilma down. She insisted we meet in a restaurant, somewhere public. The word *public* sent me a message I hadn't come to hear, having just left Eleanor and all. When the time came I was shaking inside—partly from seeing her but probably mostly from what I feared would follow. I could tell as soon as I searched her eyes that she'd made up her mind. This would take just minutes. She was cold. She was with someone else. Just the same, I owed her something because of how shabbily I'd treated her when I left Germany, not even saying good-bye. I asked her if there was anything she wanted, anything I could buy for her. I had plenty of money in my pocket. As if anticipating my question, she answered quickly that she'd like a sewing machine; in fact, a Swiss one would be nice. I bought the best I could find. And that was the end of Wilma. I played Beethoven on my cranky gramophone for weeks.

I found another surveying job, looking after construction procedures on an earthen dam project at Skins Lake in northern B.C. The plane ride to the site was breathtaking—we skimmed along the clouds near the mountain tops, missing sharp peaks by what seemed only inches, while down below Pacific breakers, pushed by the wind, crashed onto the coastline. When I got out of the plane I discovered those winds were damp and cool.

* * *

"The best thing that happened to me there was meeting you, John. Remember? I don't know if I've told you, Greta, but John was the engineer for Alcan, the company who owned the massive project that needed ten thousand workers. John and I spent our free time challenging each other over a chessboard. We set it up on a table in the field between the barracks and tents, hoping the thick clouds of black flies would be blown away by the breeze that came through the open field. That's where we became friends."

* * *

It was a gorgeous summer. The dam was part of one of the world's largest artificial watersheds—two hundred miles long. Water fell a couple of thousand feet through tunnels into monstrous turbines in a power station that had been hewn into a stone mountain near the ocean. The station was big enough to make *heavy* water that supplied electricity to the new smelter and to Kitimat, a newly created community for the fifty thousand people needed for the Alcan smelter when it began to produce aluminum from the bauxite shipped in from Jamaica.

Monstrous machines are what made the building of the dam possible. One was a D9 bulldozer that pulled a *sheepsfoot* roller, crawling back and forth to compact the clay dumped by the W21 scrapers. Compaction was essential to make the dam watertight. The *sheepsfoot* weighed about five tons. It was a large roller spiculated with ten-inch steel spikes shaped like a sheep's foot. There were rocks mixed in with the clay that had to be picked out by hand before compaction could proceed. They hired kids for that job. Lots of kids got summer jobs that way.

One day the operator of a D9 bulldozer pulling a *sheepsfoot* backed up just as one of the boys bent down to pick up a rock. Its spikes snagged his clothes, pulling him under, and compacting him into the dam. Days earlier that very operator had gotten the job for him—his own son. The RCMP had to use shovels to dig out what was left of him. After that the operator took to the bottle, eventually drinking himself to death.

The *bull cooks* had the safest jobs of all the men in camp, working inside for the cook, away from the swarms of black flies. That is, safe most of the time. Their job title came from years earlier when the cook's helpers looked after the bulls—the oxen—that pulled the old-fashioned equipment. Now their job was to keep the fire going and to help the cook with odd jobs like peeling potatoes, but that wasn't the real reason they came to camp. Most came to play cards and hustle the hard-working guys at the games that went on every night. Those *bull cooks* were professional gamblers, and most were crooked ones. One, who played with marked cards, was found rotting under the gaming tent. The killer was never found.

The camps were rough. We slept twenty to a tent. It was an ordeal similar to the railroad camps I'd just left, with constant noise and carryings-on. Some nights the loud music drove me clear outside. I decided to get a tent of my own, a real big one, big enough to show movies in so that I could spend my time away from their carrying-on. I got one in exchange for an IOU. With some sawdust on the floor, wooden benches, a projector and screen, I had a movie house. And as a joke I gave it a grand name, naming it after a famous theater in London. Part of my plan was to give people something to laugh about, and I often saw them laughing as they walked under the oversized sign: *Paladium*.

I showed old, cheap films. The men didn't care what they

saw—outdated or not—just as long as it had plenty of action. Cowboy shows were the favorite, especially with the kids of the working couples who lived in camp. They had a great time and screamed and hollered along with the actors. I didn't make any money on the *Paladium*—at best I broke even—but I learned some lessons for later on in life.

* * *

"John, I remember you telling me then that you were going to take a trip to South America. Did you?"

"Yes, we drove an old station wagon, four guys off to see the world. It was so crammed full of stuff that when we did need something, we usually couldn't find it. We drove through Central America, through the interior of Peru, and down to Chile. From there we crossed the Andes into Argentina and drove east through the red and green mountains to Buenos Aires, the *Paris* of South America. From there we sailed across the Atlantic to Africa.

"Our travel in Africa cost almost nothing, thanks to how all the countries handled foreign currencies. The first day we entered a country we would exchange U.S. dollars on the black market—where they brought a premium—for local currency. When we were ready to leave that country, we returned any remaining local currency to the bank in exchange for U.S. dollars, ending up with pretty much the same amount as we'd started with. It didn't make sense to us, but it happened in country after country. The countries had all overvalued their local currency, giving us more U.S. dollars for their local currency than it was worth on the international market. The first time it happened we laughed after we got out of the bank, feeling as if we'd just committed a robbery and had gotten away with it.

"We saw a lot of things along the way: gold mines in Johannesburg, lots of wild animals, and all kinds of natives. We went to East Africa and zigzagged back and forth across the continent, always heading north.

"We visited natives in their huts and saw how they lived and some of their problems. In one, we stayed with a boy who had a worm coming out of his belly. He used a partially split stick to twist and roll the worm out with, curling it onto the stick, about an inch a day, until he had pulled the entire three-foot worm out. It took weeks. We saw split sticks hanging on other natives too. It was fairly common—a Medina worm that came from larvae-infested drinking water.

"In North Africa we followed a column of French Legionnaires heading for Casablanca. They tolerated us until they reached a point where they expected to have a gunfight; then they turned us back. Eventually we made it anyway, and from Casablanca, we went on through Spain, France, Germany, and, finally, to England where we toured around for quite a while."

John paused. "Talking about Casablanca reminds me of a guy Estelle and I met."

"John, you're not going to tell them about that guy with the awful..."

"Estelle—don't give my story away."

"Sorry, dear."

"We were camping near Taber in Alberta in a travel trailer and got into a conversation with the guy parked next to us. He looked Australian—dressed in military fatigues, including a bush hat with the side turned up. We invited him in for a drink. That seemed to have been a mistake. He turned out to be a German from Hamburg. That was a surprise to us. He claimed that he'd gone to Marseilles to have some fun, got drunk in a bar, and woke up to find he'd been shanghaied into the French Foreign Legion.

" 'A likely story,' we thought. The later it got and the more we drank, the wilder his stories became. We figured that he was trying to repay us for the drinks by entertaining us.

"The Legion warned him not to attempt to escape. The punishment on being caught would be a week in a dark hole. If caught a second time he'd be beaten, then thrown back in the hole for a longer period—this time without food or water. And a third attempt would be fatal. They'd drill holes through his elbows and hang him with wires on a cross, leaving him to rot in the sun and to feed the vultures. But he claimed he'd escaped and had made his way to Casablanca.

"We knew better; it was a bold-faced lie. As we sat there, wondering how he could expect us to believe it, we couldn't keep our skepticism from showing on our faces. When he saw our raised eyebrows, he rolled up his sleeves to show us the scars on his elbows. They looked like tattoos to me. But we had a few more drinks and listened to some more lies, until he finally got up to leave in the early morning hours. As we stood on the steps of the trailer, he reached under his shirt and pulled out a snake, scaring us half to death! He'd been sitting there with it the whole evening. It gave us the shakes. But it also made us reconsider the stories he'd told. With that one sweep of his arm, holding up the snake, he'd given credibility to them all."

Greta look at Estelle in astonishment, and the two girls went off to do something else.

John had decided he was done telling stories, so we settled into a corner to play chess. We reminisced about our summer among the black flies and enjoyed the opportunity to spend the time by ourselves, catching up on what we'd been doing in more recent years, our stories occasionally distracting us from the game.

"Alex, you better put your mind on this game or you're going to lose it. I'll put you in check as soon as I figure out something here."

Which he soon did. We'd played most of the afternoon, so we decided to call it quits. "Let's go see what the girls are doing. Estelle, how are you doing?"

"Fine. Greta's having a nap, trying to catch up on her sleep, still suffering from jet lag, but she said not to let her sleep too long. We're going to have coffee as soon as she comes down."

A cup of coffee with friends in a warm cozy cabin was all the happiness I could imagine at that moment, and since they had requested it, I went on with my story.

“One day at the camp I confided in John that I planned to marry a girl from Vancouver that I didn’t know too well, remember John?”

“Oh, yes.”

♣ CHAPTER 24 ♣

She was young and looked honest and clean. That was pretty well all I knew, except that she belonged to the Jehovah's Witnesses. When John heard that, his ears perked up. He told me in no uncertain terms that it wouldn't work out, that I didn't know anything about them and their beliefs, and if I did, I'd realize I didn't belong with them. It would be the biggest mistake I'd ever make. But John didn't know about all of the mistakes I'd already made, some really big ones too, but he knew more than I gave him credit for about this.

Violet was like her name—shy and sweet. Her friendliness touched my loneliness. I was hooked. Being a Jehovah's Witness didn't matter to me—then. But John was still alarmed and tried to warn me that in time it would become a big problem. He told me more than once not to marry her, but I didn't listen. I was too lonely. And I've never been any good at taking advice anyway. It's a weakness that has cost me dearly throughout my life.

I was hungry for someone to care for me. I was into my third year of living in Canada. I couldn't stand the loneliness in this big, friendly country any longer. Loneliness rusts away the heart until there's nothing left. Besides, I liked the Witnesses I'd met so far. I found them to be friendly and decent. John just shook his head whenever I mentioned it. He had been fortunate in having wonderful parents and sisters. He didn't know what it meant to be alone all the time, and an immigrant besides. He just couldn't understand it. I married her anyway. She wasn't pretty or smart, but she was reliable and honest, until many years later when she lost those remaining qualities too.

Just before the wedding, I felt physically sick. I realized the wedding would make me part of the Jehovah's Witnesses religion, a reality waiting just around the corner. Until then, it was just talk between John and me. When the Witnesses found out about the emotional state I was in—my wavering emotions about getting married—a group of faithful elderly ladies came to take care of me as if I was their new *Witness* queen bee. They bathed me, gave me secret potions, and soothed me with sweet words, all to build a new moral conscience on my old one and to get me to accept their ways as the only way in life. So I got married their way. I made a pact with myself to arrange my life in a new way, eliminating the hunter instincts that had driven me thus far. But I wasn't at all sure I could accept their knocking on doors day-to-day like *goody-two-shoes* to tell strangers about a Bible I knew nothing about and wasn't interested in learning about either. But I tried. I'd made a promise.

It wasn't long before I could no longer fight my real nature. I had to find a way to make something of myself and to make some money to get ahead in the world. In the end I could only do one or the other. I decided on the other and started selling Kirby vacuum cleaners door-to-door, then neon signs from store-to-store. I did odd jobs to buy groceries, like shoveling snow for old ladies. In a very short time it became clear that their way wasn't my way. Any other religion might have been all right, but not this one. My sentiments lay with the Jewish way of understanding things that I had found in the Sepher Torah and Talmud. I found wisdom in their words, tested wisdom.

I talked to my new wife and explained my feelings—that the only thing I could do was to leave her—because of her religion and how her life was attached to it. We separated amiably and I began to rethink my life and myself.

When I was younger I'd found peace in the forest, so I retreated to the woods on northern Vancouver Island, a place of tall trees and salal as high as man, out where the cougars and bears were at home.

I hired on with a logging company to do a quantity survey of giant cedars and firs and to do contour mapping for a future railroad. As for the wild animals, my encounters weren't quite what I'd expected. One day I shot into the brush at the base of a monstrous cedar, fearing I'd seen a cougar. It was just a big raccoon that I'd killed. I felt guilty for years.

The men in camp were like the others I'd met, but they knew the country and told me I'd gotten off lucky with the raccoon. The forest did hide cougars and bears; I just hadn't see them. Some had come near the camp, even into it. One cougar took a dog out of the camp; another took a young girl. And when one guy ran into two bear cubs in the woods, he figured mama bear was close by, so he quickly climbed up an abandoned railroad trestle where mama bear kept him all night long.

After a few months of doing the same job, I was bored again—my sign to move on. But I wasn't ready to go back to Violet.

I stopped by John's folks. They lived in Burnaby in a Panabode house built of cedar logs. They raised champion boxers that his dad took to dog shows. It was fun living with them. There was a happy, upbeat atmosphere filled with smiles and laughter around them. Laughing was their way of life, from morning to night. I stayed with them for almost a year. During that year I learned not only how to laugh more easily, but that any problem had a solution.

To earn some money I decided to build a Panabode house like theirs in Abbotsford, east of Vancouver, on land owned by an Italian. We set the price. He bought the materials and gave me money for food. In a few months I had the building assembled, including the foundation, had roughed in the plumbing and electrical works, and had shingled the roof. While I was roofing, Queen Elizabeth came to visit Vancouver, always a special event. The motorcade passed within sight of my roof but I kept nailing and hammering—it was just another day of work to me. The finished house didn't sell. I'd expanded myself but had made no money. I was learning things, bit by bit, the hard way again.

I took a new job as a transitman with B.C. Engineering at Harrison Lake, surveying for a future transmission line. The job was to determine the best location for the future power line, identify any trees that would be hazardous to it, and mark them to be cut by the loggers. I admired how eloquently the loggers moved—like cats through thick underbrush—balancing on logs this way and that, while cutting off thick branches, zip, zip, zip, with razor-sharp double-bladed axes, all the while maintaining a walking speed down the length of the trunk. They cut trees so big that two men couldn't touch hands around them. They worked hard for their money, dangerous money.

My job wasn't challenging except for Easter Monday. We were following the abandoned Caribou Trail that had been built in 1859 by Royal Engineers from Britain for miners traveling up to the gold rush in the Caribou Mountains. It was six feet wide and followed the Lillooet River north through a forest of gigantic fir trees. Some showed evidence of old campsites. The scars where then eye-level bark had been removed for long-ago campfires were now ten feet above the ground, representing a hundred-year's growth.

Two Christian twenty-year-old boys were working with me that day. The night before, one had dreamed we would all die that Easter Monday. Naturally, he was hesitant to travel along the river with me that morning. I talked him into coming anyway; it was just a dream. I drove the Land Rover extra carefully along the trail in the spring sunshine. We passed over makeshift creek crossings, through pools of water and skunk cabbage swamps, and traveled on rough dirt, mud, and partly frozen gravel, passing above the Indian village of Skookumchuck that stretched out along the river below. Its name means *place of wild waters*. Just past the village we came to a rock face, a sharp-stoned cliff that dropped more than hundred feet down to the river. We could hear the pounding roar of rocks roiling in the white water that sprayed against the big boulders.

The roaring spectacle made me drive even more cautiously, as I tried to keep the wheels steady on a trail barely wide enough to drive on. The river was on my side. I watched carefully as the left wheels rolled slowly along the gravel cliff edge that, little by little, was beginning to slope and tilt the jeep gently towards the river. Still on the trail, it was beginning to slide slowly, tipping, hesitating, until finally I knew nothing could keep the jeep from going over and taking us with it.

I yelled, “Jump! Now!” One boy opened his door, then froze. In a few seconds the jeep began to roll, and its momentum rolled us over faster and faster, pounding and banging, finally dumping us into sudden darkness.

In the blackness under the water I held my breath as long as I could, then swallowed a lung full of water. A ripping pain burst through my chest. Seconds of panic, another gulp of water, more pain. I knew this was it. My mind had accepted death, but was surprised that it would be in water. I saw my mother as if in a picture, and then felt the moving weights of two bodies on me. Intuitively, as if it was the last act of my life, I struggled against the weights with all my might, pushed, then wormed my way past. A shimmer of light appeared in the dark, and I burst upwards into the light, gasping and coughing painfully.

I found I was standing on the side of the jeep in knee-deep icy water. I could see the two boys still under water, as if sitting in the jeep. I grabbed at their clothes, one at a time, gave them my hand to orient them, and pulled them up. It was all over in minutes.

We stood close together in the rushing water on one side of the jeep, coughing and coughing, stunned, then lost our balance and fell into the river. Now we had to swim for our lives to the edge of the river, through the force of the powerful spring runoff. In a flashback I remembered the ice-cold feeling of crossing the river at the Russian front. This wasn't so bad—no bullets zinging over our heads and no minefield waiting on the bank.

We made it across without any problem, and from shore I watched my paperwork float by, rapidly carried out of sight by the swift-moving water, work that had taken weeks to do. We could see where we'd come down the cliff face. We spotted the broken-off door and, more critically, our rear axle lying partway down. That door had saved our lives. If one of the boys hadn't opened the door trying to get out during the first roll, it wouldn't have broken off, and we wouldn't have made it out of the icy darkness. We would have been down and under. Heaven was kind to us.

It wasn't all that hard to climb back up the steep rocky cliff to the trail. Shaking inside and shivering outside, still hacking and coughing, we started the long walk back to camp and talked about the dream, the premonition, and the religious stuff the young boy was sure about. He'd been right all along and was going to make an offering in church.

It took us until nightfall to get back to camp. As soon as I reported our accident—as I'd expected—I was fired on the spot. I took it all in stride, thinking, "That's the way it goes." I was just glad to be alive.

I got another job on the transmission line: cutting trees with a forty-inch power saw and a double-bladed axe, just like the loggers I'd admired. There was good money in it. It was fun, but dangerous swinging that sharp axe from right to left while dancing along the trunk of the tree, zip, zip, zip. When I finished the job, I thought it had taught me more than if I'd stayed with the surveying.

♣ CHAPTER 25 ♣

With the job finished and money in my pocket, I'd begun to feel sorry for the situation I'd put my new wife in, so I decided to see if I could sort out my marriage one way or another and find some sort of a new arrangement for our lives.

I secretly hoped she wouldn't agree to what I saw as a possible solution to our dilemma. I felt obliged to propose something reasonable. For me that meant that we should both quietly hold onto our own beliefs and refrain from open participation in either one. If she agreed, it was clear that the road ahead would be tough for us both. We talked and walked and, in the end, agreed to give it a try.

We agreed to follow our own religious beliefs at arm's length, not bringing either into our home. Our future children would be brought up as Catholics to have a solid religious foundation, like the one I remembered Greta had. I never forgot her sinking down onto her knees on cold stone to pray in a Catholic chapel as I stood beside her. I was moved by her devotion. So my wife was free to read her *Watchtower* and I the Torah and the Talmud.

I decided to pick up on my study of architecture and finish what I'd started years before. That meant I had to be accepted as a student at UBC, the University of British Columbia. I was in luck; Professor Laserre, Dean of the School of Architecture, accepted my application.

To save money, we moved to a dog kennel. In return for my feeding a hundred dogs lots of eggs and white bread in the morning and evening, we got a rent-free sunny apartment alongside the barking dogs. I thought I'd try it to see if we could get ahead that way. After a month I knew we couldn't. We rented a place and paid for it somehow.

Now I had to make time to learn how to study. The Talmud says: "*Find yourself a teacher*." So I did, and I was lucky to find Peter Batchelor as my mentor. He was an honor student and *Massey* Medallist who taught me how to organize myself and showed me how he studied. Part of his plan was to keep fit, to run a few miles early in the mornings before going to school. On one of my four a.m. runs along Kitsilano Beach, four guys tried to mug me. With weeks of training it was easy to outrun them. I looked back and wagged *donkey's ears* at them.

I copied Peter as much as I could, except for his marks. He had top marks and I barely got by. My studies took everything out of me, but my grades still didn't improve.

For some reason I never knew, Professor Peeps invited one other student and me to do archaeological work with him during the summer holidays at Fort Langley, forgotten then but once an old Hudson's Bay Trading Post. We found enough material for him to figure out what the old fort looked like and how it had been laid out. Today the fort has been re-created. It was a moving experience for me to see the restored fort and buildings and palisades as they once were and to know I had a small part in it—finding pottery shards and old tools where most of the artifacts were discovered, along the outside edge of the old fort wall where garbage had been thrown.

The following year, as a student, Arthur Erickson—my professor in architectural design and later a world-famous architect—counseled me that to better develop my design abilities, I should enroll at the school he had just come from, the University of Oregon. I took his advice and applied.

To earn enough money to go to Oregon, I took on a job as a

field engineer with Bechtel, surveying and supervising a tank farm and pipeline near Abbottsford, part of a 48-inch oil pipeline crossing the whole of Canada, the *Trans Mountain Pipe Line*. The tank farm had three oil tanks, made of steel plates—a mere one-inch thick at the bottom—welded together, each a few stories high, to be used for storing 18 million liters of crude oil. Building them successfully depended on the welders' skills. Their seams had to be welded with just the right temperature so that the steel plates wouldn't buckle. A buckled tank couldn't hold oil safely.

I had one problem on the job: getting the construction supervisor's cooperation. I had to pass his test to prove that I was worthy of giving him orders on the site. He wanted to know if I was strong enough to stand up to him. He challenged me to lift a 250-pound valve as high as my belly button. That would impress him. I thought it was a strange way to relate to a co-worker on a construction site, but if that's what I had to do to get the tanks built and move on, then I would. So I lifted it for him, and after that he cooperated.

I found similar situations at other building sites in later years—a testing of authority between head men, a dance of wits to see who knew his job best and who had more experience doing things right and efficiently. The outcome established the hierarchy of command. For the benefit of smooth-working relationships on job sites, I thought it best to allow the guys I had to work with to challenge me in whatever way they wished, even if it was a silly game like arm wrestling. We still aren't that far from the animal world.

My tall Texan boss wore a Stetson and a smile. He always gave me the toughest jobs on the site. I finally asked why. He smiled, disarmed me gently by putting his arm around my shoulder, looked down and drawled, "Alex, if those jobs had been easy ones, I would have asked somebody else." How could I complain about that? At the end of the project he offered to buy me a beer. On the way in, he held open the door and said, "When you've finished school, come run a stretch of pipeline in

Montana for me." I knew then I would always be able to find a job.

Thanks to that job, I had enough money to go to school in Eugene, Oregon. We bought a tiny house with $500 down, an old Packard for Violet, and a scruffy second-hand bike for me—scruffy so that no one would steal it.

I went after my goal in my usual way, with everything I had, and soon got into the swing of studying, thanks to my friend Peter who had helped me organize myself. The daily commute by bike gave me time to reflect on how to do my best.

My route took me past an old cemetery on a hilltop. Marble statues of fallen soldiers from the Civil War stood on pedestals, watched over by tall fir trees whose tops swayed in the wind. When the tops hushed and stayed still, they reminded me of a German poem by Goethe, roughly translated:

There is no breeze in sight.
Even the birds are still.
See—even all the tree tops are at rest.
So be patient, be sure, soon you will rest too.

When I saw the treetops at rest, I pedaled harder, faster, wanting to do better, to get over the hilltop and get on with it, to get down to the university and do my best.

Architecture was five years of small classes, except for the design course. That was held in an oversized room filled with light where hundreds of students worked together as they developed architectural solutions to assigned tasks. We pinned our designs on bulletin boards near our workbenches to show our progress to the professor assigned to critique what we were working on.

This huge space was filled with laughter and talk and loud music of sorts—our commotion. I suspected it had been designed that way for a purpose—to force us to shut off the outside world from ourselves and to make us concentrate better—to think and feel architecture. We had to learn to concentrate by shutting out the outside world at will. I had to survive in the chaos. It helped me later in life to concentrate and zero in on something.

Although I never quite reached Peter's scholastic level, the university president congratulated my dad several times on my high marks, averaging above 3.5, mostly 4.0, even one in English Composition. His letters home were unexpected. I was happy to have Dad find out I was trying hard.

A special event came along—our first daughter, Alexandria. She was alert and had a sense of humor right from the start. I loved her bright ways. With her in my life I was aware a new responsibility had come my way. No more loony ways for me. But could I stop myself from being me? Could I?

It was tough being a student and a husband and a father, looking after the yard, and working thirty-six hours a week for the Department of Agriculture designing logging roads. I was allowed to work as many hours as I wanted whenever I could fit them in. Being able to choose my working hours was the best part.

All in all, I think I was at my best then. I loved every minute of it. I especially enjoyed walking between classes through the park-like grounds of tall fir trees, being permitted to be part of it and being given a chance to improve myself with a scholarship paid for by the people of Oregon. I was so deeply grateful that at times tears rose to my eyes as I crisscrossed the campus.

Behind my ability to improve my grades was help from a new friend, my English teacher, Dr. John Pratt, a Quaker. He was funny and lively, and taught me the finer points of writing prose. To him prose was music, writing prose was like composing. He taught me to compose sentences in a paragraph as if they were a sequence of notes, forming a melody, dada da daaaaa, and to use the proper instruments—effective sentence structures.

We philosophized a lot together about how nature was ruled by its own ever-repeating laws and methods. We discussed how nature's development of diverse root systems for trees of different lengths, types, densities, and in different environments, was similar to the structure of the nerves in the brain. We speculated on how man in a thousand years would be a floating head in a plastic bubble—no body or arms or legs, nothing else—floating at will, a being at its optimum. And Dr. Pratt loved medieval literature. He had a particular weakness for religious sagas. He even went so far as to have a black raven perched on his shoulder at home, while citing the words of the old man in Beowulf. Under his tutelage I won some recognition in an international essay competition commemorating Albert Schweitzer's 85th birthday.

The last summer at school I worked as a structural draftsman for Stone & Webster, who really needed structural designers, so I ended up designing parts of the new Georgia-Pacific pulp mill at Toledo. When each assignment was finished, I was given a more difficult one. My boss, a wonderful Mr. Kennedy from Boston, kidded me as he gave me increasingly more difficult design jobs to see how far my ability would take me before I failed. He found out. I couldn't design a set of bolts for a tower. It looked simple at first, but when I realized that the bolts had to withstand three-dimensional stresses from a six-foot by sixty-foot long drum spinning with varying weights and speeds, I was stuck. I wasn't capable of doing three-dimensional calculations.

Another interest I had at school was sculpture. I was fortunate enough to be able to study under Professor Zach. He had done sculptures for the world-famous architect Niemeyer who had designed parts of Brasilia. With his guidance I did some sculptures in concrete for a park in Springfield that are still in use today—kids still slide up and down on them.

The years at school were full of events. Our second child, Anna, had arrived. She laughed a lot, and was solidly stubborn, which later in life gave her the ability to wade through problems of her own making, and to get herself out of them again and again. With the responsibility of a second child, it was time to finish school.

During my fifth and last year we had to design a prison. The whole class went up to the penitentiary in Salem to see the real thing. The warden led us around to see the prisoners and their cells, the cafeteria, and the places where they worked, such as the laundry. To feel what it was like to be a prisoner, to understand the human side and come up with a good design, I had myself locked in a cell, and to raised eyebrows, I got permission to be strapped into the chair in the gas chamber. It felt eerie. I could see both my classmates watching me and the black handle that would be pulled during execution to drop the deadly pellets into the water-filled metal box behind the chair. I thought I had to know what it was like to be in the shoes of the people I was to design the prison for, to find a solution right for them—a human design.

To earn my degree I chose to design a housing complex for Indians in the Northwest Territories, similar to the railroad land where I'd worked with old Indian Jim. I'd learned to respect him and his ways, so I incorporated the Indian thinking into my design as I understood it. I found one ancient Indian band's approach to life most fascinating: instead of incarcerating a fellow Indian for stealing, the elders would just give him a new name, like *Grey Wolf Who Stole*. My project was to be made with local indigenous materials—stone and timber—and include both the winter and summer living modes inside each home, a reflection of their traditional winter and summer life. I presented my project to the faculty, who accepted it with handshakes and an invitation for a beer. My Bachelor of Architecture was complete.

Within weeks I got a job as a project designer with Peter Bilder who had a company in Lynnwood, Washington. We designed prefabricated offices, schools, homes, and you-name-it. Most designs were ingenious, often in curved and sculptured forms, and were a success on the market. That success meant a new factory had to be built.

Peter entrusted me with buying and contracting what was needed to build it, including the unusual requirements of finding machines able to carve and glue and press panels up to twenty feet long. These inventions required innovative machines that had to be tinkered together in a do-it-yourself fashion right on the site—which we did. By the time we finished, I realized that building this unique factory had cost a lot of money, and I expressed my concerns to him. He put his arm around me, gave me a big Havana-cigar smile, and told me that the way I'd bought and built the factory had made him more money than all his salesmen combined. I never forgot Pete's analysis that buying right is a powerful tool in accumulating wealth. With his being so pleased, I dared to ask him for a small share in the company, maybe one or two percent. He just smiled again, and lectured that partners he could do without. So I moved on—with Pete's blessing and a letter of recommendation.

♣ CHAPTER 26 ♣

It was Easter 1961. The Canadian government had studied my design for the Indian housing complex in the Northwest Territories and invited me to work for them there. *There* meant Edmonton, Alberta. I accepted. I loaded everything into a white panel truck—the wife, the two girls, a canary, and even a washing machine. The birdie, in its cage, swung back and forth in front of my nose all the way through the magnificent Rockies and on to Edmonton. As we got closer to the new city, the land became endlessly flat with a horizon of frozen gray grass blowing in the wind.

My hopes for our new life began to sink. I became disheartened. I longed for the lush green of Washington State. But we had to go on, into a landscape that made me feel sick at heart with its boring straight road and patches of scruffy short trees lost among the gray-grass prairie. I saw a tough land that was going to make our start here no picnic. We could only handle it if we became tough too.

"Happy Easter!" I thought, driving into a leafless gray Edmonton, which sat in the middle of a desolate-looking flatness—no place to live in. We looked for a place in the country and hoped to find a down-to-earth farmhouse with at least a few trees and some nature nearby.

We found a place owned by an old farmer who didn't want

to live in it anymore, preferring to move into the city with all its conveniences. The place was pretty crude, but we took it. It had no running water, only one potbelly stove for heat, and a chemical 5-gallon toilet that I had to empty first thing every morning—but I got used to it.

The house was set on a dugout, a cellar dug in the dirt—dirt floor and dirt walls—where gophers could dig in and out. In the early days on the prairies when a farmer first got his homestead, he just dug a hole, covered it over to live in during the first winter, and then turned it into the cellar when he built his house over it. Our farmhouse dated back to those olden days. We did have electric power though.

We got our water from an old-fashioned well with a tin bucket we let down on a rope. And in winter when the well froze, we hauled water from our neighbor's creek where a waterfall kept the water flowing year round.

We had a garage too, but it had a problem: the big doors fell off, face down in the dirt, whenever I unlatched them to get something out. It was an acrobatic act to get in. And there was another problem: a hundred feet from the house there was an outhouse that needed relocating—badly. That meant digging a new hole, moving the outhouse, and immediately filling in the old one.

All in all, the rather romantic outside of our dilapidated new farmhouse compensated for a great deal.

The nicest thing about the farm was the abandoned barn. It had a mansard roof, hay and straw, and smelled of cows. It was big enough to put a house in. I loved looking inside once in a while, not really looking for anything, just checking to see if everything was the way I remembered it from the last look.

There was a chicken coop with a fenced-in yard. As soon as we saw it, we had to get some chickens for it and for the kids, to put some life into the place. Later we got some ducks and geese too. We had a little dugout pond for them to paddle in that they shared with two muskrats. At times the geese, followed by the ducks, would waddle down the road miles from the farmhouse to be near other geese. It took part of a day to get them all back.

Inside the house there was a potbelly stove with a stovepipe that went up to the roof right through the middle of the upstairs hallway. We had to turn that pipe a deep red in the windy winters to get any heat upstairs. Tiny sparks would stick in the pipe and come out of the chimney when the wind blew. What's more, sparks seemed to stick on the outside of the glowing red pipe. How we never burned the place down I'll never know.

We took our garbage to a gully to add to the previous farmer's refuse of beds and stoves and tin cans—assorted iron stuff that had rusted down to almost nothing. We enjoyed poking around there and often found interesting treasures like old tobacco cans and odd-shaped bottles in old-fashioned colors.

The second-story windows looked out over the prairie—the real prairie with miles of nothing where one could feel the power of the prairie sky. One window faced onto a dozen or so spruce trees, the most precious part of the whole place. The first thing each morning, I looked out to admire them and the sparrows nesting and flying about in them, summer and winter. It became a ritual for me. In the winter I had to scratch the ice crystals off the tiny window with my fingernails to be able to see the trees.

There were a few significant events that happened during our first winter on the farm. First, our son Rudy was born. We gave him five names, all previously used by one line of ancestors as far back as six hundred years ago. It wasn't right that I pushed it, but I felt I might as well. This remarkable event of a male coming into the family might not reoccur. Having five names would give him an edge right off the bat when he tried to measure up to the standards of others.

Another thing happened one morning at forty below when—already late for work—I couldn't get the truck started. The radiator was a block of ice. With the energy of a young man, I unbolted the radiator, step by step in the freezing wind, with a chill-factor of minus 60, stoked up the kitchen stove and put the whole radiator in the oven—like a cake. As soon as the ice had thawed, I filled the radiator with boiling water and put it back in the truck, hose and all. To my surprise the truck started, but now I discovered it was stuck in the snow. Still with some energy left, I left the truck running and stalked over to the neighbor's—a couple of miles away—in the cold wind to ask for a push with his tractor. Neighbors on the prairies would always help each other out, so he came to my rescue. He pushed my truck out of the snow—minus the back bumper. It simply snapped off when the tractor pushed the truck forward, because its steel had become brittle from the forty-below cold. Not counting the chill factor.

Then there were the chickens. We had to move them out of the coop during the fifty-below nights into our dugout under the house. We left a bulb burning day and night for warmth for them. The knife-sharp winds lowered the fifty below temperature even more. After the coldest night that winter, even the bulb-warmed dugout was too cold for the chickens. When we went down to feed them in the morning, we found some hopping around on one leg, the night's cold having *bitten* their other leg off. Life was only for the hardy on the prairies.

The worst thing of all happened one morning when I was late for work again. It seemed I was often late getting to work in the winter. Folks living in the prairie took the weather in stride and dealt with the winter's challenges, not worrying about time too much, just doing what needed to be done. But I worked in the city for the Canadian government, so I was checked up on.

This eventful morning as I carefully carried the chemical toilet down the steep stairs, which I did every morning, I stumbled and dumped it—all of it. It ran all the way down the stairs and into the kitchen. That was the worst sight in my life. My job waited while I spent hours on my knees, gagging, cleaning it all out from the cracks in the wooden floorboards. By the time I'd finished, I was exhausted, more emotionally than physically, but I still had to get to work through the deep snow that covered the narrow gravel roads. I raced off to town and watched the snow fly into the ditches, thanks to a coffin in the back of my panel truck—filled with head-sized rocks for good traction. I got there late, but I made it.

In the same way that I cut through the snow with my truck, my co-workers scrambled to their desks when our boss, the district architect for Alberta, Saskatchewan, and the Northwest Territories, came into the office. I stayed wherever I was. After he left, they told me that I'd get a bad annual review for being seen just standing around, but I couldn't hustle for show. I told them that whatever they did, sooner or later, their real worth would shine through, whether caught standing around talking or not. I was in a free country, where I would be judged for what I could do.

Back in green Washington, my old friend Pete struggled to keep his business alive but finally lost it all. I felt bad and wondered if it might have been different if he'd given me a chance to be even a small partner of it.

Spring made up for the hard winter. The nicest feeling in the spring was seeing the snow thaw, watching the puddles find ways through the cracks of the soft surfaces, here and there, and to finally see some green appear along the side of the barn that faced the sun, near the farmhouse. I enjoyed watching the trickles of water find freedom and found it interesting to see how little the water moved after working itself free—like people.

At work, everybody thought I was nuts for living in the country on a farm in primitive conditions. Even the farmers who'd worked on those farms for generations had given them up and were renting them out to dummies like me. They now lived in the city in comfort, with the conveniences of running water and shops, restaurants and theatres.

In The Country Spring Brought Healing
Not in the city.
In the city
spring brought slush and filth,
and accumulated dirt from the winter
that wore down the city
for too many months.

Flying papers and dirty water
trickled along the curbs.
Spring was ugly to the people too.
They were tired from too much winter.
Many escaped,
if they could,
until the hardy bushes and scruffy trees
put out their green.

On the farm,
I began digging in the garden,
watching the long sunny hours of summer
perform miracles.
Plants suddenly
sprouted out of the ground
and grew quickly,
flowers and cabbages
growing in days,
nature performing miracles.

At work we also wrestled with the seasons in the Northwest Territories. We had to plan a year ahead—what to ship, what to build, and what to repair—all within a strict timetable to accommodate the natives and non-natives. We built bathhouses for the Eskimos, RCMP posts, boarding schools for the Indian children, water and sewer systems for towns, new airports, nursing homes, hospitals, and storage facilities for oil and gasoline. Everything had to be complete in every detail a full year ahead. If one part failed or was missing, all was for naught, and the project had to be shelved until the following year. Because the waterways were frozen most of the year, we had a very narrow two-month window to ship everything north by barge and get them back south before the open water in the Arctic Ocean refroze and prevented their return passage.

Much of it was flown in by ingenious bush pilots. These guys were expert mechanics who could fix their own broken oil lines and plugged-up gas lines when their planes let them down in cold desolate country. They were magicians at landing on the frozen lakes and rivers, at moving barking dog teams in the back of their planes, and at cutting through the treetops to make emergency landings. Bush pilots were the glue that held the essentials together in the vast lands of the Northwest Territories. They made the impossible possible. It was always an adventure to fly with one of them. Some had been fighter pilots in the last war. They got you there. You could count on that.

In winter the ground below all looked the same: white, with wind-swept blowing snow. The other three months of the year it was endless water: in swamps, in swooping gigantic mud slides, miles long, in rivers and creeks running in endless lazy S's, and in lakes as big as some countries. The land consisted of barren ground, rocks, mountains, and mud slides, always mud slides.

When a plane arrived, it would be greeted by dozens of natives, usually the very young and very old, who stood where the plane had cut its propellers to wait for something or someone to get out. The first time I arrived to that waiting crowd, I felt like the Queen of Sheba until I came out, walked through the crowd, and looked back to discover that they were still waiting to see what or who else might appear. It never changed.

After we landed, I would worry with the pilot about the mechanical condition of the plane and the availability of oil and fuel, to make sure I wouldn't be stuck where I'd just landed. Then I could turn my attention to whatever task had been the original reason for my trip. My job was to take over buildings, to accept completed projects on behalf of the government, and to collect the list of changes and requirements for future buildings. It was basically a boring task, but I grew to love the people and the nature of the north.

It didn't take long before I realized that my dreams of architecture for the natives would never be approved by the government. I had to do things the way they'd always been done. A good example was the bathhouse designed by the

Health Department to teach the Eskimos hygiene. A year after the building was finished, I found it wasn't used at all, except for the doors, which had been burned as firewood.

Doing my job, while taking hazardous flights with bush pilots—barely missing power lines and landing on broken-up ice fields—I became aware that the bathhouse project was a typically benevolent, but misdirected, solution by the government. I couldn't justify sticking around much longer. I knew this was going to be a job I would quit soon.

In the meantime I learned what I could: solutions to overcome permafrost problems, how to build in severe cold, what kinds of pilings supported the buildings—steel, wood, plain driven, or steamed through the ice—to hold them up like spider's feet. I learned the grip values of ice for various pilings and how to insulate permafrost from the radiating heat of the buildings sitting on the piles. The foundation was a serious problem for the builder up north. In all other aspects, the structure simply demanded more attention to detail and more insulation than buildings down south. The discharge of sewage was the most difficult challenge. Six- to eight-foot deep ditches had to be dug or blasted, hundreds of feet long, in the permafrost and filled with sand and gravel to accommodate the waste pipes—a costly way to get rid of the waste. Useless waste, except to some who kept their waste to use for gardening. Some. One planted strawberries under some thick plastic sheeting—along the bend of a river in kind of a nook in the brush—which created a temperature of almost 50 degrees Fahrenheit under the sheeting, even though it was still below freezing outside.

Getting back from a few days up North was always a relief. I looked forward to getting back to my family of little ones at the farmhouse, chemical toilet and all.

At work I announced I was going to become a millionaire. It was a challenge to myself mostly—a lark to put myself on the spot. What I had to figure out now was how. I began by asking people in the know. They all said the same thing—real estate—

so I looked for a bargain-priced piece of land.

My start came when I found the land, and more importantly, when the banker at the bank where I deposited my checks every two weeks listened to my idea. I told him I wanted to buy a farm, subdivide it, and then sell it. He opened the door to wealth by showing me how to do it.

Because I had a steady job with the government and deposited my pay regularly he would lend me ten thousand dollars. He knew I had a panel truck. That was worth a thousand dollars collateral. When I bought the farm, he would lend me half of what it was worth. The farm cost eighteen thousand, so he lent me nine thousand, plus a thousand for the truck, and ten thousand based on my regular deposits, for a total of twenty thousand. After I'd paid for the farm with the bank's money, I used the two thousand left over to drill a well. I subdivided the land and sold the whole farm for double what I'd paid.

I kept one parcel of land to build a house on. I took out a mortgage and spent the next year building and completing it, all by hand—no power. My hands were a mass of bloody blisters by the time I was done. The new house had a gorgeous glassed-in tower, and from there I could see miles of the prairie and its inhabitants—coyotes, deer, and lots of owls and gophers.

About that time, our youngest and last child, Maria, arrived—a butterfly, nothing but joy. And that's how she stayed all her life.

I flew north again; I sensed it was going to be my last time. I went to visit the Inuits who generally occupied the land fifty miles inland from the Arctic Ocean. That's as far as they went by foot to hunt caribou. From there the Indian lands ran south for a thousand miles or so. I hired a plane to fly past the divide and watched the very tall skinny pilot, known to all by his nickname, *Dipstick*. He was a German ex-fighter pilot who'd been shot down over London. He sat—silent and purposeful—as his eyes skimmed the terrain below, the clouds, then the instruments, back and forth, while at the same time he seemed to listen to the hum of the single engine, ensuring it sounded right. I felt safe and enjoyed the trip. He landed me safely at the Arctic village of Coppermine. After the usual landing worry about fuel and oil, I went off to visit Jim.

Jim was now ninety years old, my oldest Inuit acquaintance—completely tattooed. He lived with his third tattooed wife, now in her eighties, in a tent set on barren soil and stone. They were the only inhabitants of a rock island where the natives buried their loved ones. Jim hoped for some cigarettes I'd promised him weeks ago. It was spring.

A flickering kaleidoscope of northern lights illuminated my walk over the ice on Coronation Gulf in the Arctic Ocean. Looking down into the clear bluish-green ice was like looking into glass. I could see paper-thin lines running like scars at different angles for a depth of ten feet, an unusual beautiful sight. I couldn't see Jim's tent, but I could hear him coughing and chipping ice for the tea his wife would make to honor my visit. By the time I got there, it would be ready. Hidden by a snowdrift, I didn't see the caribou-hide tent until I got within shouting distance.

The wood door to the tent was tiny—less than two by three feet—and made from old crates from the beach. Weathered caribou straps held it together and formed the hinges. To get in, I crossed my arms, leaned my shoulders forward and bent down as far as I could. Then I shuffled my feet to carry me slowly over the frozen, barren ground, seeing nothing but my feet at this point.

Once inside, I had to stand slightly bent. Light came from a kerosene heater. Jim and his wife stood upright, smiling, in decorated, two-piece white caribou outfits. They stretched out their hands to me after I gave them mine, which was their custom.

Two bunks lay in an *L*-shape made from peeled crooked sticks. Other sticks formed an overhead frame to support the brown caribou furs. The tent was covered with two layers of fur, skinned sides together, which formed an air space of insulation.

Long winter living had dried the inner fur and released single hairs that floated around inside like odd flies.

We smiled and nodded in silence, agreeably pointing to ask or answer questions. Jim's wife served tea in chipped enamel cups filled to the rim. The tin cup was too hot to drink from. It looked like tea, except for the floating caribou hair. Now it was my turn to ceremonially hand Jim the anticipated cigarettes. He smiled and bowed and smiled and bowed.

Smiling and nodding, we warmed our hands on the mugs. Jim's wife offered rock-hard biscuits complete with caribou hair—not unexpected. We smiled and nodded some more. The wait for the tea to cool determined the length of my visit. Jim nodded; it was time to drink and eat. Then Jim indicated it was time for me to go by lying back on his bunk and closing his eyes, still smiling. I thanked Jim's wife by bowing my head a few times. I looked at Jim. His eyes were still closed, saying good-bye. This memorable moment of leaving taught me that it was possible to say much without words.

I walked back in the flickering northern lights across ice that continued to make eerie cracking sounds. I was grateful to get back to camp to bunk on fresh linen.

The next day, after I had checked out some buildings and made my report, *Dipstick* took me up in his Otter. Before take-off…

I Scraped a Clear Patch
on the frosted plane window
to bid good-bye in my mind
to ever-smiling Jim
with his aged wisdom.
I caught a quick glimpse of him
holding the rope of his sled,
standing, still smiling.

Pounding and shaking,
the roar of the motor filled the cabin

as the powerful single engine took off,
freed at last from the frozen land.
From the air I could see
other small tents and scattered dark cabins
in the white expanse below,
Jim's now a dot.
Then everything faded
into indistinct contours of bluish-white.
As we rose,
The bluish-white gave way
to a shapeless mass
of one white vastness.
Jim was gone, for good.

We flew over never-ending white
for hours
until at last,
tiny dark spots appeared,
winter bushes,
marking the beginning of the tree line.
We flew through banks
of swiftly moving white clouds
that cast weirdly shaped shadows below
until, in the distance,
we saw a valley floor
and a city that seemed to float
on a bed of greyish velvet.
No snow this time.
Sometimes Edmonton in the early spring.

At home, the grass wasn't as velvety
as it had appeared from the air.
It was just plain gray.
In my absence a badger,
snarling and wild-eyed,
had moved in under my panel truck.

He didn't want to budge,
so I left him.

Soon life returned to the prairies. As the weeks of spring passed, more wildlife appeared. An owl nesting near the house swooped down on me, clawed at my hair as it passed, and hissed shrilly, as it tried to keep me from going past its domain on my land. The wildlife was part of the reason I had learned to love living on the prairie.

♣ CHAPTER 27 ♣

I decided it was time to open my own architectural firm and begin working for myself. I accepted an offer for a fifty-fifty partnership from a contractor who'd worked for the government up north. I was the architect, and he was the builder and owner. That way, he saved half the architectural fees and I had a chance to challenge myself and put what I had learned to work.

My office was a small empty space in my new partner's building. My new partner asked a painter to paint my cubicle in exchange for a two-car garage design for the painter—not exactly what I'd dreamed of while studying architecture. I drew up the plans in half a day.

After that I doodled imaginary building sketches as I sat next to the telephone in the corner, snugged away, waiting for it to ring, not knowing what to do if it did, and secretly hoping it wouldn't. I had nothing to worry about. It was silent for days, for weeks.

I had to wait until my partner brought me a job. He was going to build a forty-suite apartment. I was to draw up the plans for him. While in the process of doing them the project floundered and was canceled. More waiting.

Word got around somehow that I was a smart architect, looking for work. Why smart, I never knew, except that some people thought any immigrant who'd become an architect must be smart. Two professional wrestlers, who were also real estate agents, didn't figure I was too smart however. They figured I was an easy mark, which I was. I designed an office building for them and they only paid a small portion of the fee. The rest I never got.

To get the rest of the money—so they said—they first needed some drawings for a warehouse, so I did them and, in the end, never got paid for that job either.

It went on like that and got worse. Word got around that I was to be readily had. In came a friend of the wrestlers who wanted plans for a twelve-suite apartment—but it had to be done in a hurry. He promised to make me a partner. I had three days to do the plans. I'd do anything to get a job, so I worked every hour of those three days, finished the complete set of drawings in time, but again didn't get paid. It was no way to make a living, but now what? All I could do was wait.

My partner was going to build a hotel in the town of Peace River. I did the drawings, and he saved half the architectural fee. In the process of visiting the site for the hotel, I met people in real estate and insurance and others who spread the news that there was an architect in town looking for work, and promising finders' fees, which was illegal for an architect to do. If found out, I would lose my license.

But I had to risk it. How would an unknown immigrant, with no friends or relatives, get commissions? If I could just get one job, I would offer the client something more than other architects. I had to be better and smarter and design innovative, attractive buildings, superior to what was on the market. And the cost per square foot had to be less. I promised all those things to prospective clients. And in the end, that's just what I did.

An insurance agent in Peace River, in return for a finder's fee, told me about a motel that had to be enlarged. I got that job. Then I found out about a hotel needing improvements and that the town needed an attractive health department and a fire hall. I got all those jobs, one after another.

I studied and analyzed the recently built buildings designed by other architects. I listened to complaints from the contractors about how the instructions were presented on the drawings, and complaints from the owners. Elements such as different-sized doors and windows in the same building cost extra money and detracted from the overall aesthetics.

To improve on what other architects had designed, I standardized details and elements. Where cant stripping of the roof edges was done with five building elements, I used three. I achieved reductions in cost and construction time in various ways while never abandoning the aesthetics. Solutions came easily to me; most shortcomings in existing buildings were obvious. Maintenance costs could be kept down by applying wear-resistant epoxy coatings to the walls and floors. Heating needed to be economical but reliable, and the space I saved could be used by the client for other options. In general, the cost of a heating system depends on the type of heating as well as the design. The brand depends on choosing wisely from those available and analyzing details. The how and where, cost, reliability, and options are often matters of design. I placed my heating units on the roof, in zones, so that if one unit failed, the others were available. Placing them on the roof was safer and made them more readily accessible for maintenance work, plus it freed up space inside. And the hot air units gave the client the option to use the system for air conditioning as well.

There are many other criteria that need to be mastered through analysis and experience in designing a building, including how and where to insulate the building against cold and noise, etc. More importantly, I took my finished drawings to a couple of reputable contractors and let them tear my designs apart. Their criticism helped me improve my drawings, understand their construction problems, and make the lowest bid on public contracts. As I developed my design philosophy over the next two years, my buildings became less expensive, more maintenance-friendly, and most importantly, not only pleasing to look at, but enjoyable to live in.

The time was right to present myself to other prospective clients and to sell my ideas, using my finished projects as examples. On publicly tendered projects, my prices came in astoundingly low, yet the buildings were attractive. I just had to continue on in that vein.

Now I needed staff. I stopped paying commissions for job referrals, and, to please my banker, I now charged the higher, established architect fees. My license was no longer at risk. Because of my success in Peace River—appealing designs, prices, and quality—I was invited to compete with other architects to design a number of schools near Fort Vermilion in northern Alberta, the coldest part of Alberta.

As I sat in a waiting room filled with competing architects from the largest firms in Edmonton, one established architect asked me if I was sure I had everything necessary to present my case to the school board. I nodded. He shook his head, doubting me, and laughed. Smiling, he opened his briefcase to show me an expensive bottle of whiskey. I laughed it off as a joke. No, he assured me; if I didn't have a bottle, I'd be out of the running.

I slowly began to think he was right. After all, he was an old hand at this. During the prolonged wait I looked at his profile, trying to see what he was and I wasn't. He was silent, looking ahead, probably deciding how he would do it, bottle at the beginning or at the end? But the more I looked at him—although he seemed smart, very smart—I sensed that he was a fool. He wasn't the shoo-in he thought he was. He went in. An hour later he came out, smiling at me, pointing to his briefcase.

My turn came. Suddenly I was standing in front of the board of about twenty men. I began by apologizing—for not bringing a bottle of the best. They looked stunned, then smiled and chuckled. After that I felt I was making my pitch in friendly territory. After telling them about my experiences in building up north for the government, I sensed I'd touched the right nerve. That was what they were waiting to hear—finally—someone with experience building in the severe cold. I elaborated as much as I dared, after which I felt maybe I'd get the job after all, and without a bottle at that, which is exactly what happened—to the amazement of the big architectural firms. Now I'd established myself both as an architect and as a threat to my competitors.

I hired more staff and decided it was time to find a bigger home for Violet and the kids—in the city. We found a large house, built at the turn of the century, with a large garden and big trees. The trees decided it for me. I would buy it somehow. I had lots of work completed but the money hadn't come in yet, so I went to see my banker. As he'd done before, he took out a piece of paper and worked it all out. He would give me ten thousand dollars because I had my own firm and payments forthcoming, and for the balance he advised that I should take out a mortgage on the house and then told me where I could get one.

We now had a gorgeous old house. Things fell into place nicely. We bought a new car, furniture, and appliances—no more second-hand stuff. We even hired a housekeeper. We planted flowers and more flowers in the yard and got a little dog for the kids. While renovating the house, I discovered an old photograph on heavy cardboard, brown and faded from the light: it was a picture of a very young officer in the Confederate Army in 1863 during the Civil War, standing proudly, one hand on his belt, the other holding faded gloves. He was the father of the man who had built our house and had once lived in it himself. I hoped he wasn't the one who'd left the empty whiskey bottles lying in the dark corner of the attic near where I'd discovered the picture. It seemed we were living in a Confederate mansion.

The house was humming with the four little ones, so now I could concentrate more on my work at the office. I had to work harder and smarter to run my office. I had to keep the stream of new contracts flowing smoothly—new projects at just the right pace and intervals. Too much work for the office was as bad as too little.

The school designs for Fort Vermilion were coming along nicely. The sewer system had to be carved out of the subsoil in a similar way to jobs I'd done before further north. The inside of the school needed some soul for the children, so my artist friend, Harry Heine, created murals depicting the history of the region. He painted them on the walls in the halls and the library. I helped with the actual painting, mainly filling in spots. We painted late into the night, then slept for a few hours on some hard, wooden school benches we'd pushed together. We used plastic coating to seal in the pictures which included early missionaries, caribou and buffalo herds, and bush pilots with the planes they'd used to open up the region many years before.

After the approval on opening day from the sparkling-eyed kids and their teachers, my friend Harry and I gave all future school projects, whether new or renovations, this kind of soul. It turned out I would design almost fifty more during my many years as an architect.

I learned that it was important to visit school boards in new districts to develop a good relationship with them and to let them know I cared about their community. I started my visit by first going to the local cemetery to find out the prevalent ethnic background and nationality of the people I was going to see. I'd remember a few names—like Johansen or Polski—from the gravestones. By the time I went to see the board, I had some idea of who was sitting around the table. When I was introduced to individuals, I would know whether his relatives had been in the area for a long time or not. From that I could almost tell how much weight someone carried on the board. In short, it helped me in presenting myself and often resulted in me getting jobs.

Typically, doing things my way, I developed my own style of addressing the audience at the opening of a newly finished school. The occasion usually involved lots of speeches from elected school board members, local officials, and maybe even the Provincial Minister of Education. They all sat on the stage in the gym and took the opportunity to do some *politicking* as they talked to the parents.

As the architect, I would be asked to say a few words too, but I didn't speak to the parents. The politicians had already done that, droning on about what good things they would do for them. Instead, I talked to the kids and revealed the mistakes I'd made in designing their school and what I'd done to correct them. I told them I hoped one of them would one day become a better architect than I obviously was. By letting them know my generation wasn't as smart as they pretended to be, I suggested that perhaps their generation could put mine to shame and that they should go for it. That got a lot of smiles from the kids, and later when I conducted a tour to point out the special features in the new school, the kids swarmed around me as if I was the *Pied Piper* and followed, listening eagerly to every word I said. That confirmed to me how important it was to put "soul" into the schools and made me think of them as "my" children.

Over the years, contractors here and there kidded me about going into partnership with them. I would design and they would build, and then we'd rent the building out. What they really meant was that I should do the drawings for free in return for a ten-percent interest in the building.

I'd already been burned on one of those deals—the twelve-suite apartment I'd never been paid for, but I still had the drawings. They were my legal property, so I decided to use them and get a contractor to build the apartment. I picked a reliable builder, and we agreed that each would own half the liabilities and share half of any profits thereafter.

I got a mortgage. I knew quite a few mortgage companies by then. This was my second real estate venture. I bought the land—a weed patch—dirt-cheap. We built the apartment with the mortgage advance and then rented it out. It was a success.

In time I learned that partners could not only be difficult to get along with, but they could also suck you into poor risks, which I needed to avoid. I was difficult too and made my partner uneasy with my questioning ways and in how I kept myself apart. Although I always trusted my partners initially, I watched them closely as we worked together to see whether or not I should continue trusting them or whether it would be stupid to do so. It always turned out to be stupid. In the end I sold my shares to my partner and looked for ventures on my own whenever possible.

As work at the office steadily grew, my credit at the bank grew along with it. My banker suggested that I should buy some profit-promising real estate. He would lend me the money. My friends in the Synagogue Beth Israel provided me with some additional options to do so. More contractors persuaded me to go into partnerships with them, even though I was leery of partners.

When some retired neighbors, who lived near our Confederate mansion, put up their well-treed place for sale, I jumped at the chance to buy it. I signed the contract, again without knowing how I'd pay for it, and went to see my banker who found the answer. Lot by lot, I bought all the houses on our street using the recipe I had learned from my first banker.

I got more daring. I got testy with city hall and tackled the zoning department. While designing buildings in the city I had learned all about the building code. I used the fine print to my advantage to get permits to build where they thought it wasn't possible to build. Because of their thinking, the land was dirt-cheap. Buying cheap land and putting a good building on it—one that created revenue—made me popular with my banker.

My balance sheet grew. I had made the million I'd boasted of years before, but becoming wealthy too quickly can be treacherous. I soon got myself into a box financially. I had built too much too fast and needed ever-increasing amounts of cash to make mortgage payments. I had to either sell a property or earn the money at the office. Between the mortgage payments and the cost of running the office, I needed $100,000 every month.

It was a constant struggle to come up with that much cash every month. Staying ahead of the due dates just became one quandary after another, a constant juggling act. I woke up every morning worrying about where and how to come up with the money, and when I'd solved that month's problems, I worried about the next. Once in a while I went to my banker, but whatever he loaned had to be paid back quickly. He generally gave me two or three years, but it was still a deadline. I was getting into a real rat race, taking money from *Peter to pay Paul*, and always trying to figure out what to do next. The monthly amounts escalated until, one month, I found myself needing half a million dollars for one of my companies. It was due within weeks or else *finis*. So said my banker.

I'd never seen that much money in my life. I could come up with part of it but never the whole amount, so I had to find some other way.

I knew the president of a small public company was having political problems and that his company had cash and assets. Maybe he would be interested in selling his shares. If I bought his shares, then I could become the president, but that still wouldn't get me the half-million dollars I needed. I needed to buy the whole company, but that would take even more money and maybe some of the shareholders wouldn't be interested in selling.

A reverse takeover—where I would buy the larger public company with my smaller companies—would work but it would be risky. I could lose everything if the majority of the present shareholders didn't want to swap their shares for shares in the new company I planned to create, a company that would merge all my existing companies with their old public one. They could vote against a merger if I didn't hold the majority of the shares. And it would take a very complicated dance to carry out the necessary legal procedures of a reverse takeover, yet right then I didn't feel I had any choice except to try it. If I didn't take the risk, I'd lose everything I had anyway—only sooner. The banker wanted his half-million dollars—and soon.

I locked myself in the dining room, glued my ear to the phone, and promised myself I wouldn't come out until I found out what I needed to know to accomplish it. I started by calling the company president to find out if he would sell his shares. Yes, he would. For the right amount. Would he recommend to his board that I should take his place as president? Yes, he would.

Now I had to figure out how much the shares were worth so that I knew how much to offer the president and other shareholders. I got a list of the shareholders from the company branch and called a cross section of them, offering them the opportunity to buy shares in their own company. Through those conversations I found out how much their company was worth. Some told whiny stories and said they would rather sell than buy shares. By asking what they would sell for, I eventually determined a value for the shares and, consequently, the value of the company. I kept a closely written record of all my conversations to hammer out my attack for later.

Next I went to see my banker to get a large credit line. This time I had to deal with a banker at head office. He listened to my plan. My figures made sense to him, so he agreed to lend me the money.

I bought out the president, paying him double what his shares were worth, and then I bought all the shares that I could in a particular sequence that I'd come up with from my earlier notes. Now I was president of the public company, but no closer to the half-million dollars I needed.

I had to do yet another dance to satisfy the Securities Commission. I had to make a public offering to buy out all the remaining shareholders or swap their shares for new shares to be held in trust in my new company, the merger of my private companies with the public company. Luckily, most opted for the swap.

As president and majority shareholder of the now larger public company, I could borrow the half-million on its properties and under-mortgaged assets to pay off the loan owed by another of its properties—the one needing the $500,000 payment. The new public company was financially sound, and I could grow from there.

I took the family to Hawaii for a vacation, but I couldn't help looking for buildings and properties to buy. It seemed to be in my blood. We ended up buying a dream of a house on the beach in Kihei on Maui. In hindsight, we needed this house like a hole in the head. I bought it for ten thousand down and a thousand a month.

Suddenly gas and oil shortages affected the world's economy, bringing new priorities and demanding higher prices on real estate. Inflation sneaked into the land. Alberta was lucky—the oil and gas province of Canada—so the city boomed and real estate prices with it. I was lucky to have lots of real estate on my hands. My architectural practice was flourishing, and everything and everyone was busy. Now, more than ever, the quality and loyalty of the people in the firm became paramount to my success.

I was fortunate in having good people around me. I was especially fortunate to find Susie. Susan Erb. She was a bundle of energy, reliable, and, on top of that, she was nice. She was my right hand, on and off, for longer than it takes to make a generation, through all the ups and downs in my life. She was there when I had only a foot to do what a hand was supposed to—sometimes.

In practicing architecture, I became more and more aware that designing spaces for people—young or old or handicapped—demanded more knowledge of psychology than I had, so I enrolled in some graduate classes in the Psychology Department at the University of Alberta, including some seminars given by Dr. Nelson, Chairman of the Department. I enjoyed learning for its own sake, as well as the benefit of being able to add new elements to my designs.

More and more people moved into Edmonton, pushing the city to expand its boundaries by building new subdivisions. I knew where thousands of farm acres were ready for development in one big parcel. I approached the farmers to ask if they wanted to sell, when, and at what price. To develop those thousands of acres, I needed more equity than I had; I needed hundreds of millions of dollars. I hoped to earn a fee out of my idea if I could only find someone who wanted to do it. I found someone who might. I showed them my plans in detail and took them up in a helicopter to point out my proposal, location by location. They were interested, but all they offered was a job to develop the land for them at a hundred thousand dollars a year. I didn't even have to think about it. I turned it down flat. I made more than that working for myself, lots more. And besides, my freedom wasn't for sale anymore. After I turned the billion-dollar company down, they told me that their own land people, unknown to them, had been working on the same idea and planned to develop it the way I'd proposed. That was another lesson. After that I was careful not to tango with anyone much bigger than I was. That's all I got out of it. Years later the chairman of the company put his arm around me and said, "Alex, we made a two-hundred-million dollar profit on the deal you originally showed us." How nice.

It was time to see something more of the world. My partner Joe was not great as a partner, but he was an interesting guy and lots of fun. He was planning to go to Mexico and South America, and I thought it would be fun to go along.

♣ CHAPTER 28 ♣

We got a taxi in Mexico City. The driver asked where to. I needled Joe, who spoke no Spanish, and said, "Just put an *'o'* on the end of any English word and tell him where to. The Mexicans will understand you. Just watch."

At that point the driver was having trouble getting the car to shift into gear, so Joe, utilizing his new Spanish language lesson, hollered into the front seat, "Heyo, youro clutcho noto worko?" The driver leaned back, smiled, and told Joe, in good English, that it was an old clutch all right, but that it would get us wherever we wanted to go. Joe was teed off. He told me to tell the driver where to go and that I could go to hell.

That was my start of my trip with Joe. Mexico City was chaos—noise, hustle, hollering, and speeding vehicles that missed pedestrians by inches—and laid out in a hideous maze. Electrical wires hung loosely at entrances, going nowhere. If they did lead to a power box, the box had no door. But the city seemed to work and the tourists kept coming.

We went to the belly market where pork bellies and other kinds of bellies were sold. The people there were colorful in their dress and manner but poverty-marked. The sellers gestured smilingly at both their bellies and the potential customers who turned the bellies over, smelled them, and held them up, looking at their undersides. I didn't know what they were looking for, but swarms of flies followed the bellies as they were turned and held up, while bystanders gathered to hear the customer's judgment. Throughout the transaction, everyone smiled: the seller, the buyer, and the onlookers. Always. There were hustlers too. They moved quickly, like ants, hustling to grab at any opportunity, crumb, or leftover they spotted. I was quite overwhelmed by the poverty. I was glad I'd had a chance to see it but relieved to move on to see something else.

Entrance after entrance along the busiest street had electrical wires hanging down like spider's legs that grabbed at anyone who entered. At times they almost blocked the entries. Joe and I were curious about sounds we heard coming from one, so we walked up a glaze-tiled stairway and found ourselves in a large, loud hall filled with people laughing and making cakes and cookies. They immediately looked up at the strangers who'd appeared in their place. We laughed our way closer to them, and Joe went even closer, bending down to smell the dough trying to identify its ingredients. He shook his head and laughed which made them laugh. From the way they all looked at him, he suddenly seemed to be in charge of the whole place. He took a cloth-collared metal funnel from one that was filled with icing sugar and then made an eloquent rose on one of the cakes. They looked at it, then at him as if he was a magician. Now he was in his element. He decorated all the dozens and dozens of blank cakes with roses, quickly—really like a magician. They were all laughing hilariously by the time he was finished. We left as we'd arrived, still laughing. We'd had a good time and had given them something of ourselves. Joe had once been a baker.

We took a bus east to Vera Cruz on the Gulf of Mexico. We took a couple of bottles of Coca-Cola with us to drink along the way, mostly just to help pass the time. We shouldn't have. We both got the *runs* on a non-stop bus without toilets. We made it to Vera Cruz, but I won't say how.

Wherever we looked, we saw something fascinating. The next day, eager to see more, we got up while it was still dewy and wandered down to the harbor to look at the big rusting ships and the rail lines with their long rows of freight cars. We saw a boy wearing rags crawl clumsily out of a freight car. He had deformed feet and huge dog-like brown eyes. His body was covered with boils and rat bites.

As we approached him, he cowered back in fear. I gave him a few pesos when, suddenly, a tall black guy appeared out from behind the car. Apparently he'd been watching. He pointed back to where he'd come from to show us there were other men watching and told us as soon as we left, they'd take the pesos. We saw them sitting on the edge of a platform, dangling their feet, and laughing as if they knew they'd soon have some tequila. I motioned for the boy to come back. I took back the pesos and asked him to come with us.

We found a taxi and took him to buy some clothes. He'd peeled his old ones off in the taxi; he was as naked and as ugly as a frog. We had to slice open his new shoes so that they'd fit over his deformed feet. His whole body was covered in bites from sleeping in the rat-infested freight cars, so we knew we needed to take him to a hospital.

The taxi took us to a monstrous, monumental pyramid structure. We saw a few medics but had to wait in a line, and wait, and wait, for a half a day, along with the rest of the locals. Eventually they treated his boils with tar-smelling stuff and covered them with sloppily applied bandages. Then we wanted to find him a place that he could stay for good—a hospital or church. We weren't sure.

As we left the hospital and started down the hundreds of pyramid-like steps, a beautiful young Mexican girl appeared, knelt down in front of me, and kissed my hand. She held onto it and wouldn't let go. I could see that she didn't need medical care, so I patted her head and told her to stand up and stop it. She began crying and ran away. I couldn't understand what that was all about.

We searched for priests and hospitals to find somewhere the boy could live permanently. We showed them our money and offered to pay for his care in advance and by the year. We went to place after place, but nobody wanted him, not even for our hard green cash. I couldn't understand it. I got angry. What purpose did these outwardly well-meaning institutions serve?

We shared a last meal with him—all of us were depressed—and took him back to the only *home* he had. His eyes turned darker and sadder. In the end I gave him some money, making sure no one saw it. He turned his dog-like eyes on me, full of obedience, and waited for a sign that he should follow me. When we finally left, I wondered if this was how man generally misplaces his help.

Our recent episode on the bus was still on our minds, so we returned to Mexico City on a train—with toilets. It dragged up the mountainous terrain and stopped at every hacienda just long enough for me to quickly sketch in water colors what I saw: once proud, now rundown, white-washed adobe plantations where indolent natives in Yankee overalls and oversized straw hats walked behind archaic wooden ploughs hitched to three donkeys. Joe supplied the necessary water for my sketching from leaky newspaper cones, running to and from the toilet compartment to get it. Only the natives could have thought of that too.

We Went On To Visit Temples
tourists usually search out.
Up into the mountains from Mexico City
and then south to the Mayan temples.

Stepping up and up
to the top of a temple,
I was overwhelmed
at the monumentality of stone,
and at the top,
I understood,
but even more, experienced
the feeling of absolute power
the Mayans must have had

over what lay below in the flat lands.

I sensed brutality buried in these stones.
I looked at the natives,
at their faces,
and saw they were ready to duck,
expecting to be beaten,
any second,
for some reason they couldn't understand,
but waiting for it anyway.
I somehow sensed
how their ancestors
must have been through hell.

We went on.
We flew to Guayaquil, Ecuador,
where the butterflies were as big as birds,
and where ten-inch pieces of walking bark
on the pavement
turned out to be bark-carrying spiders.
And where islands
floated down the Rio Vinces
through its mud-brown waters,
laden with banana trees.

People gathered
in its open-air market,
eager to sell,
some to buy,
in front of high white-washed walls
securing a cemetery
that was filled with dollhouse monuments
which the poor claimed
as homes at night.
Those stark white walls
stood in contrast

with the bright colors
natives wore in the market.
When I studied their costumes,
they turned their faces,
hiding them,
whispering together,
then turned to face their fresh fruits and vegetables
so much the hues of their wovens.
When two tomatoes
sailed past my nose,
landing on some yellow potatoes,
I looked around quickly.
I saw shy faces.
"Customary greetings,"
I thought,
and went on.

We went on to Lima,
the old colonial city.
It seemed beleaguered
by the poorest of the poor.
Peasants who had once grown their own food
in the high valleys of the Andes
now merely existed
in cardboard boxes.
Their shelters blocked any view
of the old stone buildings
and walls behind which
lived the proud ones
with watered-down Spanish blood
who claimed a heritage
linked to the earlier glory days of Spain—
where natives sat stoically
behind their laid-out wares
with an air of acceptance
of their fate

of not being wanted.

We flew south to Cuzco
for hours
in a dilapidated plane
that shook slightly
as if afraid to cross the Andes.
And we got the shakes too
when we looked at the vibrating fuselage
and wondered about
the general condition of the plane.
The steward,
who saw our worried faces,
handed us oversized red tanks
to suck on and
pass on to others
who'd nodded—yes,
they needed oxygen too.

At the highest point of the mountains
above the clouds,
I felt a falling
in the pit of my stomach
as the plane dropped
out of the sky
to land on a quiet field,
but before disembarking
with our heads still dizzy from the red tanks,
a man in blue overalls
ran over to the plane
with a wooden garden ladder
and a screwdriver
and climbed up under the motor
to fix it.

We were in the ancient Incan

city of Cuzco, a wonder:
huge walls built from
monstrous blocks of stone.
Not one Incan hair
could have fit between those blocks
laid so many generations ago.

We walked along a stone way
to a church
that had been built
under the swords of the Conquistadors.
Inside, I immediately sensed a oneness
between the feminine curves
of the stone interior
and the soothing hymns
that rose from the devoted
to fill the whole space
with hosannas
to the glory of God.
We stood in awe for some minutes
as we admired the past,
of stone lain upon stone,
and them.

As we walked through the ancient city,
I couldn't resist glancing inside openings
to see behind the walls
that lined the narrow streets.
A young lady resident who saw me
insisted that she show me her home,
so that I could see for myself
whether or not
she was descended
from a royal Incan family.
Curiosity made me accept.

Her residence surrounded an inner courtyard
into which each room opened.
Every room was large
with high ceilings
and had soft diffused light coming in.
I felt as if I was being allowed
into ancient royal spaces
not shown to commoners.
So it was.
The rooms were cool and musty,
each devoted to one specific ancestor.
It held his belongings—
furniture, musical instruments,
and personal effects—
with some in glass cabinets.

After I'd toured two rooms,
I began to think,
"Seen one, seen 'em all."
I worked my way
through a few more rooms
before I started to wonder
what this was all going to cost.
How would I be expected to pay?
I was invited to have dinner
with the family,
but I declined, humbly,
extra humbly,
afraid something else would come up.
Maybe the pretty Incan lady
would be presented to me.
Who knows?

We visited a real museum
filled with shelves and shelves
of nothing but utility-style pottery

that had been stolen from graves.
It was all the same:
pottery and more pottery
in the same reddish colors.
It bothered me for some reason.

After an uncomfortable night
in a bed filled with fleas,
we were glad to leave the hotel behind
when crowing roosters
woke us up early enough
to catch the day's only train
to Machu Pichu.

The train swayed
and meandered
its way up the mountains
as if its sole purpose
was to slip off the track.
It felt like it could go
at any moment
during the half-day ride.
As it took us high into the Andes,
it passed rivers
lined with old trees and wild orchids.
It made odd stops at old settlements
where the natives eagerly offered to sell
what they themselves treasured.
Out the window
we saw one poor man
who had been hit by the train.
He had been rolled out of his blanket
and had landed butt down
on the street where he now sat,
stunned and naked,
but—thanks to fate—

still alive.

The train to Machu Pichu
was filled with Indians
returning from the Cuzco market
where they'd sold
some of what they'd carried down
from the mountains.
Having left Cuzco hours ago,
we arrived in the mountains
where masses of clouds
held watch
over the many valleys down below.
This was where
the Andinos made their living
on stony soil.
Tiny, wiry people,
two-legged donkeys,
with bodies bent from oversized burdens,
and minds spaced out on coke.
They fascinated me.

Driven for centuries by their spirits and demons,
and given the unpredictable moods of nature
in this land in the clouds,
they lived in valleys with
paper-thin grass and dry moss
where clouds touched the land
and milked its moisture.
There was nothing else
above the clouds,
except the seat of the gods,
where Incas had once lived closer to the sun,
in temples now called Machu Pichu.

Below, along the Urubamba River, the gigantic steaming

rainforests brew fertile soil, producing fruits that were carried up to Machu Pichu during Incan times by the ancestors of those tiny Andinos now besotted by coke. Now, above the clouds, I was mesmerized by the sight of Machu Pichu. I spent the entire day sitting on one rock, looking—not painting, not walking around—just looking, inhaling the sight. The next day we were back in Lima.

We flew south past Santiago, Chile, across the red Andes, over its crevasses and deep dark canyons, and over mountains so high that we feared the plane couldn't climb them. After we had crossed the peaks, I saw shiny red places where water ran down into crevasses and red lines my aunt had once described to me as the place where my uncle—prospecting for even more copper than he already had—had survived falling into one, donkey and all. I watched one of the red lines as long as I could.

We landed in Buenos Aires. I felt a sense of Paris in the buildings that had been built from memory by the immigrants who had come there. The harbor was different—utilitarian. The giant ships coming and going determined how buildings and things had to look—the usual docks and cranes and warehouses. Nearby, I had to stop in to take a look and drink a few rounds at the infamous *Mouse Club* that has attracted sailors from all over the world, even Aristotle Onassis, as a young sailor.

On the walk back from the harbor, we initially passed by an area of dark blank buildings showing no entrances from the narrow, crooked streets which then changed to exotic sights that pulled us along from street to street and store to store, giving us, more and more, a sense of Paris as we strolled past healthy-looking people—very tall people. Dirty white buildings of various sizes and shapes and wooden huts sat next to luxurious marble buildings, the odd reflection of Paris. And then we came to a magnificent sight: a curtain of sculptured concrete, a gigantic piece of sculpture that, in reality, was a building with massive curves and exotic swirls in concrete, a design that hypnotized the eye: the *Banco de Londres*.

We went inside and asked if we could see more. Olga guided

us around. She fit right in with the building: gorgeous and exotic, with the same elegant lightness and grace. Her steps were like dances. She was very intelligent and spoke five languages fluently. Standing near her in the elevator, too near her exotic scent of mystery, I felt my body freeze in a combination of fear and expectation. I didn't come on this trip for romance. I suppressed my reaction to her by keeping my mind on her tour, on the shapes and forms and colors she graciously pointed out. Joe thought otherwise; he wanted to tour her. I was surprised to learn he'd made a date with her. That evening at dinner we got to know her. She was open and friendly and offered to show us more of the country. How could we say no?

The next day was March 26, 1967. She took us to Punta de Este, the eastern-most point of Montevideo. There the fury of the Atlantic pitches house-high waves against the shore, engulfing everything and anything. I felt drawn by it and walked closer to see the fury for myself. Olga raced after me to pull me back from my own stupidity—just in time. Her eyes were angry, and her wet hair was plastered against her head and neck. As she glared angrily at me, I saw the soft look of love in her eyes.

The next day she called me a *chicken head*. That day I was following a mile behind her as I walked along the wide beach of Montevideo. I saw her write something in the white sand while I was busy joking with the lifeguard, telling him I had to check his whistle to make sure it worked. When I got near enough to see her message—*I love you*—I added my own: *not*. I went on adding *not* to her repeated notes, and then caught up to her, out of breath and laughing. She laughingly stuck her writing stick in the sand, and I stuck mine next to hers, to stand together in an embrace against the incoming tide. We walked on together and looked back often to see if they still stood. I thought about the sticks all night. I'd fallen in love.

We enjoyed the next few days. One day she coaxed me into a music booth at a record store to hear a song she'd chosen, then sang it to me in the tight confines of the booth. I breathed her in, as I watched her lips gaily whisper the words inches from mine. My body was evaporating in front of her lips and whispers.

The next day was our last. I held my breath and stared at her, knowing I'd never see her again. The day was gray and the sky poured tears from then into the next one. The day seemed to be sad along with us.

By the time I was in the sky on my way home in the plane that had taken off at late dusk…

She Was Gone
When the sun set into deep red,
majestically,
giving the sky to a new night.
My eyes were red from the glow of the sky.
The sunset was gone,
like her.
Peace, peace.
Please come like the dark.

Back in Edmonton, she was too far away; it was hopeless.

♣ CHAPTER 29 ♣

The Alberta Ministry of Education asked me to study existing schools in the province and then write a report to form the basis for future school designs. Flights in Otter and Beaver planes throughout Alberta to visit schools weren't new to me, but they were to Jim Bilder, Peter's son, whom I had taken along. He remembered when I'd worked for his dad in Washington. At the time, through the eyes of a young boy, he'd admired what I'd done for his dad. He'd come for help I wasn't capable of giving. He was sick—a schizophrenic. I treated him the same as anyone else and tried to instill in him the idea that he shouldn't copy me, but be himself.

He wrote later, thanked me for the good time, and asked me to send him money for drugs he needed badly. I wrote back:

"My dear young friend,

Please be yourself. Find your roots. Please try. It might work. You are part of today's hippie generation, which wants to be different and better than mine. Why not? But to seek only pleasure is not being better. It doesn't fit into the real nature your generation longs for. All living things have to fit into their own nature."

I wanted to kick his hippie butt a little, so I wrote a fable for him.

> *"Jim, I've written a fable to explain my feelings about your generation. Imagine a donkey—my generation—who generously gave you money to study photography, but you used the money instead to buy drugs.*
>
> *The donkey met a bunch of hippies—your generation—who asked it to carry their bags. The donkey gladly accepted. At nightfall the hippies explained to the donkey that although it had done well that day, and they needed it to do the same tomorrow and in the days ahead, at the moment, they were hungry, so they would have to butcher it in order to survive until the next day.*
>
> *That is how I see your generation—demanding that it 'have its cake and eat it too.' The pioneers who built this country knew they couldn't build their future your way. Those were your folks, your parents. You must know it's true.*
>
> *Please be a little bit like me, but above all, try to be yourself. And remember, it doesn't matter what people tell you about yourself as long as you trust who you are."*

Jim rested heavy on my heart. We both knew I couldn't help him. We had both tried.

When I finished my report on the schools, the Minister of Education asked me to do an in-depth feasibility study of my *air-right* concept. It presumes a high property value, but otherwise is simple enough: it gives the school board a free school. A great idea!

An *air-right* is a grant over a property—a private caveat between two parties. One party could be a school board that owns an expensive piece of property. The other could be a developer who would build a high-rise apartment plus a school at his cost, in return for the fifty-year *air-right* to collect rent on the high-rise.

Bylaws would need to be passed to make *air-rights* legal if the Ministry of Education found my concept sound. To check it out I went to a place with the highest possible land values—New York. I found that my concept was already in use there and worked well.

And I learned something else in New York. The collective fantasy of millions of people, both the good and the bad, living together over a period of time, only results in bad piling up on bad while the good evaporates. I was shocked. I was disenchanted with daily life in a big city.

Back in Edmonton, I promised myself I'd show the world what could be done by designing a pavilion for the Canadian government in Osaka, Japan. It was a competition that I was invited to participate in. I was pleased with my finished design and naturally thought it was the best submitted, but my old teacher, Arthur Erickson, won. I won honorable mention, which meant my design would be exhibited in his pavilion two years later.

For some reason, the Alberta government then asked me to participate in a *think tank* with forty others to analyze problems the government would or could face by the year 2002. They initiated the study to find intelligent, useful interpretations of events that they could use as economic flags prior to any erosion of the prosperity being enjoyed in the province at the time. They wanted to find out the ramifications, options, and relative risks by having us look for patterns, circumstances, and criteria that would provide clues to the future. Various disciplines—economic, social and political—were involved. Computer-generated graphs of plausibility and timelines were developed with both major and minor graph curves.

My field was finance, specifically, expected mortgage rates and production factors in the building industry and related fields. I found it fascinating to search out tools that could be used to look into the future, to prognosticate. To understand the problems and directions of mortgage and interest rates, I looked for a correlating factor between labor efficiency and high mortgage rates. Labor efficiency, or lack thereof, correlates to the rate mortgages should be set at.

With that philosophy in mind, I studied the correlating factors in London. I had chosen London because at that time it had the highest mortgage rate in the world—17 percent. Normally, a person cannot make a return on an investment in construction if the mortgage rate is much higher than 10 percent. I wanted to see if the high mortgage rates correlated to labor efficiency—where and under what circumstances red flags for both factors appeared. The data I collected confirmed my suspicion.

After I finished my study, I had the opportunity to observe my theory in action while I waited for my flight home from Heathrow. I watched some renovations being made to a corridor. Two worked, three stood around watching those two, and a sixth occasionally came around to make sure the three were actually watching the two working. That was it. Considering that those watching were the highest paid of the bunch, the labor efficiency on that job was no more than thirty percent, two out of the six, which tripled the labor costs.

Nothing worthwhile came of the *think tank.* It was a waste of time and effort. Its results were used by the opposition party after the press gave them hints of what we were working on. I felt the current party would soon be out of office, so it would be best not to get involved any further—best to dance nearest the exit door.

Somehow I'd gained the inner ear of the government. At one point, I told the Premier he'd be smart to try to promote the selling of goods from Alberta—like Alberta beef—to Japan. He ought to go out and promote Alberta before the next election. And, furthermore, he would be smart to keep the date he'd chosen for the next election to himself right up to the last minute and not divulge it to anyone. I knew that there were leaks in his cabinet. Canadian election dates are decided by the ruling party. They can choose a time most advantageous to them. I was embarrassed to see that he was noting my points down on a pad. I knew that meant he was weak.

When the Premier had decided on the date of the next election, he told only two people: a cabinet minister and myself. The day I learned of it, the leader of the opposition walked right past me as I stood near the fountain in the legislature. He was on his way up north to do some politicking. I thought, "If you knew what I know, you wouldn't be leaving town just now. You'd stay here to push the alarm button." But he won anyhow, so it didn't really matter.

In the end I was glad the Premier had lost. The province needed some fresh blood after thirty years of the same party in office. Prairie people aren't big on change. They stay with what they're familiar with, in much the same way that they stay home during the coldest days of winter.

Serving in politics was wasting time I should have been using to attend to urgent business. It was time to get away from the political theater.

But I wasted more time—by going on another trip with Joe. This time we went to Calgary to look at nursing homes. His Jewish friend, Mr. Kayser, who owned quite a few, wanted Joe to build another, and Joe had asked me to design it. I suspected it might be a waste of time because Joe's projects usually seemed to fall by the wayside, but I went anyway.

We flew to Calgary early one morning and went see a buddy of Joe's to borrow his car. Joe got the keys and I got a shock—when I saw the car. It was a piece of junk—an old blue Pontiac. The door padding was gone, the window crank was missing, and the sharp springs in the driver's seat stuck out, so Joe had to watch out for his pants. The back seat was filled with junk, which wasn't too surprising because his friend owned a second-hand store.

I asked Joe if we really had to take that car. Maybe we should take a cab. He said not to worry. His friend drove it to work; it would get us where we wanted to go. Besides, it was cheaper than a cab. I had only one thing on my mind—get the day over with as fast as possible.

First, we went to meet Mr. Kayser. As soon as we entered

his home, I could see how wealthy he was. Standing guard just inside his front door was a full suit of armor, dating from the Middle Ages, complete with a rose in its visor put there each morning by Mr. Kayser's butler to humor those who entered. The house was big enough for his butler to bicycle through, and his chauffeur stood waiting for him beside a sparkling gold Cadillac. He was a well-known multi-millionaire in town.

We followed behind them in our borrowed blue car, until Mr. Kayser asked us to park it downtown somewhere while he waited for us to join him in the extended limousine. We visited a number of nursing homes, one after another, until it was time to catch the last flight of the day back to Edmonton. Mr. Kayser wanted to show us one last nursing home. We still needed to return the car to Joe's friend, so we didn't have enough time. Mr. Kayser assured us that it was no problem, that he'd personally return it. He knew the man anyway. We protested that the car was awful, but he said it didn't matter. It was more important to him that we see that last nursing home. Then he would drive us to the airport and return the car. We agreed, smiling to each other, as Joe gave him the keys to the car and the location where we'd parked it.

The next day Joe asked me to come see him at his hotel in downtown Edmonton. He had something to tell me. He was laughing so hard he could hardly talk as he told me that when Mr. Kayser had returned the car to Joe's friend and had thanked him for loaning it to us, Joe's friend looked at the car and said, "I'm sorry to have to tell you this, but even though that's a blue '56 Pontiac like mine, that isn't my car."

Imagine what Mr. Kayser was thinking, having broken into a car with keys that fit any '56 Pontiac. The car he'd driven from downtown to return—as a favor—belonged to someone else who was likely looking for it by now. He'd stolen a car. He had to return it fast, hopefully before anyone discovered it. The whole time he was driving the car back in the busy rush-hour traffic, he was scared and kept one eye out for the police. When he finally got back downtown, he was relieved to find the parking spot still empty, so he re-parked it quickly and went off to find the right car and then returned it—with the steel springs poking through his pants—in rush-hour traffic along with the rest of the working people, at a time of day he was usually at home relaxing with a drink.

That was the end of that project. Once again, the time I'd spent with Joe was wasted; I'd gotten no more than a laugh out of it. It was springtime in Edmonton, a sad time in the city. The tangled grounds around our home needed so much work that I was glad when a late snowfall covered everything and made it look clean again. That spring I was especially sad because I was missing Olga. I couldn't get her out of my mind. I wrote to her and played sad songs on my organ.

By chance I saw an interview on TV by an Iranian who announced an auction of Persian carpets. He showed a twenty-thousand-dollar carpet that he said was a twin of one hanging in a London museum. The auction was that night. I had to see it. Maybe I'd bid on it. And I did—getting it for a tenth of its supposed value. I was shaking by the time the bidding closed. To get insurance on the carpet I needed an appraisal. The Iranians promised to get one and also promised that if I wasn't satisfied, for any reason, they would gladly return my money. My insurance company was willing to insure the carpet for whatever the appraised value was, but couldn't do it without the appraisal.

I waited for the appraisal. Then I phoned. For two years I phoned. And heard nothing. Finally, I took the carpet to an auctioneer who appraised it at half of what I'd paid. Now I wanted my money back or a letter of "their" appraisal, or else. A reputable carpet chain, Jordan Carpets, who also sold Persian carpets, had heard about my dilemma. They were suing the same Iranians for misleading advertising. They asked me to join them in their lawsuit. I figured they'd launched it more because of lost business than because of the misleading ads, but after a few more months had gone by, and I still hadn't heard from the Iranians, I joined them.

Out of the blue, Joe called one day and asked me to come down to his hotel. He had a member of the same Iranian family waiting to talk to me. He was an Iranian Jew, named Eskander Ghermazian. He wanted to buy my carpet back. That suited me just fine, because he finally admitted he couldn't provide an appraisal for the amount that I'd paid. Besides, a Jew doesn't fight another Jew, so I withdrew from the lawsuit. I got my money and Jordan's lawsuit was dismissed because they had no case without me.

Eskander had lots of money to invest from his carpet sales. The rapidly rising real estate market in Edmonton looked like a good place to put it, so one discussion followed another, until Joe, Eskander, and I—the three stooges—formed a company to buy land around Edmonton. We called it De Milo Investments.

One evening we made a down payment on a few hundred acres of valuable land along the Saskatchewan River that cut right through the heart of Edmonton. The land was worth millions and millions. We gave the seller a company check signed by all three of us, but Joe went back later that evening and substituted a personal check, without our consent, to buy the land for himself. That was the end of my business association with him. Somehow we remained friends, but I did no further business with him. My good buddy, John Polunak, who was a planner with the government, had warned me long before, "Stay away from that guy. He's bad news."

Eskander, who was always on the up and up, put more carpet money into buying land. We'd shown him how to go about it by talking to the farmers, giving them fifty thousand down for whatever price they wanted, and then letting them stay on the land until the time came to develop it. At that time the balance would be paid. In time, Eskander moved his family to Edmonton, and I introduced him to my banker.

Together with his three brothers, he amassed large land holdings. Wherever a shopping center was proposed, Eskander was right there on the spot, buying out the proposal, and with it, each anchor store to put in his own shopping center, which was already on the drawing board. He repeated this process three more times. With the city still booming and expanding around its circumferencc, Eskander used those anchor stores as the basis for building the largest shopping center in the world at that time: West Edmonton Mall.

* * *

"I later realized that if I hadn't watched TV that night, Edmonton wouldn't have gotten the biggest shopping center in the world, John."

"Crazy. Or fate?"

"I wonder. Did I ever tell you about Mrs. Glocky?"

"No. I suspect this is going to be crazy."

"You're right. It's a story Mr. Glocky told me. Every year Mr. Glocky bought his wife a new Rolls Royce in Calgary. He was the guy who talked me into buying one by telling me it would be good for business.

"Anyway, on the way back to Edmonton in the new Rolls, Mr. Glocky sat in the passenger seat with his wife's two poodles on his lap while Mrs. Glocky tried out her new car, driving way too fast. Then she saw a flashing red light appear in the rearview mirror. 'What should I do?' Mr. Glocky said he didn't know. He was a smart man. So she kept going. 'The light is still there, dear. What do I do now?'

"He knew enough to repeat that he didn't know. It was one of those moments in a marriage to say nothing. If he told her what to do and it didn't turn out right, it would be his fault. Finally, she roared into a gas station, ran into the bathroom, and locked herself in. The RCMP car followed her and rolled right up beside the bathroom. For a few minutes, nothing happened. Inside, Mrs. Glocky was busy trying to think of something to say. She knew the police were waiting to give her a ticket and some points on her license. After accumulating a certain number of points, she could lose her license. She finally came out smiling, and said, 'Whew! I didn't think I'd make it with this diarrhea.' The officer just smiled and let her go."

"That just goes to show you that most women know just what to say at the right moment."

"Don't I know it!"

* * *

Life went on comfortably for the next few years. I enjoyed the yard and lying out…

Under Our Poplar Tree In Summer

While I lie under my poplar tree,
way below those poplar leaves
and fluffy clouds above,
I close my eyes and listen.
I throw my arms back
and touch the grass
to welcome what I see.

"Listen."
There.
Gently one, two, three,
and now millions of leaves,
dance with each other.
They swish,
touching, rubbing, chafing each other,
becoming a rustle,
swinging, singing in concert,
a concert in the breeze,
with millions of them singing in harmony.

How they swish,
How they rustle,
swinging, singing in concert,
to the clouds above,
way above.
Suddenly,
in quick response to the breeze,

there's a silence in this tree.
The leaves hang motionless in the still air,
as if listening for a breeze,
listening to the fluffy clouds above,
listening to each other.

"Listen."
There again.
Gently one, two, three,
and now millions of leaves,
dance to each other,
swishing, then rustling,
from touching, rubbing and chafing
with each other,
swinging, singing in concert again.
Those poplar leaves play with the breeze,
tussling, swaying, swaggering, sagging,
while the clouds move on above them,
clouds no gods can stop or turn back,
clouds in shades of white in light
moving in one single plane.

Still now.
Let me breathe.
Let me inhale with all my senses
what I feel, what I see, what I hear,
and then let me go.
Let me embrace this lovely tree,
around its whole trunk,
as if to say thanks.
And then let me dance and sing myself away
while the leaves are still and listen again.

The time was right to realize another dream—owning my own office building to house my office and staff—so I built it, but I didn't really need it. Before long, I'd sold it. And I sold the house in Hawaii too. We didn't need that either. We were only able to get there for a couple of weeks every other year.

Besides, I needed the cash to pay off mortgages on apartments that I was renovating to attract new tenants. By that time I had a few hundred apartment units and that meant people—people chasing me all day, every day, about something. It was getting to me.

The continuing economic boom—caused by rising prices for oil, gas and real estate—filled the apartment vacancies which brought the cash flow up to where my banker had wanted it all along, and the value of my apartments had gone up with it. Now was the time to sell them all. But that takes time. I got an agent and told him whom to offer various pieces of real estate to. I'd learned that I needed to direct agents the same way I directed my lawyers in order to get the results I wanted. Soon I'd sold all my real estate. I now had millions in cash. It seemed that *Lady Luck* was sticking with me.

I needed a breather. And it was time for a change in our lives, for the whole family. I'd been so busy the past few years that I'd missed a lot of the kids growing up, so we moved to closer to where some of them were going to school.

♣ CHAPTER 30 ♣

I bought a moving truck, put everything we had in it, and pulled up roots to move near to where two of the kids were going to prestigious boarding schools on Vancouver Island. We drove west as far as Canada went: to Vancouver Island, where I'd bought a piece of land on the Georgia Strait. I began raising white Charolais cattle for something to do. It was just a lark to match the white cattle to all the white buildings and fences on the property. They were the only cows on the island who had a sea view where they could watch ships sailing by from all over the world. The kids could now come to visit us and the white cows on the weekends. The place was heaven.

The estate was visible from the highway that ran from Schwartz Bay to Victoria. From there, the scene was of a white fence enclosing an expanse of green, dotted with white cattle and four huge white buildings with high black roofs. The whole area was surrounded by trees. From Georgia Strait it looked like a park on the edge of a cliff.

Three Giant Poplar Trees
stood like sentinels at the main gate—
heavy black steel set into self-built pillars,
somewhat crooked, of used brick.
The drive into this paradise
was lined with dense cedar and cypress bushes

filled with birds at dusk.

The old white house
sitting amidst an expanse of ferns and flowers
was bordered in the green the land gave.
Way at the end of the drive,
and beyond the old house,
a huge, overgrown bamboo
signaled one to stop and look around.

To the right lured a park
with an ivy-covered tree holding a swing,
and a clear view of the sea beyond
that charmed me with all its different moods,
in rain and mist and pitching winds
or in warm sunshine on flat water.

To the left beckoned flowering bushes,
and decorative green trees,
and nearby black benches,
gracefully curved to invite sitting
to enjoy the surrounding beauty.

There where ferns bordered the big house,
next to the snowball bushes,
wide, green worn-out steps
invited anyone near to sit down,
to look far out to sea,
to watch ships pass by,
to inhale this heaven on earth,
to listen to the sea and the cries of its seagulls.

At daffodil time,
when the crocuses were just gone,
and the late spring sun glowed red
through the needles of the firs,

I would listen for someone
who had once whistled for me
about the time the sun set.

* * *

I busied myself raising a hundred Charolais. I hired two men to look after them. Soon I had to buy two more farms to get enough hay to feed the cows. It quickly became too much. And at calving time, along with worrying night and day, I helped take care of them. It was absurd. I sold the cattle to be free again. I lost money to buy that freedom, but I made it up by selling the land they'd grazed on. All in all, it was an experience I wouldn't want to repeat.

Before long, I was looking for trouble somewhere else. I'd get myself into a box with some new venture, initially to learn something from it, and then when I became bored, I'd have to find some way to get out. I've repeated the same pattern over and over throughout my life.

This time it started with Mr. Steve Savodelli, a real gentleman, who represented Howard Hughes's Summa Corporation in Las Vegas. Summa owned a dozen casinos, a TV station, and the large ranch Mr. Hughes used to live on. He offered to sell me The Landmark casino for a good price.

A casino is a complex business. Today corporate businesses control most of the casinos in Las Vegas. A lawyer working for Mr. Savodelli let me have the casino books to study the profits and losses from various types of gaming—roulette, black jack, baccarat, and slot machines—as well as the shows, dining, and hotel rooms.

Then he took me on a complete tour and showed me the place room by room. The casino was on the ground floor with the hotel rooms in the tower. On the top floor I saw a big machine Mr. Hughes had installed—an earthquake sensitizer that monitored atomic tests in the Nevada desert.

In the basement I asked the lawyer what the stern-looking black fellow watching us was doing. The lawyer smiled,

One of three oil storage tanks that I supervised construction on in 1956 near Abbotsford, B.C. The small figures of the men on top give some idea as to its size and to the importance of the welds holding the sheets of one-inch thick steel together.

One of the many bush pilot planes I took when flying "up north."

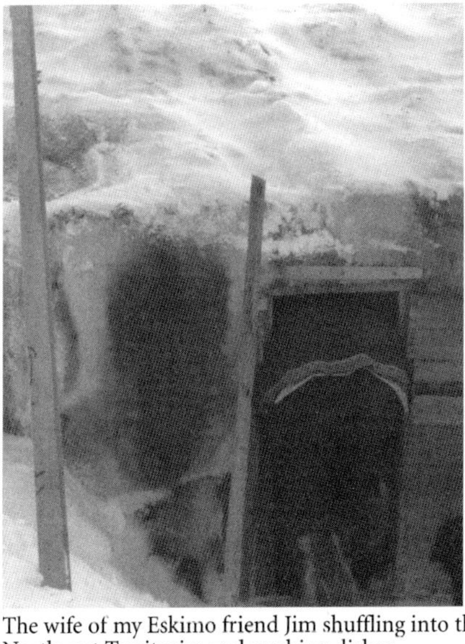

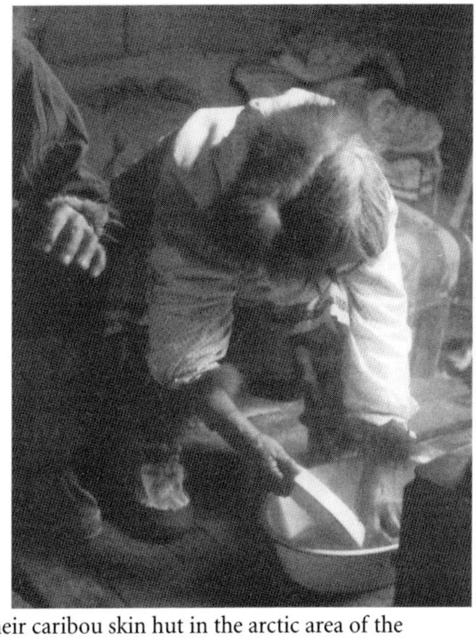

The wife of my Eskimo friend Jim shuffling into their caribou skin hut in the arctic area of the Northwest Territories and washing dishes.

Making my presentation for graduation at the Univ. of Oregon in Architecture.

The first house I built for the family, entirely done by hand in 1961.

My favorite project of all I've ever designed: St. John's Catholic church in Fort McMurray, Alberta.

No longer content to just design, as a major shareholder, I put together my own proposal for the Westlawn project in Edmonton, Alberta.

One, two, three, four—the kids, my wife, and myself in typical Alberta weather.

Our move to the city, Edmonton, to a large old mansion with a "Confederate" in its past.

(left) My former teacher, Arthur Erickson's winning design for the Canadian Pavilion of the 1970 Osaka World's Fair. To me it seemed mechanical in form.

(below) My design was more reflective of what Canada is—a country with more water than land, formed and helped along by a diversity of cultures still within nature's environs—and all, as yet, unfinished.

To reflect these unique characteristics, I created an organic design, not a mechanical one. My design won honorable mention and was exhibited in his two years later.

Pensive Olga from Argentina.

I was jokingly checking the whistle of the lifeguard on the beach of Montevideo.

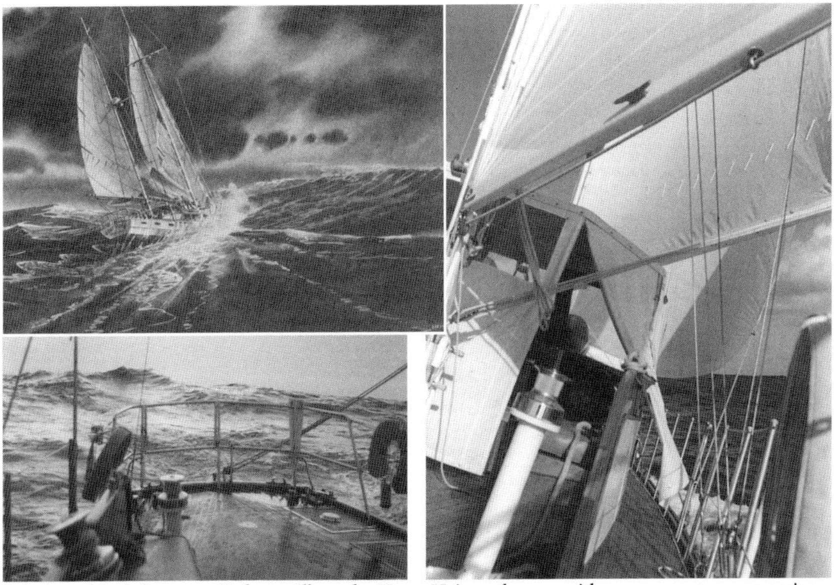

Painting of *Ladyfame*, my 60-foot sailboat, by Harry Heine, who was with us on our stormy crossing from Hawaii to California, and photos taken during the 1000-mile long storm that left us disabled.

Ladyfame, my first mistake, anchored in Hawaii before crossing the Pacific.

My second mistake, the *Seafarer*, was a one-hundred ton Rhodes with all the latest electronic bells and whistles.

(above) The Munzel family was growing up. Our four children, *(from l. to r.)* Maria, Anna, Alexa, and Rudy.

(above right) Our gorgeous 6-bathroom mansion in La Jolla, California.

(right) Meirah, (Maria) on the day of her wedding to my good *mensch*, Dr. Joel Labovitch.

(bottom left) The office building I designed and owned in Houston, Texas.

(bottom right) The 500-unit apartment complex in Houston that I bought and revitalized.

Greta and I, taken when we finally met after forty years.

"Two souls had found each other again—
for no more than two hours."

Greta and I at the Roman villa, *Dei Papyri*, recreated at the Getty Museum in California.

Yes, my Paradise was postponed until now.
Now I am committed to her
with all my emotions in my life with her—
my private heaven in the now—
my heaven ahead of time.
Yes. I could accept total darkness forever
after this heaven.

The stream on John Braams' upstate New York property.

She and I sat down
on a soft carpet of moss
near the stream.
The water swished by,
slithering over slices of shale,
making itself into thin sheets,
slapping down on the flat water,
to spray,
to settle,
to become one
with the stream.
It was like music.

"Nothing."

"Nothing?" I questioned. He explained that the casino had a contract with the Teamsters Union, which had put him there to watch things. My interest in the casino evaporated right then. I thanked him and went to see Mr. Savodelli.

Mr. Savodelli had a typical Las Vegas big-shot office filled with glitter and glamour, occupied by big guys in flashy suits, who claimed to be his assistants. They were leaning back on cushioned couches, playing with their hands to show off the gold they wore. They talked loudly, wanting to impress anyone within earshot with how important they were and how much wisdom they had to offer. To me they were goons—fool's gold. They knew who I was and that I was waiting for Mr. Savodelli. To them it was a chance to hustle me—not only to buy The Landmark, but also to get me to pay a high price for it.

"Surely it's worth it." They repeated it often, hoping it would sink into my brain. It was the same way they convinced each other of things.

My voice was, by nature, too loud. I was thankful for it during those times I had to deal in big money or when I had to stand up to goons like these or to bankers from big banks.

I shrugged off their talk, as I waited to see Mr. Savodelli, by telling them I would discuss what I had to say only with Mr. Savodelli. They were stunned by my answer and slumped down together. They went on talking to each other and tried hard to make themselves look like businessmen. They continued to talk extra loud to get across to me that they were *in the know* and to make sure I heard every word they said. I studied their faces and smiled at them. I read them to be insecure deep down, almost questioning themselves, as if they wondered if maybe the ideas that they spouted so loudly might not be right. I figured the time would come when the people around them would find out they didn't know much.

At last Mr. Savodelli entered the room, bringing in a traditional finesse and endearing style just by his appearance. He had intellectual grace and hard work written all over him. He had an easy manner—purposeful, quiet, and understated. I told him right away that there was no deal. The goons got so loud—as if standing up for Mr. Savodelli—that I could hardly hear him thank me for looking the place over. The goons looked surprised that that was all there was to it. No fight, no hustle, no argument.

* * *

"Why did you decide to pass?"

"The Teamsters Union which had put that stern-looking black fellow on the job was a type of labor I could do without. It was a non-productive cost to the casino. Who knows what else they had in place. I couldn't run a business with a union telling me who would be employed to do what. I kept my eye on the casino though, out of curiosity. Two fellows from Kansas bought it and lost a few million dollars, and then someone else bought it from them and made quite a bundle.

"All businesses work like a yo-yo. The trick is to know when to get in and when to get out. Anybody can get in, but few can get out. You just have to know when. Money in any deal is just *energy* to do whatever you want to do—like power in a battery. The trick is figuring out where and how and when to apply the *energy*, the money."

"You seem to love being in trouble, don't you? You love the challenge of it?"

"Yes, John. The most fun is getting out of it. I love building myself a box. When I'm done I'm eager to crawl into it, and after I'm in there for a while, I frantically try to get out. How to get out is not only the fun part, but also the hardest—the big challenge in business. That was my *modus operandi*: in and out. Dare to get in and dare to get out. But no longer. Today I stay away from boxes."

"Alexander, while you were talking, I sneaked out and made some sandwiches for us. Let's have them right here. Greta, try some of my homemade pickles. John, put a few pieces of wood in the stove, please. So, Alexander, what did you do next?"

I was surprised to hear her ask. I thought she'd left to pitter-patter in her kitchen because she was bored.

"Estelle, I bought a sailboat—*Ladyfame* cast her spell on me. She was a sixty-five ton sixty-footer, all steel; I had to ship her from Hawaii. I bit off too much to start with, but that's the way I've always done things."

* * *

I'd never really sailed before, except once on a twenty-footer on a river in Heidelberg. And that one I'd keeled over trying to turn it too quickly. That was the sum of my sailing experience. The *Ladyfame* was Dutch-designed and built with a seven-foot draft, steel hull, and capable of ten knots. It had a twelve hundred square foot mainsail, a mizzen and a genoa, a dining and kitchen galley, two heads, nine berths, a 180-horsepower Caterpillar engine, a generator, bilge pumps, and a dry exhaust system. And it was finished beautifully in mahogany.

Next I had to get a crew. I got the best sailmaster California could offer, at three hundred dollars a day. My artist friend, Harry Heine, his fisherman brother, and I were the rest of the crew. Well almost. My daughter Anna and a cat came along too. Anna got me into trouble with the sailmaster. I should have just taken the cat.

I had the crew flown to Hawaii. The sailmaster inspected the riggings, and the ship was checked out in dry dock. Then we stocked it with supplies, including fresh lettuce sealed in plastic bags. The maiden voyage took us to Kauai. From there we sailed east. Night came quickly and we soon became part of the endless expanse of the sea.

After a few hours of nothing but water to see, I started wondering what I was doing there—heading out towards the horizon, bobbing up and down, with no end in sight.

My old sense of survival resurfaced. I'd gotten myself into this, so I'd better get a hold of myself. The first thing I had to do was get over feeling seasick, so I stared at the tip of the swaying mast until I felt like throwing up. Then I forced my eyes down to my feet, and back to the mast, back and forth, pushing my threshold of feeling seasick up until eventually I felt I might get my sea legs. Then I had to master something even more important—learning to sleep in the rough water.

I finished my first four-hour watch at the wheel. In four hours I would be on watch again, so I had to be able to sleep in the pitch and roll of the moving water. The waves crashed against the porthole with an audible force, as if trying to get in to where I was holding onto my bunk. Desperate to get some sleep, I soothed myself by imagining that I was being rocked to sleep by a giant mama with big boobies. It worked, and I fell asleep. When I woke up, I was surprised to see how wild the waters had become. We were moving around in a hellish sea. I now felt confident that I could eat and sleep and endure the following days and nights it would take to cross the ocean.

We threw out a line with a one-foot spinner, a six-inch red fly, and a hook, but no bait. After a few hours, fly and hook were both gone. A shark, we guessed. With a new fly and hook we caught a nice six-foot silver-gray wahoo, a large warm-water mackerel. It tasted like steak. The next day we hooked a four-foot tuna and a silver-gold louvar. It sparkled like a rainbow until it died.

"That should be enough." the sailmaster told us, so we stopped fishing, but got more anyway—flying fish that landed on the deck during the night.

The prettiest sight I saw on the trip, during the first six days, was the multicolored spray of water pushed aside by the hull, which was caused by plankton in the wake of the bow. And we enjoyed watching the dolphins let themselves be pushed along by the bow of our boat. We whistled at them, but they didn't seem to hear or notice us.

I learned to shoot the sun with a sextant to find our daily position for longitude and latitude. We marked and compared that finding with our route by *dead reckoning*, which was penciled in on the charts by measuring our hull speed. The two markings on the chart were usually just a couple of miles apart, so we knew pretty well where we were, which was important to me. My heart and soul needed to know that. After days and days on the water, it became even more important.

One day I was astonished to see a mosquito-looking creature, in the middle of the ocean, swaying on top of a wave. How did it get there? How did it survive? Another day, far south of Japan, we ran into a mile-wide trail of floating garbage, sluggishly making a circle miles in circumference.

The radio announced a storm a thousand miles wide, south of Japan. We appeared to be riding near the edge of it already. The sailmaster figured we were making ten knots an hour on wings from its wild winds. That was full speed, the fastest the ship could do. The wind pushed us from the aft.

Then we were upon the storm and riding its edge: ten-foot waves in monstrous thousand-foot-long, house-high swells came at us, one after the other, for days on end, in fierce, wild howling winds. It was unreal. It was hell. It went on and on: up and down and up and down—house-high—without end. We lost the mainsail in a squall, and soon after, our engine. We tried to crank it up, but the pistons had already rusted from sitting in salt water. The purpose of the dry exhaust was to keep water out, not let it in. But the storm had driven the waves in through the dry exhaust and let salt water into the engines. We'd lost the generator the same way, so now we were in trouble. The batteries wouldn't last long, so the fridge would be off soon.

When I got something from the fridge, I opened and closed the door as fast as I could to keep the food from spilling out onto the galley floor, where it would roll around and become hard to catch. Getting dressed in the rough sea was a real challenge. Once it took me ten minutes just to get my socks on.

I saw a freighter in the distance. It was the only ship we saw. By then we'd been eighteen days on rough water. Anna was seasick for days and terrified. I was very angry with myself for having put her in such danger. I really should have just taken the cat. After eighteen days, I swore I'd never cross an ocean again.

Just as suddenly as the winds had come, they were gone, and

we were becalmed. We searched the horizon for clouds, and waited. Finally, gray clouds rolled in and brought the wind with them. We hoped for enough wind to fill the sails. It lasted one day. Two days of swearing at the disappearing wind followed that. We tried singing for it. That didn't work either. We were adrift, helpless, floating in the current until, at last, we contacted a trawler by radio and got him to tow us into the harbor at Santa Barbara under the watchful eyes of the harbor police and a crowd of bystanders. I knew I had dared more than I should have. Never again.

I stayed alone on the boat to look after repairs to the sails and the motor while the others flew home, including Anna. They'd had enough.

When repairs were finished, I skippered the yacht by myself, along the coast, past Catalina Island to San Diego, home to our gorgeous Spanish villa with a warm bed on dry land. What a relief!

For the next few weeks, I sat in the sun among the lemon-scented bushes and watched hummingbirds hover busily over the bell-shaped yellow flowers near the fan palms. I thought, "Only idiots would spend weeks in pitching salt water." I vowed that I would never take to the open ocean again. I hoped that I'd gotten that longing for openness out of my system. It was the freedom I loved at sea, that endless openness, no boxes to crawl into and try to get out of, just man against nature.

* * *

"Hold it, Alex. What you did there was box yourself in too, one you could only get out of by getting back into the harbor. Don't you think?"

"I guess so. Yes, you are so right. And, believe it or not, John, I soon found another box for myself."

* * *

After a few weeks in our San Diego paradise, I was off again—to purchase a bigger sailboat, a one-hundred-ton

Rhodes. It had all the bells and whistles and the latest electronics.

It had two propeller screws that allowed the ship to turn on a dime. The bow extended quite far out making it tricky to berth. It was powered by two 250 HP *Gimmys*. It had two big Chrysler generators to supply its electrical needs, including the electric heating system on board, and it had an electrolysis system to counter any corroding of the hull. The sails were just for stabilization to help the mechanical stabilizers. The ship was too big and heavy to sail.

The first time out, I pushed one screw and pulled the other to direct the bow of the *Seafarer* against the morning breeze trying to get out of the slip in the harbor.

To my dismay the large eighty-foot-long surface of the hull acted as a sail in the breeze and pushed me back, again and again. People began to gather, trying to figure out what I was doing, and while some began to worry about their nearby boats, most were laughing.

I kept going back and forth against the breeze, back and forth, but I was making no progress. I became fidgety and frustrated, so I throttled the engines up to full power and just went for it. I clipped the rudder off the adjacent boat as its startled owner stared at me from his deck. I couldn't stop, so I shouted over my shoulder, as I sailed out of the marina, "Don't worry. I'll pay for it." And smiled to myself as I thought, "That is, if I make it back from riding this tiger."

I'd made a name for myself in the harbor in a hurry. It was only the first of many adventures with this boat that my friend Harry called a battleship. Not too long after that I took out a bunch of pilings in the harbor. Someone on deck had left the *sheet* on, a thick rope wound around the pilings—after I'd called for it to be removed—and when I took off, 500 horses all pulled at once, dislocating the piling. After a while I had the impression boats got out of my way when I started out to sea. It was as if word had gotten around about the damages I'd done in the harbor. But there were lots of other harbors along the California coast for me to visit.

My dad came to visit us about that time. He had become a frail old man. I took him out to sea against some moody winds, and he sat behind the wheelhouse watching me with our little dog on his lap—making the dog feel safe, he said—so, in order to keep from worrying him, I kept him unaware of it when I was having problems.

One evening at twilight, I ran into a big problem, trying to get into a harbor at the location where the chart said it was supposed to be. Going with the swells was like riding a roller coaster into the harbor. Then we passed some pointed, black cone-shaped rocks that appeared and disappeared in the swells. We seemed to be pushed by the devil himself into the strange harbor, pushed past the black heads that were coming and going. They seemed to be the devil's own heads, watching and diving, giggling, and waiting for me to soon join them under the cold water. Surrounded by rocks, I finally saw the harbor I was looking for—still a mile in the distance—and two fishermen jumping off their trawlers as they saw me coming at them. They knew the harbor wasn't wide enough for my ship, especially with them in it already. Seeing the speed I was coming, they stayed away from their boats. There was no other safe passage into the harbor—just more rocks.

Then I realized what a mess I was in. Now came the moment when I had to get out of the box I had put myself in. I forced a turn past the black rocks with all the speed and power the *Seafarer* was capable of, and bucked the giant swells trying to push me into the arms of the fishermen who had jumped off their boats. I inched slowly, very slowly, against the powerful swells back out to sea where I spent all night standing at the wheel and on into the next day. Vigilant, I listened to the engines and watched the horizon, continuously on alert for one of the massive white breakers that could keel us over—mighty waves from earthquakes in the sea or from storm surges.

I saw smoke puffing vertically on the horizon, something I'd never seen before. Smoke always appears slowly on the horizon.

I headed towards what turned out to be a Russian trawler, working quickly to pull in its nets. This was an area I had heard rumors about. It was rumored that American listening devices had been laid on the sea bottom there as part of the American defense system. I smelled a rat when I saw the Russian ship over it, and being an American-licensed vessel, I called the Coast Guard to report a foreign ship that was, perhaps, in an unauthorized area.

I knew it was Russian from the ID on its hull. There was no doubt about that, and I had heard no radio messages, no talking on the radio from the Russian ship. Ships always gabble. Messages come and go. Not this one. It was like a bad boy in hiding, mantled in silence. The Coast Guard asked for its nationality and ID. The silence from the Russian ship told me it was listening—closely. This was during the Cold War. I decided to have a little fun with the cagey Russians. After a long while I told the Coast Guard that the hull was so rusty that I couldn't make out its ID, but I'd say it was Russian. Yes, considering how rusty it was, it could only be Russian. I told them I needed time to check it out.

I took my time, then told them that, yes, it was Russian and I gave the ID.

The Coast Guard radioed back and reported that they'd checked with Washington DC and found that the Russian trawler was licensed to do research work in the area. And then radio-hell broke loose. The Russians hollered over the radio at me, over and over, "Gat out of way. We work. Gat out." I was five hundred feet away from whatever they were doing, the required international distance to be kept from any working boat. To irritate them a little more, I told them over the radio that they should just relax and carry on with whatever they were doing; I was just going to take a few pictures of them. They quickly turned and took off. I followed but they were soon gone from sight with their thirty knots against my fifteen. My Dad, who spoke Russian, was all ears, listening and watching—enjoying the encounter.

One other adventure with the *Seafarer* remains clear in my memory, an awkward event. We anchored outside Catalina Island harbor and took our Boston whaler off the *Seafarer* to head to the beach. My son Rudy and I pulled the boat up on the sand and went beachcombing, looking for anything unusual. We couldn't believe what we saw: a treasure chest, a real wooden treasure chest with worn leather parts that was partly exposed in the mud of a creek bed that ran steeply down to the sea.

Carefully, making sure nobody was watching, we loaded it into the whaler. We were bursting with excitement, so we opened it just enough to peek inside. It was filled with pearls, antique jewelry, and more pearls. We closed it quickly and looked at each other, speechless. The motor wouldn't start, so we had to row the Boston whaler back to the *Seafarer*, but we didn't care. We laughed and sang pirate songs; we couldn't wait to get back on the *Seafarer* to check out the treasure where no one could see us.

When we finally got on board, we began laying it all on deck, piece by piece. With each piece our enthusiasm waned a little more: cheap replicas and a handful of pennies. We saw our own letdown expression reflected in each other's face. We kept a few pieces for souvenirs and threw the rest overboard.

Some weeks later, I read a story in the social section of the *LA Times* about a family who had collected cheap replicas from uncles and grandmas to put in a treasure box that had been lovingly built by the father, and then hidden on Catalina Island for his little boy to find. That day wasn't coming. I didn't know what to do. By now they'd already been disappointed. Maybe I should have tried to get in touch with them or built another box, but I didn't.

♣ CHAPTER 31 ♣

"Didn't you write a book about a little boy?"

"Yes, I have a copy of it with my stuff in the envelope."

"What was it about?"

"I called it *B-611—Way Out There.* It's a story about a little boy and his star."

"Would you read some of it?"

"Okay, here are a few lines, Estelle."

> *...I can see way over there a glittering sea of stars, they sparkle like water ripples in the sun...All night out here in the universe these clouds of stars look at you. I know at night I don't look at the stars, they look at me. Grownups don't know this. Those stars look at you from all directions, all at once. I wished I could see like the stars, from all directions, all at once. I can't.*

"It's like a song, a song for children and maybe for grownups who can still dream like a child."

"That's what I was trying to write, Estelle."

"I don't understand it at all. I think it's gibberish."

"John, you just don't understand it."

"I'll leave you a copy, Estelle, so that you can read later if you like."

"Thanks. That would be nice."

* * *

I stayed away from the stress of wheeling and dealing with people for a few years, and I enjoyed the *good life* by spending time with the kids and working in the garden, planting vegetables and flowers and pulling weeds at our place on Vancouver Island, but I began to miss the challenges that got my blood pumping and my mind racing. Then, as if reading my mind, my banker called and suggested I should look at a deal in Houston, Texas.

Within days I was meeting with the bank's representatives at their lawyer's office in Houston. This firm had an army of lawyers, over three hundred partners and employees. I was there to negotiate the purchase of a 500-unit apartment complex from my bank. The lawyer's office was stuffed with heavy leather furniture and walls filled with antique shotguns and paintings of ducks. At a glance I wondered if the guns were meant to impress with or to shoot with. And there were duck decoys sitting on piles of files. Was it to remind the lawyer of the upcoming hunting season or that the clients in those files were sitting ducks? I knew I wasn't going to be one.

The boys from the bank numbered six—*six-to-one* odds I was used to—plus their lawyer. We went through the proposed contract with the *do's and don'ts*. The bankers represented one of the biggest banks in the world, and I respected them for their position. But that was all. It sure wasn't for their *know-how* or *smarts*. The older ones I treated gently, out of habit. With them, I used a quiet manner to discuss the pros and cons in an understated fashion. I took my time in answering their questions, which gave me more time to think. In the end they thought I was weighing things—which is what I hoped. Towards the younger ones, I showed sharp edges and occasionally jumped over and beyond what they were getting at.

Their head man was completely different. He was trying,

during the course of the discussion, to show that he was the only smart one—a very smart one—and that he knew it all and decided it all. The more he showed that side of himself, the more positive I was that I could get a good deal. At one point, as if by a secret signal amongst themselves, they tried to scare me with remarks about their power over the bank: how much money I would or wouldn't get to buy the project, how much interest I'd have to pay for the loan, and how much that interest would amount to—a few million. Things had to be their way and no other.

I let their remarks pass without comment, and using poignant arguments in my favor, I piloted my financial direction slowly and easily past them. I had concealed my inner resolve on the points most contentious to me. Outwardly, I had to be like a cloud and let them guess where I really was and what I was up to. Otherwise, they would nail me down to their way of operating. The little things that they were willing to concede were the very things that were important to me.

When the head man asked me if I minded him smoking his Cuban cigar, I begged him not to. I'd been expecting his request for quite a while because he'd been playing with a cigar for quite some time. From the time he'd started it, I'd been thinking about how to reply. I had watched his hands all along. I had decided that my begging him not to smoke would make him edgy. He was probably addicted to smoking, so it might weaken him and prompt him to end the meeting sooner, thus conceding on the points I saw as important.

I continued to gently reshape their opinions. We all maintained poker faces. I was trying to understand what was behind their faces, looking at the visible to read their invisible selves. It became a chess game of thought and counter-thought as the discussions became more complicated. The bank's representatives weren't simpletons. The bank had sent its best. They were tough and filled with *know-how* they showed off more to each other than to me.

Up to this point their lawyer hadn't said a word. "Did that

have anything to do with the decoys?" I wondered. What they all lacked was flexibility in their thinking. That raised red flags in me and left us deadlocked on minor points—minor to them, but crucial to me. Not getting my way on one minor point, I decided it was now my turn to take them for a twirl—to tell them there was no deal. That way I would get the deal the way I wanted it later, because I knew they would get hell from the big boss for failing to make the deal just because of one small, unresolved detail. So, to everyone's surprise, I called the whole deal off and went back to my hotel. I knew what would happen.

Late that night the *decoy man,* their lawyer, appeared at my room and apologetically conceded on the contentious points for the bank. The deal was completed the next day. I now had 500 apartment units on my hands, all located in Texas.

I'd locked myself in a box with new obligations, the box the bank wanted me to be in, but I had learned a little throughout the years, so I knew how I could get out of this one.

Now I had to make enough money to make payments on the apartment project, pay the staff, and do any needed renovations, plus pay for whatever other ideas I came up with along the way. But I had to do all this in a strange town in a foreign country. I needed the assurance of feeling safe to have the peace of mind to begin working, so I decided to do two things: pay a retainer to the biggest and best local law firm and make a sizable donation to the union of the local police force—both legal and effective ways to feel safer doing business on foreign soil. I still remembered how vulnerable I'd felt as a stowaway. In a foreign country I could get dumped into a river, and no one would miss me. But not now.

First, I saw the local banker and, with his help, bought all the properties surrounding my project before their prices went up, which they would do after I'd invested in the new apartment complex to make it more attractive. Within a year I had completed extensive renovations to all five hundred apartments to make them more attractive to prospective tenants. I had designed large brass logos for the entrances, transplanted exotic trees and bushes from another property I'd purchased expressly for that purpose, bought a bus and established shuttle services to places frequented by the tenants, added more competent staff and raised the morale of the existing one, purchased attractive uniforms for all of the staff, and worked out an advertising campaign to attract up-scale tenants. The money began rolling in, faster and more than I'd expected.

After being on the road for a week, I arrived home late one night to my penthouse in the Houston apartment with a suitcase full of dirty laundry and no laundry detergent. Midnight found me in a Safeway store searching the aisles for a certain kind of soap. I seemed to be the only one in the huge store. As I studied the detergent boxes, I felt a hand on my shoulder. Startled, I turned to see a tall good-looking Texan, Stetson and all, dressed as if going to a ball. He drawled, "What ya looking for, boy?" I explained. He went on, "Where ya comin' from boy?" I explained again. Then he put his arm around me and said, "Don't worry, boy. We'll make a Texan out o' ya yet."

I found Texans to be generous in spirit, and they gave me the feeling of being at home wherever I was, even in the stores where the cashiers said, "Ya'all come back now, ya hear." I loved the Texan people and their ways. When I sold the project a few years later, I earned a bundle due to improving the buildings, better-than-expected cash flows, and by selling the surrounding land I'd purchased in the beginning.

I was making too much money, but I spent it too. I spent money like water, buying buildings and adding to my collection of antiques. I bought another penthouse in Houston I didn't need, new homes in various cities in North America, and a new office building in Houston. Within a short time I had seven beautiful homes to live in. I spent over a million renovating one home alone, the one in La Jolla, just above Ray Crock's place, the Ray Crock of McDonald's. The expense of keeping them all up added up too. By then, the kids were growing up and living in Canada most of the time.

Some of the homes I lived in only a couple weeks out of the

year—like the one in La Jolla where I forgot the security code to get in, so I had to stay the night in a hotel. When I finally did get in, I apologized to the housekeeper for making footprints on the freshly vacuumed carpet.

Whenever I had to recuperate from illness or fatigue, I'd go back to La Jolla. The weather was always nice, and James, my butler, was there to look after me. Furthermore, my two sailboats were docked nearby, with people working on them all the time. There was always something needing to be done.

Before breakfast I would stroll out onto the beautiful grounds and enjoy the flowers and the humming birds, while I picked fresh oranges for James to make into juice for my breakfast. It was a paradise.

On this particular day I looked at James more closely. His tailcoat was pulled into wrinkles. It had fit much better a year ago. He had eaten steak every day while I was gone, which was most of the time. I'd eaten steaks when I'd worked up north building the railroad and had never put on weight because I was working hard physically all day out in the cold, but James lived in a warm climate and spent his days inside watching TV.

A critical moment came soon after, the turning point when I re-examined my sense of values. Here I was, at the apex of my career, making more money than I needed, and having more than I should have, when I suddenly realized what was happening to me. I asked James to take away the roses he'd put on my desk. I was tired of them so close to my face. He gave me a dry, as-you-like-sir look.

That was the instant when I knew, right then and there, that I had everything money could possibly buy and too much of it, far too much. Surely life would find a way to take me down a notch or two. It was foolish to accumulate so much. Slowly, I took stock of myself. I had to come back down to earth. I couldn't wear more than one suit at a time.

I Humbly Knelt Down Somewhere
slowly,

conscious of every moment in me.
I didn't know when
I had folded my hands over my head.
When I looked out into beautiful nature,
I knew my part in it was barely a spark
in all that integrated beauty outside.
Total nature I could never fathom,
could never fathom how many sparks it held,
could never fathom what it all meant.
I closed my eyes.
I stopped breathing
to listen to myself inside,
to my millions of friends,
all no more than a spark.
My thought repeated
that I am just a spark in it all,
and that for such a short time—
never even to be noticed.

I felt it wasn't hard to realize how small you are when you're down and out, or near to it, but for me to realize it when I was standing on the peak of what I'd accomplished in my life made me very lucky indeed.

My luck with the bankers seemed to keep coming. After they saw how successful I'd been in turning around a money-losing project, and knowing my willingness to take on the challenge of such projects, they called with a new project, hoping I could once again turn around a losing proposition. They slipped me one this time, promising to provide whatever amount of credit I needed to pull it through for them. They had some land near Edmonton that was going to be developed, and they promised I'd make a few million on the side. They had all the paperwork to back up their claims.

I soon found that the land sat—not on silt, which would have been bad enough—but on silty water, so there was no way to keep the subdivision service lines in place. I tried to stabilize the ground by laying fifty-foot-wide fiberglass sheets in the bottom of the trench, covered them with gravel many feet deep—to keep the silt down—put the pipes in, and packed them with sand and soil. The pipes still wouldn't stay in place, so the town wouldn't accept the elevation variances of the pipes.

In the end the bank had slipped me one I couldn't solve. I lost a bundle, and the town had the last laugh when they installed pumps to stabilize the silty subsoil, something they hadn't allowed me to do. They got serviced land for almost nothing, just the cost of the pumps. And because it was against the law in Alberta to sue a town, all the money I'd put into the project became theirs. Could it be that Lady Luck had stuck it to me this time?

The bank wasn't fair and the town wasn't fair, but so what? I set out to recover the money. And I needed to move quickly. But there is no *quick fix* when you're in trouble.

I tried anyhow. I bought two high-rise towers to convert into condominiums in Edmonton. Unfortunately, the economy heated up just then, raising interest rates to 21fi percent. Now I was paying five million dollars in interest each year on the two towers, and I couldn't sell the condominiums because the high interest rate discouraged any prospective buyers. I lost over ten million dollars on that project.

Another call from my banker. This time he wanted me to buy the biggest ranch in Canada, the Gang Ranch near Kamloops. He said the value of the timber on it was worth more than what they were asking. I hired a helicopter to take a look. It consisted of over a million acres that included both owned and provincially-leased land, part of which was in inaccessible mountain country.

The helicopter pilot scooped along the meadows, missing rocks by only a few feet in showing me the whole layout of the ranch. It had acres of abandoned machinery, five thousand head of cattle roaming over its hills, Indian people with their homes and store and post office, and the timber—about enough to make toothpicks with. When I landed to talk to the foremen, they said it needed new irrigation pipes put in, miles of it, and new machinery; in fact, everything needed to be replaced. Nothing worked anymore. The Indians would look after the new machinery. I thought it more likely the new machinery would soon be added to the hundreds of machines already sitting around rusting.

That was all the information I needed to pass on the deal. As I flew home I wondered if the bank was trying to get rid of their poor investments or if they were trying to bankrupt me. It was one or the other, for sure.

Fortunately, I didn't need to buy just anything to make a fast buck. I still had land in Texas and in other places, so I took my time and built up a car leasing business. In the end it just held its own.

I decided it was time to offer my help and advice and give back some of what I had learned, so I ran in a civic election in Edmonton. I had good contacts with the Italians because I'd written a weekly column for the *El Congresso*, and I should get the Jewish vote. It was a lot of work to make speeches, and it cost quite a bit too, but I didn't get elected. That was that.

It was a sign that it was time to look after my loved ones and myself.

♣ CHAPTER 32 ♣

My dad was visiting again. He came every year for over twenty years to see what crazy things I had tried to do next. He loved me so much that it was embarrassing to me—yes, and to him. He used to stroke my hair, look at the ground as if embarrassed to show his love, and then shyly glance up at my face, smiling, and whisper in a melancholy tone, "*Mei jung.*" "My son."

I was still the little boy he'd asked for advice from the time I was seven. That day I'd gone with him to meet his lawyer, and we were on the way home, waiting at a crossing for the train to pass, when he asked me if the lawyer was the right one to look after his case, if he was smart enough. "No, he wasn't," I'd told him. Years later he wished he'd listened to his little boy.

> ***My Dad Was Such a Modest Man***
> *I liked that part of him.*
> *I always wished I had some part of it in me.*
> *I wasn't modest enough.*
> *I tried.*
> *It just never worked.*
>
> *Then came the time*
> *I held that sealed envelope.*
> *I already knew what it said.*

My hands felt it,
felt what was in it:
Dad had died.
In that moment
I moved into a trance,
forgetting to open the letter.
My hands were right.

I couldn't sleep during the nights that followed.
Every detail around me was magnified.
I hated the ticking of the clock in the hall,
the chime that sounded every hour.
Muted stirrings outside
at light's dawn offended me.
And then the sudden early morning bursts,
bursts of singing from the birds
outside the windows—
I couldn't stand it.
I'd never heard birds sing so loud before.

Early the next day
I looked at the chair he had last sat in
to watch the birds
hide and play in the bare branches.

I would like to be a little more like him,
show less than I have,
give more when there is little to give,
and to reach out to help
when I needed it myself.

Within days I became someone else.
I had lost a bit of the old me in me—
but life, as it is, must go on.

Things come in waves at you. My mother had died some

years before. I had sent a generous amount of money to a relative to have my mother buried as she had asked, near her father, with a nice stone. But the relative had hidden her remains in someone else's grave, and squandered the money on beer and who knows what instead. I was devastated. I had no choice but to fly to Germany—a place I never wanted to see again—to bury my mother a second time, this time where and how she'd asked to be buried. The urn with my mother's ashes was shipped to Bremen.

I Held the Plain Grey Tin
She was as light as a feather—
no—less,
weighing nothing,
I felt as if I held
all humanity in my hands,
as if the whole world was depending on me
to do this right,
to carry her for a few steps
to her final resting place.
Walking carefully,
I was deeply conscious of her,
from whom I'd once come,
now only seconds remaining with me,
too soon out of my hands,
put into the dark forever.
I handed her extra slowly to the pallbearer
who placed the urn into the dark hole
to remain in it
as long as the urn would last.

She now rested in the family plot
with those she had once known,
with those she had both loved and despised,
under a heavy granite block.
All those under it with her

were now closer together than ever before.

All night the image of the tiny urn
floated in front of my eyes,
keeping me awake.
I waited for morning to wake the birds.
I couldn't wait to get back to her grave,
anxious to be near her one last time.

On the way through the cemetery
I looked at the beautiful park-like setting,
the ponds and bridges and ducks.
It wasn't a bad place to be left.
I pulled my collar up
and stared into the gentle rain
as I listened to the drops
rustle the fall leaves.
It was cold enough to snow.

Christmas came to my mind.
Mother used to sing carols
at that time of year
when most places had
more lights inside than out,
long ago,
when I had secretly hoped for some warmth,
some love—
anything less tangible than
the pain of not being wanted—
under the Christmas tree.
Yes, she used to sing.
I admired her singing
about a cherry tree and a cuckoo
long before I went to school.
Oh, how I admired her singing!

I suddenly stood before the place I'd just left her yesterday. I closed my eyes. I could see her in my mind. I hung onto her vision. Slowly, I opened my eyes. "Who'd put those flowers there?" Oops. That wasn't her grave. She was one over, three feet under the left front corner of the heavy red granite block.

Surely she lived on in me. While I stood there, I thought of how everyone alive is a puzzle unto himself, a puzzle made up of the millions of voices of all the ancestors who have come before and have also left their imprint in one single living person.

Ancestor Voices
Sighing,
Crying,
Shoving and coaxing
Until they get a chance
To be brought out
By an act of a new birth.

It was 1984. I was fifty-nine years old. I'd lost my cocky trust in the ever-present *Lady Luck*, though I was luckier than anyone I knew. I'd traveled and seen much; I had lived much, and had been allowed to dare much, but I didn't wanted to live in the memory of the past any longer. I hoped for something new, a safe place to live in during my time remaining, some happy pasture to graze on.

As I took the first few steps out of the cemetery, I realized Bremen wasn't just the place where I'd buried my mother. It was also the place, where almost forty years ago, I'd departed with my pony, Alex, clopping along the cobblestones heading towards Krefeld. It had taken almost two weeks.

I looked at a map to find the road I must have taken. It was about 200 miles. Today it's a three-hour drive by car. I smiled when I remembered how long it had taken me to get Alex off the pasture, into the harness, and onto the road, seldom before mid-morning, and by early afternoon I was already looking for a pasture for him. I began thinking it out: three miles an hour for five hours a day equaled fifteen miles a day for maybe two weeks, yes, 200 miles.

I couldn't resist looking for the old route I'd taken, but everything had changed—new roads, new houses, and new towns. I was soon forced onto the Autobahn. I was disillusioned. I wanted to see the places where I'd stayed a lifetime before. Nothing looked familiar. Suddenly I saw a cold blue metal sign: Krefeld. For the first time, my thoughts turned to Greta.

* * *

"Thank heavens. I'm going to hear about Greta at last."

"Yes, Estelle. You're going to hear a lot about Greta now."

"Great."

* * *

I wondered if she was all right. Was there anything I could do for her? I had the money to help her if she needed it, so I inquired as to her whereabouts from the German authorities. Germans are good at keeping records—keeping an eye on everybody. Even though her name and address had changed, I got her new address within minutes.

As I neared her address, the apartments, I noticed, on both sides of the street were dull and drab. I said to myself, "Poor Greta." Then the street number I'd been given appeared on an old house. "Not too bad," I thought.

It was around nine-thirty in the morning when I rang the bell. It brought back memories of the times I'd rung the bell for her before and how I had shaken in my boots. I felt it again. A woman opened the door. I smiled at her, thinking, "She couldn't have changed that much." I asked for Greta. She turned to speak to people behind her who wanted to know who was at the door. Suddenly, from behind the door, there she was—her hair askew. She'd always been so meticulous. I was stunned anyway, just at seeing her. I could see that she was shocked to see me, a long-forgotten guy that had suddenly appeared out of nowhere. A tall man, likely her husband, stood at the top of a marble stairway, looking me over to see if I meant trouble. He looked at me as if he was taken aback by my boldness to appear at his door. I didn't belong in his world.

I could see what he thought and I sympathized with what I saw in his face, so I smiled at him for a prolonged period.

"You know who I am, Greta?" I asked.

"Yes, of course. You are Alexander. Please, you must come in."

Her husband, now standing slightly behind her, stepped aside, reluctantly.

So Many Years Had Passed
Now inside her house,
we sat looking at each other,
trying to fathom each other,
smiling,
wondering about the what's and where's
and why's of the other,
having fallen with these into silence
for a couple of minutes.

When an hour passed,
she asked me to walk with her,
to the place where we'd walked
with our young dreams,
in the park.
Yes, it was a dream again
for a short while,
among the trees,
older, fuller, taller,
just as we were.

She held my hand,
bubbling over with words,
magically re-creating

the intimate feelings of long ago.
At the pavilion we watched white swans.
We paused,
as old memories tied us to this spot,
wordless,
remembering.

I looked at her from the side.
She was beautiful.
My thoughts flew back to her seventeenth birthday
when she girlishly asked,
twirling around,
what I thought of the dress she'd just made
out of a bedroom drape.
Even more.
If she had nice legs?
Yes.
I couldn't tell her then,
and I surely couldn't say anything now.
She was married.
Happy.
No sir.
I couldn't tell her how beautiful she still was.
I couldn't tell her how I wanted to hold her.
I never gave her any signs
of the love I still felt for her.

We began to walk. She asked if I remembered when we'd stood at this spot before. I nodded. I asked if she was happy, if life had been good to her. She hesitated. I sensed that something seemed to be troubling her, something she didn't want to talk about. She nodded that she was happy, but her face was solemn. Then her face changed, as if a new thought had changed it. She looked relieved and began to talk. No, she wasn't happy. She'd been through hell. Her husband was an alcoholic beyond reach. She'd sent him to clinics and hospitals to get dry, many times, but it hadn't worked. And there was more. He had a fat blond girlfriend, he called his *Birdie*, whom he saw in the evening and took on trips. Greta didn't know what to do.

It explained her unkempt appearance at the door. I was sad to hear how she'd suffered and had been unsuccessful in helping him. What could I say but that I wished she was happy. That meant I had to tell her to try again to work things out with her husband. I told her that she should make herself attractive to him. She'd done it before and could do it again. Forgive and forget. She wondered if she could do it. I told her there was no other way. She seemed surprised that I suggested she try to reconcile with her husband.

I told her, "Do your best, more than your best. You can do it. What comes after you've done your very best doesn't matter. Results don't matter. What matters is that you've tried your best. That's all. Whatever happens in the end is irrelevant. You will become a better person because of what you tried to do. You have to."

She said it would be hard but that she'd try. We agreed that if it didn't work out, we would help each other try to figure out what to do next. I had to leave to give her the chance to do what was best for her and her husband. There was no other way. I had to distance myself.

So I left as I'd come—quickly. I needed to get back to Canada anyhow. Germany meant nothing to me. Greta was the only bit of Germany I had any interest in.

A few months later I called to ask how things were going. She said she'd taken my advice. It had worked for a while, but now everything had gotten worse. It was no use trying any longer. Would I please come? To help as I'd promised? I hesitated. It would mean a lot of trouble and heartache waiting in the wings for both of us. But I had to try. To try my best as I'd told her earlier. I met her…

At the Duisburg Railway Station
It was Tuesday afternoon at 3:52.
My heart was pounding
though I told it not to.
This was no love affair.
This was a crusade.
I walked along the platform,
searching for her
in the gray light of the glass arches
darkened by a century of steam-engine smoke.
I walked on.
No Greta anywhere.

Then down the oversized stairway
I saw her,
leaning shyly against the handrail,
halfway down the stairs,
smiling,
with her arms outstretched.
A feeling of happiness came over me.
We embraced.
I felt the pulse in her throat.
I felt like I'd come home.

We smiled and looked at each other.
Her fingers traced along my cheek up to my eyes,
then down along my nose to my lips.
What a pleasure her fingers were.
We were overwhelmed
by the circumstances
we'd found ourselves in.

In the Porsche she shifted gears, then covered my hand with hers, gently, while her fingers moved to and fro, as though wanting to make love. I pulled my hand from hers. She stopped the car and said, "If we come to any disagreement, we should part immediately so that we don't cloud the memories we have of each other. We owe it to our past."

I agreed at once and mumbled that we both had what it took to do that if we had to. She smiled and said nothing. She seemed to be at ease about us being together now. Seeing her again, I sensed that this time I wasn't just passing by. This time I might stay. Might.

She dropped me off at a hotel. Later that afternoon at the house, I saw her husband. He was wearing a morning coat, his body stooped. He looked stupefied, a man who had failed. I felt sorry for him. He looked as if there was no hope for him. He went back to bed with a bottle of wine. No one knew where he'd gotten it. He was still a big man. In looking at pictures, I saw that he'd been very good-looking once. And I learned that he'd been funny and smart and kind. What a shame! What a waste! After a few visits, I grew to like him and wanted to be able to help him, even if that meant reuniting him with Greta. I tried to give him dignity by taking him seriously. And I tried to help Greta in any way she asked. I commanded myself to help her and to do whatever she wanted done, but to always keep my distance. But I knew if she ever gave me even one sign that she cared for me, I'd never give her up. I would be totally committed to her. However long that might take was okay with me.

Whenever we were away from the house, she held my hand and became a happier, more cheerful person as she chattered away. Meanwhile, my legs would turn to rubber, but I never gave her any sign of my feelings.

The mental and physical appearance of her husband deteriorated further. Greta's friends advised her to have her husband declared insane for the sake of their three daughters. They told her it was long overdue. At the very least she should take him to live in a clinic. He didn't belong in the house with the children. She couldn't find it in her heart to declare him insane, but she agreed to take him to a clinic for alcoholics in Switzerland.

The chauffeur drove them there. Greta called me en route. She sounded upset and said they hadn't spoken a word to each other all day. She got him checked in and taken care of. In the meantime, I'd followed them in case she needed any help. When she came from the clinic to meet me at the hotel, she was very stressed out and asked me to take her to a place that she had always found comforting—her favorite Romanesque chapel at Ottmarsheim. She wanted me to share it with her. She stood outside the chapel and admired the clean simple lines of the structure. She explained how they reflected the simple and honest devotion of people long ago. In the rotunda, an old man tended plain, but beautifully colored, flowers. We entered the chapel and immediately I felt how this simple space, guarded by massive blocks of stone, called for silence, called for a holy feeling. The subdued light issued a subtle invitation to prayer. The visit seemed to bring an inner peace to her.

With her husband looked after, she came back to Canada with me so that I could show her Edmonton and catch up on some neglected business matters. She stayed at our house and met Violet and the family and looked for what she called my *footprints* in the house. While I was immersed in problems at work, she would wait for me to return. We'd embrace together, my wife and Greta and I. It was nice to have her in our house. I had to attend to some business in Vancouver for a day, and Greta wanted to see more of Canada, so she came along.

We came back to find disaster had hit. My wife had gone berserk over Greta's visit and had thrown all of Greta's things out onto the street, where they were being run over by cars. That was no way to treat the living remnants of my childhood. In that hour, I left and never returned. Greta and I went back to Krefeld. The next days went by so fast it was if we were riding a carousel, riding it round and round. In no time at all, a new day was waiting. The intensity of our feelings contrasted to the quiet times we shared when we were together.

♣ CHAPTER 33 ♣

I had a call from my oldest. Alexandria had married a brilliant plasma physicist. He was approached by a microcomputer manufacturer to mathematically evaluate the rationale of designing a scheduler for telephone operators—to work on a microcomputer. He found it mathematically possible. He told me what he'd discovered. I asked him if he himself could design the software for such a scheduler. He thought that most likely he could. That was enough for me to form a company based in St. Louis where my oldest and her husband, Jim, lived.

I knew Jim was a tenacious worker but had no business acumen. Although I knew nothing about software programming or how to get a client for it, I was willing to handle the business end and the selling—selling the *nothing* we didn't yet have, a scheduler for telephone operators. While Jim tried to produce the scheduler, I knocked down doors, financed the start, and presented us to telephone companies throughout the world. The scheduler was software designed to save labor costs for the telephone companies, savings amounting to millions. Greta provided additional investment capital and joined the company while I knocked on more doors.

British Telecom was my first success. For years, they'd begged their mainframe programmers to create a scheduler to run on microcomputers, but nothing had been done, so when I convinced them that we could do it, I knew we had our first customer. We had a wobbly program for a scheduler to start with, but after a year we had a contract that paid a million Swiss francs a year. In one year alone we saved BT ten million pounds on labor costs. Sometimes it pays to try to do the impossible.

My travel schedule was growing. I traveled from country to country, city to city, hotel to hotel, with just a carry-on.

With Christmas a week away, I rented an apartment in Krefeld to be near Greta around Christmastime. On Christmas Day, when I moved in, she gave me a big hug that felt like more than a hug. Her arms were flung around me, greatcoat and all. That hug told me I'd stay a while longer in her life, perhaps forever. But fate had other plans.

When I had to return to Edmonton for business, Greta and I parted in the busy airport, hugging and kissing like teenagers. My heart didn't know why I was going back, but my mind told me I had to.

Back in Edmonton I rushed through my business, doing just the essentials. Other places were waiting for me to present our scheduler. I had to go on to St. Louis, then Basel, London, and finally Canterbury to continue selling.

In Canterbury I stayed at the historic fourteenth century Three Tuns Inn, where I was privileged to be shown something they'd found. After a few glasses of ale and some lively conversation with the bartender, I was shown a pair of shoes they'd found in the inn behind a wall they'd removed for renovations. They looked like moccasins with a strap missing on one shoe. I held them. I couldn't believe how it felt to hold something that old. They were so light, like a handful of feathers, and had been worn hundreds of years ago. In museums I have to hold things with my eyes. Here, I held something with my hands.

On I went to Dusseldorf to say good-bye again to Greta. I was on my way back to Edmonton. This time I returned to problems that I could never have imagined. I thought I'd dealt with every kind of problem by then, but not this. My youngest daughter wouldn't let me into my own office. She yelled at me that I was crazy and threatened to call the police if I tried to come in. And there was more. From the beginning I had always put all the shares from my companies into the names of my wife and four children to avoid future estate taxes for them. I was the president, the maker, and the doer. I didn't need any shares. Led by my *trustworthy* wife, she and my children, holding all the shares, had voted me out of my own companies. They'd stripped me down to nothing. I was out—and down. With a single stroke from their pens, they had millions in their grabby hands.

Staying married to the person who'd engineered this coup no longer made sense. A divorce would be best for all, so I proceeded to arrange it. I loaded the moving van with some old furniture and headed for St. Louis. I drove straight through without stopping. In the mountains of Montana, I nearly crashed when moody mountain winds tried to tip me off a narrow road, causing the wheels on one side to become airborne. For a second I thought that this too was part of the whole lousy hand I'd been dealt in Edmonton.

I put a notepad on the steering wheel and wrote a letter to Greta. I sneaked past open weigh scales, not knowing if I was overweight, but not wanting to take a chance that I'd have to unload furniture somewhere and return for it later. I got by with it—and I shouldn't have—just for the sake of convenience.

By the time I got to the suburb of Clayton, near St. Louis, Greta was there, waiting to help me move in. She directed and I positioned the furniture. From the apartment I could look down on Main Street and watch the people crossing it, cars driving by slowly looking for parking spots, and the flashing red lights on speeding police cars.

Greta stayed on while her husband was in the clinic. After he began feeling better, he returned to Krefeld, along with Birdie who'd talked him into disowning Greta in his will, so Greta flew home to see what Birdie had accomplished.

I understood why she had to go. She promised she'd be back some day, but I didn't really expect her to return. Within a short while, I felt suspended and alone. I was dreaming myself into a dead end—not getting ahead, but not capable of backing off. By now I'd gotten used to the idea of being with Greta, that this was how everything was supposed to be. But now couldn't be. I hung onto the trance of my love affair and filled the apartment with blue music day and night. I went to…

Places We'd Both Been
to find her in them.
They were empty.
I went again and again
to get used to the emptiness of them.

The place where the magnolia blossoms fell,
spread generously,
looking so much like flesh,
no stains of aging.
It hurt to see them just lie there.
What now?
The short time she was gone
had to be forever.
It felt like forever,
like some unexperienced feeling of death.
Unbearable,
yet emanating a variety of feelings,
like singing from far away,
luring,
bringing aches inside
to both our cheated hearts
who knew not what to do now.

She phoned. It seemed strange that she was so far away. In the first call, she'd said she couldn't live alone any longer with her kids and the strange man that her husband had become, and then, in the next call, she'd said her kids really needed her, maybe her husband too, and that I'd have to get by without her.

I understood that her life was there, that what we'd shared was now in the past and had been for only a short while. The letters that followed told me otherwise.

> *"It's evening. Night slowly falls over us all this twenty-first of August. Hello. I listened to the tape you sent, filled with poems and thoughts. Tears walked across my cheeks, and I felt you caressing my hair. It felt nice, the way I felt when we first met, holding hands, the first moment in our love. And later when we found each other again, after so many, so many years, when our slumbering tender love was woken out of a forgotten land, like an unfolding flower, swaying, releasing scents and colors. Our desire to be together was unstoppable, the happiest time in my whole life. I thank you with my tears, for this good fortune to have come my way.*
>
> *Now, somehow, reality sneaked into my dream, cold and hard, into my real life, demanding old rights. I have tried to push that reality aside, struggled fiercely to hold onto you. I don't want to hurt you, but my reality—where I am now—is here to stay.*
>
> *I thank you for your love and stroke your kind face, which has suffered much. It was comforting to hear you will always be in my life, somehow, not knowing how. And I reply, you should know, that in every breath of my life, my thoughts embrace you, that I'll hold you safe in my hands, as long as I live."*

How could I come to terms with her reality? My rational mind told me that I should no longer listen to my feelings. It was time to let her sleep quietly within me, to remain numb, feeling nothing. A few days later she called. Hearing my emotionless response, she asked if I'd fallen in love with someone else. I was dumbfounded. Was it what she wanted or what she feared?

I decided to see her new reality in Krefeld for myself. I flew over and took a room at a hotel. She visited, wearing a business-like pantsuit. I looked at her and she looked at me. The suit symbolized a new control, control of her situation and everybody in it, including me. She took me home for a cup of tea. We talked about nothing. She had to go out for a brief appointment. She kissed me in passing, leaving me alone in the old house. The house felt like a shell. Her husband had been sent to a clinic again. I was to wait for her to return so that we could talk about nothing some more. I tried to make sense of it all. She was trying to show me she had no feelings for me anymore.

I watched her through the window as she parked the car. I struggled to be at my best and to show no emotion. She would enter at any second. When the door opened, the voices and noises of the Christmas shopping rushed in with her—a cheery commotion of child-like voices, rustling papers, and boxes falling to the floor. I wondered what would happen now. Nothing. She and her daughter walked past me as if I wasn't there, continuing on in their happy Christmas mood. I returned to the chair I'd been left in, busying myself with some books. I fell asleep in the chair, then woke up and read until the birds announced a new day. Then left for St. Louis.

I worked the next few months on my dissertation in psychology and finished it. The summer was gone, and it was time to check things out in Krefeld one last time, to make sure I was right in how I saw things unfolding between myself and Greta and her new affairs. As I changed planes in New York, I watched a tall lady with long hair, which swung with each step, pass me like a shadow. When I boarded the plane she was seated next to me. She was an interesting companion during the long flight. I found her style and mannerisms fascinating. She smiled all the time, as if her face knew no other way.

In Krefeld, Greta made it clear that she and her husband had reached a new understanding. Greta would get some much-sought-after shares in his factory and, in return, he'd get some of her old love and, he hoped, freedom to visit his Birdie. That left me out. Greta had gotten what she wanted and was content. To seal it, she asked me not to call her again and then left for their house in Italy, where her husband had promised to celebrate her birthday with her. He never showed up. His Birdie had shown up with some much-needed liquor combined with her lovemaking skills utilizing needles and rubber bands and more.

Greta waited in Italy while he had his orgy elsewhere. And I was in Toronto, trying hard to forget her. By chance I met Helly Rothman, my mother's Jewish secretary in those old days in Vienna and Berlin. She was now a widow. Fate had intervened with a diversion for me, an opportunity to show an old lady a good time. She'd always wanted to see New York, so I took her.

We stayed in swanky hotels, went to Broadway shows and visited enough museums to give her sore feet. She had a good time while I tried to get my mind off what my heart wanted to remember—visions of Greta.

I saw Helly off and went back to St. Louis to dream of Greta. In my dream she told me I was a butterfly and that she'd searched everywhere for me. To her surprise, I was sitting on her head and had flown off without her even noticing me. The next morning I remembered the dream and thought "my flying away" was a bad omen.

Soon after that Marianne came into my life—the girl I'd met on the plane. She called from Germany. Two days later Greta called. She said, "Hello, hello, hello. I love you."

I was more confused than ever, so I threw myself into my work; namely, studying psychology at Washington University between my trips on the road trying to sell our scheduler to telephone companies. Back in St. Louis a card had arrived from Greta telling me that she loved me.

I couldn't cope with the on-again-off-again messages I was getting from her, so I escaped to Edmonton. No one would look for me there. I visited an old Jewish friend, Joe Weinberger. Naturally I told him about Greta. That seemed to be the only reason I went there. I thought talking about her would get her out of my system and let me get back to living again.

I read him the poems I'd written about her. He listened, tears rolling down his cheeks as he told me I had an old Jewish soul. I was moved. I'd expected him to tell me I was just being ridiculous. Instead, he cried for me.

A year later he died in a car accident. No one had set him a stone—his wife was Catholic and didn't want to bury him in the traditional Jewish way—so I drove back to Edmonton, talked to the Rabbi at the cemetery, and arranged for the setting and engraving of a stone. Joe Weinberger had an old soul too. Peace would be with him now.

Back in St. Louis I got another letter from Greta—indeed, the letters kept coming—telling me how sad she was without me but—even though we loved each other—we had to live our separate lives. Any whispered promises she couldn't fulfill, and furthermore, I should understand that all the curtains she'd hung between us were in the name of sensibility—a promise she had made to herself to bar me from her heart. Then she wrote again, and I didn't know why.

> *"While I sit here I see how a silvery moonlight streak disappears behind heavy-looking clouds. The clouds have caught the moon. Around me, I'm alone. I sense the trees and bushes I cannot see. The night isn't resting. Crickets chirp, a tired frog calls a goodnight to his sweetheart. I'm so tired.*
>
> *Let me put my head on your shoulder, take my hand in yours like when we were young, and forget what happened.*
>
> *Love, Greta."*

This vacillation was tearing me to pieces. I didn't understand myself anymore. I let myself drift into the days ahead. I let everything happen as it unfolded. My heart was hungry for her, seeking to lay itself down peacefully with words of longing, while, in the meantime, I hit the road again to visit yet another telephone company.

Somewhere in Beautiful America in 1984
Isn't this beautiful?
Isn't this beautiful?
Isn't this beautiful?
Right over there,

I just saw it
right from where I was driving
in the blistering heat of this summer,
chasing landscapes in this big country,
on wheels among whizzing-by traffic.
There, over there I saw an expanse of gold,
a sun-colored field of bursting wheat,
swaying, swinging, dancing
in the tender breezes of the summer heat.
I just had to be there.
At once I slid from in between
chasing bumpers to seek solace in this gold.

Standing in front of it,
I was spellbound.
What a beauty of gold.
At once I remembered,
another field of gold I'd shared with her,
when she'd held me in her spell—
the one with the tiny ladybug near our eyes.
That was far from here, far, far away.
I asked myself in front of this gold,
could I find a tiny ladybug here like there?
Slowly, and very, very carefully,
did my feet slip into this other world,
passing the greens of sunlight-seeking grass,
for me to see, to feel.

From the dark luscious grass

hopped multitudes of gray-green grasshoppers
to show me the way.
Steps ahead of mine
chirping crickets
announced to the world my coming.
I stood still amidst the gold
where the sun had lain on my face.
I saw white and yellow flowers here and there.
Could I feel here what I felt there?
Could I find a tiny ladybug here?
There, over there, a yellow-brown butterfly
swung from flower to flower,
dancing, swaying in my company.

Everything grows so well here,
but nowhere did I see a ladybug,
not anywhere.
I saw millions of stalks in gold.
They were swinging, ever swinging,
swishing, touching each other all together
in the breeze of the hot air,
showing in waves,
as if they loved each other.
How well these millions of stalks
fit together with the sun,
and how peaceful it is right here.
For all this I closed my eyes.
I felt a deep peace where I stood in the sun.

Yes, I'd begun to feel her here.
I began to hear her whisper now
as she had when she'd shyly asked
in the midst of a golden field
far away from here:
Isn't this beautiful?
Isn't this beautiful?

Isn't this beautiful?

I didn't dare to leave.
I clung to the sun.
My eyes closed.
I felt a breeze
and heard swishing,
and—yes—a faint voice
coming from the swaying field:
Isn't this beautiful?
Isn't this beautiful?
Isn't this beautiful?

Another postcard from Greta waited under my door. It didn't tell me much:

> *"Hello, hello, hello, my dearest. How sweet it was to hear your voice on the phone. My only heart. Always.*
> *Your soul."*

Days later, I found another letter. She'd drawn a large, detailed red leaf with a note:

> *"Hello, hello, my Alexander. This leaf is my gift to you. I found it while walking in the forest. It glitters green in the sun. I imagined taking you on my walks, pointing out to you what I saw: 'Isn't it beautiful?' I feel your love wherever I am. Please help me not to be sad if you can.*
>
> *I hold you tight near my heart, and I trust in what you call fate. My hand in your hand.*
> *Your Greta."*

More letters—these telling me unmistakably that I would have to make my own life. Nothing could become of us. Obviously Greta was fighting with herself, with what she believed she should do out of duty and loyalty to her family, and what she wanted in her heart. Duty was winning while I was running around shattered.

Now I just prayed for someone to be there for me, to talk to and relate to. That turned out to be Marianne. She asked me to visit her in Cologne as soon as I could. I didn't know why, but considering the way I felt, I said, "Why not?" And went.

She met me at the Dusseldorf airport. It felt strange to be met by someone other than Greta. But I was grateful to be around somebody soft, someone who just wanted me too and didn't ask questions. Marianne was comforting to be around. We went to a concert, to dinner, and then to her place.

Finally I was talking with someone. We just talked. Then I went on to Stockholm to talk with a telephone company. Erickson Software was there too, listening to my presentation, but only to learn what we had developed, to spy, so the visit was a failure.

♣ CHAPTER 34 ♣

I desperately needed to see someone who understood me, so I asked my old friend Francois from the *Kerguelen* if I could come visit him. He said he'd be delighted to see me. From Paris I drove south to Montargis, a charming town, and on into the countryside where Francois was expecting me. I was ready to open my soul to him, knowing he'd understand.

I arrived in the late afternoon. He stood waiting at the mailbox, tall, smiling, leaning casually against it with one hand. He hadn't changed in the half-century since we'd last met. Not one bit.

His wife owned a medieval estate built of stone—a whole village. The electrical wires and plumbing ran along the exterior of the ancient stones, and everything was wanting. The farmers in the village supplied her with vegetables and such but had no cash to pay any rent they owed her. She was a large-boned woman, the type who was suspicious of strangers. She fit well into this part of the country.

The next morning, at a breakfast of white bread and tomatoes, his wife went on and on about what a failure Francois was. Because of her complaining, he was anxious to get away quickly to show me the local sights, in particular the Cathedral of Bourges. We slipped out and went off to the cathedral, marveling at the unusual red color of its stained-glass windows—a moving atmosphere far removed from insult.

We bought some local white wine, some goat cheese, and a real French baguette and found a bench high up on a knoll that overlooked the beautiful Loire Valley and then we talked and talked. It was a magnificent landscape: endless—a place to let our minds run and run—as never-ending as the valley.

Feeling relaxed and mellow from the wine and cheese and bread, we talked about the women in our hearts. He loved someone who was married. That sounded familiar. He wanted to leave his wife but decided not to because his Paris apartment would then be bare; all the antiques and fine furniture belonged to his wife. What a reason to stay married: nice furniture. I'd never heard of anything like it. I confessed as much to poor Francois. He sure was no risk-taker. Francois was like Greta. Everything had to be safe.

After our visit, I went to Krefeld to see Greta. She was furious and cried that I'd betrayed her by being with another woman. Marianne's husband had questioned Greta about his wife and me and had told her that his wife had left him for another man—me.

Marianne had apparently gone to Paris, but for reasons I knew nothing about. Greta demanded that I meet with Marianne's husband to talk with him and that I urge Marianne to go back to him. I left immediately, telephoned Marianne's husband, and then her. She told me her husband had beaten her beyond recognition and had bruised her so badly that she didn't want to be seen on the street. And she would never go back to him. Never. She was going to Florida to her mother's. There was nothing further she wanted to say or that I could do.

Greta could do nothing further for her husband either. He just smiled when she caught him with Birdie, yet she felt obligated to stay to try to save whatever she could for her daughters. I understood, but it was hard to accept. I went back to St. Louis.

Much later Marianne visited me there. It was my birthday. I had dinner with her that evening and the whole time I found myself wishing it was Greta sitting in her chair, so the next day I took her to her sister's somewhere in Connecticut. On the way we stopped for a picnic near a lake and left the car parked on the road.

As we sat eating, we heard voices and twigs breaking and saw two men looking around. We saw them, but they didn't see us. We understood from their conversation that they were looking for us, but we didn't know why. We hid in the underbrush and listened. We learned more: they were game wardens looking for people fishing without a license. My parked car was what had made them suspicious. They couldn't see anyone along the lake or us picnicking in the underbrush, so they finally left.

Marianne had found the whole thing so exciting that she began laughing and then, before I knew what she was doing, she'd peeled off her clothes and had jumped into the lake. She swam way out and called back to me, trying to coax me into following. She was a tennis ace, so I wasn't surprised that she was such a strong swimmer. She later told me that her mother had been on the Olympic swim team.

She was good company: crazy and happy in her own way. I dropped her off at her sister's and never saw her again. She was very likable and had made me laugh when I had needed it most. She told me no one had ever been as kind to her as I had been. We had helped each other during a time of confusion in both our lives.

I needed to begin a new life, so I moved to Vancouver to get away from the place I'd shared with Greta in St. Louis. Alone then in Vancouver, my heart and my letter-writing hand still reached out to Greta. I took a trip with the Rotary guys to an island near Vancouver and found that it didn't matter where I went…

She Was Still With Me
I'm flying this Easter,
on foaming water,

swaying on the Pacific.
The motors of this boat race,
piercing my ears,
forcing the thin plywood hull to shove water
and bounce on the crests of waves,
punishing this tiny boat in the sun,
far too small for the Pacific,
spraying its water all over.
We break foaming wells of water.

Where to? I don't know yet.
To be honest I do not care,
for I have more important things to attend to,
to think of you,
and to think of when I might see you.
Wet from the spraying salt waters,
we got to where I didn't care that we got to.
It was an island,
one of the many islands near Vancouver.

Walking it, exploring what it is made of,
we trod on gray-brown grass,
past jumping rabbits.
Those rabbits were something to hug all right.
They jumped all about
in their brown and light gray coats,
although some were pure white or black.
And there were real Easter bunnies too,
in all colors,
jumping pieces of fur.
What Easter bunnies!

We saw birds of all kinds.
They jumped too,
more than they flew,
and when they did,

they glided silently,
smoothly,
some landing near me.

I saw thick underbrush there,
with bell-shaped flowers, real show-offs.
And I saw majesties of the past,
what was left of them,
once-monstrous trees,
far too tall,
lying along the pebble beach,
gigantic trunks, partly rotten,
dying giants in wood.
Others still stood,
somehow.

Some were burned by time in the sun,
and by wild waters
into white-gray,
peeled naked by the patience of time,
instantly reminding one of dying,
waves now teasing them to death,
helped by ever-present winds,
who can shape stones.

Way to the left, along the beach,
were large plots of meadows in too much water,
now a swamp, smelly and green,
and near to the right,
kelp and seaweed,
swaying up and down on the waves,
harmonious together—
reflecting queer greens in the sun—
up and down.

The path to the left lured me on,

past the smells of the greens there,
to hundreds of ghost-like trees—
candlesticks in gray,
leafless,
once brown-green—
standing around lonely.
There, too, were other tall trees,
still holding green crowns,
looking sad,
quietly still hoping to grow.
I smelled magic air next to flowers,
tightly hugged together,
pointing to the sun.

The path walked us up and down
past monstrous rocks
seemingly put there by giants,
next to yellow patches of Scotch broom.
I dared to steal a blooming twig from one for you,
a little yellow wonder.
Twig in hand, I came along the winding path,
in the pleasantly cool dark world of silent trees,
just past a lake with water lilies,
as if carefully placed,
where I smelled peculiar grass,
making this dark treed world smell sweet.
Along its ground I found large propeller seeds,
that had floated down to the path,
twisting down,
turning in circles and dances.
More came down,
to lie lifeless next to my shoes.
I picked one up,
opened its kernel and stuck it on my nose,
now longer,
just as you and I did a long time ago.

I must confess to you,
you're lucky you didn't walk along with me here,
for I would have tried to stick one on your nose too,
and then I would have danced around you,
and laughed and laughed,
and then I would have run away
and you would have chased me.
Yes.

O my, how much I would have given
to have shared this place with you,
where I saw such a sweet banquet for the mind.

Then the unexpected happened—Greta's husband died. Greta was in shock, and I was stunned. I stayed in Vancouver to let nature take its course, to let Greta grieve as she must. Six months later she called, telling me she could no longer live without me. She was coming to see me to stay with me for good. I couldn't believe it. I was afraid to believe it.

Shaking, I waited for her at the airport in New York. Would she really be on the plane? Then she was there, with her arms outstretched, smiling, radiant, a youthful-looking figure in white. I was overjoyed. Speechless, dazed, my eyes wide, I thought it must be happening to somebody else. I embraced her, "Oh Greta, oh Greta."

I slowly found my bearings by talking and talking, telling her how happy I was. We drove to the Albanese Hotel. New York was a good place to start down the road together in paradise.

That night she told me a secret she'd kept since she was seventeen. A month after the day in the garden when we'd kissed, she'd missed her period. She was sure she'd become pregnant from what she'd felt—from the dampness on my pants and through her clothes—during our long, passionate kiss on the bench of her sandbox. We shared more thoughts and stories that tied our pasts with the present.

Everything was just right about her in every way: her

delicacy in doing things and her mood. We felt so close. We danced in the dark, body to body, while our souls held each other.

My Paradise Postponed To Now
Now I was committed to her
with all my emotions.
Encounters with her were like melodies
I couldn't forget,
humming them,
living them.
Life with Greta was my private heaven,
my heaven ahead of time.
I could accept total darkness
forever
after this heaven.
My paradise postponed.

Greta had been in the back of my mind throughout my whole life, throughout all the years we'd been apart. Now it seemed that all the time I'd been without her had been just a series of steps that had been necessary before I could be with her for good. It had taken almost half a century.

After a few days of sightseeing, we headed south to spend time in the sun. She looked so good in the sun and was so happy—she was a new Greta, a free Greta. I felt my own body when I held her hand, a hand sculptured with arteries from the wear of so many years of giving.

We stopped in Atlantic City to stroll on the Boardwalk, and paused to listen to some gospel singers in front of the Golden Nugget, performing in the wind and sun. Seagull shrills cut the air in between their notes. Then we went on to Cape May with more of the same seagulls, and to Washington, DC, to talk to Abraham Lincoln as he looked down at us from his pedestal above his monument's endless steps.

In North Carolina we visited with my old friends Peter

Batchelor and his wife, Barbara, and then on to Savannah, where moist air draped the live oaks in moss and red brick plantation mansions with rose gardens still stood as a reminder of Confederate times.

A few days later, we arrived in Palm Beach to stay at The Breakers. As we drove in, we passed some shrubs along the road which had sharp stems crowned with perfect white cups—something we'd never seen before. We drove back to admire them again and got out to look at them up close. The perfectly shaped cups were cut out of Styrofoam egg cartons. America—what a place!

Curved sticks floating in ponds looked like crocodile snouts, and waitresses demanded a fifteen per cent tip when they found out we were foreigners. Helicopters zoomed us across and out of the Grand Canyon, formed two billion years ago, while we listened to the baroque music of Bach. In California we discovered a copy of an authentic Roman villa—*Dei Papyri*—from Herculaneum in southern Italy. There we leaned back on a graciously curved stone bench to admire the bronze Roman sculptures and authentic colonnades that enclosed the pond, which was surrounded by Italian flowers and plants—all at the Paul Getty Museum in Malibu. And we saw the Hearst Castle on a quarter million acres of land. Only in America.

We had taken the *scenic route* from New York to Vancouver, a very long scenic route, and only days later were in Greta's Porsche driving south through the Alps into the valleys of peace, to Greta's place near Sienna.

When we crossed into Italy, the first building I saw was a shack built from all different-sized stones, tucked away in a green gully that somehow softened its appearance. I saw love in the stones. Loving hands had carried and sorted the rocks that had been placed into the inaccessible-looking terrain. I saw love everywhere, radiating from the faces of the people in their mountains of stones, and under the olive trees where they sang and laughed during harvest time. It was probably a reflection of the love I was now feeling.

* * *

"We lived like Gypsies—going from one place to another—just happy to be together at last. That's it, Estelle. I've told you all I remember about my Odyssey-like journey to find Greta again after a lifetime of waiting for her.

"You're very lucky to be together now. I'm glad for both of you."

"Thank you. I can't believe how long I've been sitting here going on with my story. Thanks for your patience."

"I loved hearing it, but I think my butt has petrified. I don't know if I can get out of this chair or not. John?"

"Come on, Choo. I'll give you a hand."

"Thanks, John. I think it's time to head for the kitchen to fix us a snack."

John and I were alone. We could hear the girls in the kitchen—their voices happy. Maybe this would be my last chance to grab John for a man-to-man talk. We were like young boys sharing treasures hidden in our pockets.

John busied himself with the stove. Maybe tomorrow would be better when I was going out to help him find the hammer he'd lost in the brush.

The table was piled with food. In the end we had too much to eat. Greta and I excused ourselves to go for a walk before it got too dark. We headed down…

Down Towards The Stream
slowly, hand in hand,
enjoying the fresh air coming off of it.
Having told my story,
I felt I was at another peak in my life.
I'd climbed many.
Greta was the last.
I am sure.

She and I sat down

on a soft carpet of moss
near the stream.
The water swished by,
slithering over slices of shale,
making itself into thin sheets,
slapping down on the flat water,
to spray,
to settle,
to become one
with the stream.
It was like music.

Greta smiled the radiant smile
only she has,
humming some sort of melody
she'd made up.
Watching her,
I couldn't help thinking that
I had yet to learn to handle myself,
living in a heaven on earth.
Keeping her
would be the hardest part
of staying on this peak of happiness.
I must not lose her—ever.
I took a deep breath
and inhaled the breeze
coming off the running water.

In time we got up, touched from sharing this special moment at the stream, and walked back towards the light from the cabin, past the crowded stick-like birches snugged tightly together, as if they loved being near the stream.

As we climbed the steep steps to the attic, John hollered the old refrain, "Don't let the bed bugs bite."

It was our last night at the cabin.

♣ CHAPTER 35 ♣

The next morning, as I went down the steep steps for the last time, I heard the stove door click. I knew John was making the morning fire. It had a sharper sound this morning. We all smiled at each other a bit more.

John was eager to show me the problems he'd had with the pond in the spring. We stood at the pond, both experts at building things. John looked around his self-made pond and waved his arm across it with an apologetic smile.

"This is it. I have to do this over again every year to keep from going nuts. The pond keeps me sane. I work on it every summer, never getting it right. It keeps me busy. There's nothing else for me to tackle at this stage in my life. The pond is my challenge now. All winter I think about the problem, as I try to figure out a better way of preventing the stream from filling the pond with debris in the spring when it floods and the whole area is underwater. Each year I try something else. And each year it doesn't work. I get nothing for my efforts except lowered expectations for the following year. But it keeps me going.

"Every spring the pond fills with overburden. It's hard work cleaning it out. I wade into the mud in hip boots and shovel it out by hand. Fighting the slime's suction is the hardest part. And it stinks. I figure I'm at it a couple of months every year. By the time I get the pond cleaned out, summer's almost over.

I've been thinking of building a channel so that the water will flow in differently, but I don't know. Any ideas, Alex?"

"You could cut an opening further upstream to direct the force of the water in from another direction, but then that water wouldn't clean out the real belly of the pond. It would probably just clean the section bordering the stream. I don't know. But frankly, John, if I did give you a solution, you wouldn't have anything to worry about all winter and nothing to do all summer, so then you'd really go nuts. I wouldn't want that to happen. I'll tell you what my stepfather used to tell me, 'You'll find a way. I'm sure.' That's the best I can tell you, John."

"Gee thanks. Should I tell you thanks for nothing, pal?"

"Sorry. You'll just have to think about it again next winter. Same old procedure."

"Same thing? No ideas?"

"I wish I could help you."

John looked into my eyes as if wondering about something, "Are you happy?"

"Yes. Now that I'm older and feel weariness setting in, I know I've been enriched by a life that has taught me some things and left me with a grateful memory that I've lived life to the full."

With the words *to the full,* my ears were drawn to the sound of the stream—gurgling sounds that seemed joyful, and I thought, "Those waters can sing! Yes. They sing!"

"Yes, I've lived a full life because I dared to chase my dreams and make the most of the opportunities that came along. The most wonderful things to me are my kids, especially my grandchildren. They're the ones who will live on. I often think about my kids in Neve Yaakov, Israel. My son-in-law Joel is my silent teacher by the way he does things and what he stands for, even though I don't agree with a lot of things he does or believes in. But I look up to him. He's intelligent and devoted to his Jewish beliefs, and his children are sweet, always laughing and giggling. I love being with them.

"I have fond memories of taking my grandson, Gershon,

on walks into town. One day we looked at big monstrous tires on the parked trucks and buses, and he stood with his nose right up next to them to measure their size. And we made the electronic doors at the grocery store open and close—by going into the store and then leaving before we really got inside—until the manager caught us. We walked for hours and then started home. He held onto my hand and wondered when we'd get home. I'd tell him, 'Just over that hill.' He'd reply, 'Okay' in such a sweet little voice, and when we'd walked to that hill, I would tell him we just had to get to the next one, and he'd say again, 'Okay,' his sweet voice making me forget about my own sore feet. I can hear his tiny magic voice right now while I'm telling you about him. And there is Yohevid, so very smart. She loves asking me to say *green* and then laughs and laughs at my strange pronunciation.

"If my life is judged to be a failure, I feel these wonderful children are the plus on the bottom of my balance sheet. I'm grateful to be around them and to be a silent part of them. Yes, I'm grateful to be a silent Jew deep in my inner being.

"What about you John?"

"My last name, Braams, came from my father, of course, but on my mother's side I'm an Insinger, Dutch, clear back to the time of Peter the Great who lived on royal property next door to the Insinger's. Over a period of time, a neighborly friendship developed between the royal family and the Insinger clan who were in the banking business. The last Insinger was my grandfather. He went to Egypt to treat his tuberculosis, and while he was there, he immersed himself in Egyptian archaeology, working with Mastpero. Some of his discoveries are still in the Museum of Leiden in Holland.

"My mother was born in Egypt, as you know. She met and fell in love with my dad, who was full of crazy ideas even then. One was to go to Canada. My mother had the money, and my father had the ideas. They lost plenty of both after breeding horses and then raising foxes in Alberta. That's where I was born. Then they moved to Vancouver where you met them."

"After the project at Skins Lake, did you go to Brazil?"

"Yes, I built a factory for Alcan there. After that I did a similar project in Quebec."

"Alcan is a heck of a big company. They must employ thousands and thousands. You've done a lot in your life in a quiet way. And now you're pushing a wheelbarrow and rebuilding your pond."

"That's life, Alex. What crazy things did you do that you didn't tell us? There must be some things you held back. Did you ever steal from anyone?"

"No, John. I'm shocked that you'd ask. I did everything with my own hands, and always against the odds. Come to think of it, I probably did steal something. I stole the opportunity from my children for them to learn the satisfaction of achieving things through their own efforts. I prevented them from growing strong by giving them too much."

"What about your son? You gave him too much too, and then he stole it from you. Didn't he? That's the way I see it."

"Well…"

"He squandered away the money from the trust that you had set up to take care of the whole family. I see that as stealing."

"I'm sad about how things turned out and hope things may still be made right one day. I just hope he himself doesn't fail."

"I'm wondering why you always moved around in your jobs: here a few months, there a few. Why?"

"I've asked myself that same question, John, but then I wonder if anything stays the same and never changes. I haven't found anything yet. I'm the type of person who always wants to learn new things. After I've learned all I can of something or somewhere, I get bored and have to move on to learn something else. Remember when I mentioned the job offer from the railroad for me to drive a putt-putt up and down the tracks? I already knew the stretches I'd be travelling, so it held no interest for me. I guess curiosity drives me. That's my motor. It's how I grow and maybe improve myself a bit."

"Was there more to the software scheduler story?"

"That's another sad story. Jim got greedy. I let him take it all because I didn't want to fight him in court over it. I don't fight my own family. Although he's a mathematical genius, he has no business sense. Greta is just glad I got her investment back out of the company."

"What about Greta's kids?"

"She has three gorgeous daughters."

"Like their mother?"

"I don't know. They're pretty, and nice, but they were spoiled—like my kids. That alone makes them different from Greta."

"Bringing up kids is tough. I don't know the right way."

"We teach our kids the wrong things because we're thoughtless."

"What do you mean?"

"When two children are fighting over a toy, screaming at each other and trying to pull it away from each other, we intervene by grabbing the toy and yelling, usually, 'Stop that! Give it to me!' We do the very thing we're telling them not to.

"Anyhow a child under five doesn't understand the word *no*. No isn't organized to mean anything in his brain. A child paints pictures in his brain—one picture after another until he ends up with many pictures. The brain is a library of picture books. Pictures in one book relate to pictures in another—a book for this, a book for that, then a book about books. You have to try to understand the child from his perspective, what he has to work with and feels safe with, and what he needs to feel safe."

"What about religion?"

"I think any traditional religion is good furniture for a child to sit in and feel safe in. From there he can reason out the *why's* and *how's* of what might be right or wrong—to learn to give and take. I tried to teach it to my kids by having a family *court* where we had to listen to whatever complaints one had about the others, and that included complaints about me. We discussed it together, arbitrated it, and voted on what and how it should be corrected, and how we could help each other to do better. We held court around the dining room table. It was mostly the kids and I. My job was to stay in the background to see that it was done fairly and that they weren't too harsh with each other. They were generally too harsh in their judgments. It's odd how harsh kids usually are with each other."

"That was a different approach all right, but you've always liked to be different and were willing to take risks. Are you still willing to take the kind of risks you took when you were young?"

"Hell, no. Besides, even then I set my limits. A risk had to be worth it. I was trying to find light among some of the shadows in life. I failed whenever I set my sights too high. I had to learn the best way to bail out and not complain, and then analyze why I'd failed. When I really crashed, I usually ended up laughing at myself for going so far out on a limb—the only fool clear out on the very end of it."

"But if you're never foolish, you never risk and then you don't get ahead. Failure is only another challenge."

"True. It's a matter of measuring how much to risk."

"You're so right."

"Besides, John, we need the right to make poor choices. The important thing is to have the right to choose and the right to achieve happiness through those choices. I find happiness each day in doing my best and having fun at it. I spend more time resting now, listening to music, enjoying books that teach me something new, or spending time with a friend, like I'm doing now here with you. It's all in the present. I don't concern myself with the future much anymore. Oh, sure, I aim for this or that, but the future's not here yet. The past carries the seeds of today's thoughts and happiness—when I'm patient enough to let things develop on their own by working on the present. That's what I think."

"But that means changing all the time."

"Who stays the same? None of us, John. We all change—for better or for worse. When you come right down to it, we all have to change. Nature is changing everywhere, every second.

Look at the universe. It changes at the speed of light! How we change depends on what we do along the way. You need to keep improving to keep from being a failure. Besides, it helps you to keep friends because they move and change too. You need to change with them. If you keep your friends, you haven't failed in the end."

"What about enemies?"

"Well, I've had plenty of those."

"Like the people who criticized you?"

"No. I see critics as friends, although disguised ones, because they reveal my faults. They give me a chance to improve myself, and hopefully, to do better the next time around."

"Do you think you've learned anything really important in life?"

"Whew, John! You're asking me awfully deep questions. Why?"

"I'm trying to find out what kind of goofy ideas you collected while I wasn't around."

"I have plenty that seem goofy to some. Some people really think I'm goofy when they see how I laugh at myself. If I've learned one thing, it's that. Laughing at yourself is like looking in a rearview mirror. And I've learned that you need *Lady Luck*. She has often turned dismal failures into giant successes for me. But the thing that is most important of all is—to love more. You should do everything with love."

"Do you think you're smart?"

"No. I've worked my whole life to build a shelter for my final years and, somewhere along the way, I managed to burn part of it down. Now I have to live in what's left. I don't think that's very smart."

"But you hung around a few places of learning: universities where you studied psychology and architecture, and you ran lots of different kinds of businesses where you learned about financing, and you're a Jew. Most Jews are smart."

"I'm sure not one of them. Any orthodox Jew would call me

a *mumser*, not a Jew. Although I'm Jewish and Russian and German, it's the Jewish way I feel most at home with. When I look back at what I did, I'm one of the dumb Jews. And I tried so hard to be one of the smart ones."

"I wouldn't say that. All the Jews I've known seem to be smart *shufflers*, and you've certainly done a lot of shuffling in your life and did well at it."

"Yes, I shuffled all right, but most of the time I kept at it so long that I ached so badly that I just wanted to give the whole thing up to be free again. Now I'm free to give time to wondering and pondering and enjoying being alive—more every day."

"What do you wonder and ponder about?"

"Mostly about life. I think life is a loan, a loan from nature that in time has to be repaid. We do that when we return to nature at the end of our lives. The laws of nature always prevail, in your body as well as in the universe. Both start and end with a big bang."

"You die with a bang?"

"Yes, bangs are the birth-death cycle of nature in general, a cycle to keep everything growing, going forward, including the whole flat universe."

"The whole flat universe? What do you mean by *flat*?"

"It's one of those things I've pondered, my *disk-universe theory:* the universe is being driven by the same laws of nature as the billions of disk-like galaxies and their solar systems, and therefore it must have a similar disk-like configuration. The lack of matter in the universe in itself proves it to me because the entire universe contains only ten percent of the matter necessary to form a spherical universe. I'm puzzled as to why most scientists still speculate in a spherical configuration of the universe.

"Oh, sorry, John. I see your glazed look."

"That's okay. I know you well enough to know that you have plenty of crazy ideas."

"I keep coming back to nature. It really fascinates me.

Nature only permits something to survive if it is balanced within itself. Nature is a balancing act of forces moving along with an affinity to mutations. Mutations seem to be the seeds that keep it in existence."

"You might be right. I don't quite understand what you're getting at though."

"Mutations existing inside time are where life is and how it continues. *Time* is the true force. Mighty. As mighty as your God. Without *time* there can be no mutation. Mutation and time create new life forms. Look at you, you came to life with a bang—semen to egg—that triggered an explosion of cell mutations with uncountable affinities, and you became a self-sufficient intimate universe, all on loan to be repaid at the end of your time, when those same affinities are reversed in one big bang. It begins with a big bang and ends with a big bang."

"Boy. John, the Big Bang!"

"Take your brains. They make your *bangs*."

"Haven't got any."

"Yes, you have two brains—split ones. One spies on the other day and night. The two wrestle with each other for control of your body. Either one, the emotional brain, or the other, which I call the unemotional one, dominates your body. That act of wrestling is what I call wrestling with conscience. Conscience is a delicate equilibrium of our thoughts in play between the two brains—going to and fro—stimulated by dopamine boosts and executed by the fascinating *photon phenomenon*—a theory I have—postulating how the brain communicates."

"Oh, sure, that sounds simple. Now you've really lost me."

"Nature is simple to understand if we think of it as making and taking."

"Alex, are you saying that in nature, including us as part of it, there are makers or takers?"

"Sure. Love is an example. When you're most vulnerable, either very young or very old, you give all you have. Love is the only thing you have to give, thus you are the giver, or maker of love. A toddler gives his all to you when he jumps into your arms, trusting you to catch him, to take his love. The maker depends on the taker to survive. It's like people trusting in a God they've created, trusting everything to him."

"We haven't created God. Although God is a mystery, He's understandable to most."

"Well put. God is a mystery to most. I am sad that I'm not one of *the most*. My mind stands in the way of believing in the wonderful myth of God."

"Maybe you'll change your mind one day. It's happened to other people at the end of their lives. Maybe you'll get there too. Do you think man created God?"

"Yes. I'm afraid so. Man created God to have somebody to love and to be loved in return. It's love that keeps us sane, and love knows no regret, no hate. True love is too smart to hate. Hate comes from an anxiety of not being able to possess. It's that and nothing more. Why try to possess things when you can't? Does any part of your body possess the other parts? No. Parts of you wrestle with each other to try and dominate, but in the end you are a whole of the parts of the interdependent, symbiotic relationships of unseen things. The more things are unseen, the more real they seem—more real than real."

"What you're saying is confusing. Do you think we can avoid what seems to be our mismanagement of the world—and, instead, do anything to improve it?"

"I have no answer for your question, no utopia to offer. Any utopia is doomed to failure. Man has tried it many times, but it has always failed. There is no place in nature for a utopia. The days for man to try to create a utopia are long gone. Pluto tried it. Marx tried it. And back then, there was more space between men; there were walls and boundaries. A utopia needs tight borders where nothing can penetrate. Today man interacts globally within seconds. Everything that happens today happens in the present, allowing no place for utopias to be tried, no borders within which it can grow."

"So what should we do to make the best of things today? Play dead?"

"Just do your best. Live. Do your best for your loved ones and for whatever else is alive to you—reverence for life as one entity. I've come full circle back to what Albert Schweitzer said all those years ago—a reverence for life."

"But you need a place to do it in. A free country."

"Yes. And I can think of no better place than the whole of North America where governing is part of a continuing experiment, just as man is. But don't let others get power over you to stop you from being yourself above all. There are plenty of them around, who want to make you theirs. And they have their own prayer of worrying about you once they have you under control. I know it by heart...

Their Prayer For Suckers
Lord, we beg you, we besiege you,
All of us, with all of our hearts,
Safeguard and grace them,
All those who serve us,
All those who do our bidding,
All those who sweetly swear false witness for us,
All those who gladly go to the pit for us,
All those who give us a jingle at our wink,
Who beg us day by day to do it to them.
Lord, we graciously let them do
what they can't help themselves from doing—
holding us supreme over all.
Our Lord, forgive them for they know no better.
Our Lord, don't let them fade away on us—ever.
Our Lord, you know we depend on them day by day,
For heaven's sake, protect them,
At least for our sake.
Amen.

"You're right. We are suckers most of our lives. And we're suckers enough to pick those who take advantage of us, like politicians who have only the power we gave them, and then we do their bidding and dance to their tune. Damn. So how do we avoid it."

"Try not to be sucked in. Do your own thing. Really living life means having muscles that ache from work, not play, and a mind that aches from trying to do things that extend beyond your personal needs, and never blaming anyone else when you fail. You failed—not them."

"It's not that simple. Don't you blame your parents for some of what they did to you?"

"No, I don't see how I could. They did things the only way they knew how, and they somehow made something out of what life gave them. They didn't have much time for me, but that gave me a chance to learn to do things my own way. Everyone should try to do things his own way, although being mindful of those around him. That's important. Then you will end up with…

A Little Paradise On Earth
We're all given a chance
to make a little paradise for ourselves,
to create some happiness for ourselves.
Some get a chance in the
earlier days of their life,
and others later in life.
My paradise was postponed.
It came later,
when Greta came back
into my life,
and I put my head on her lap—
happy to age with her.

Painting is what matters to me now,
sunsets on canvases
that echo my passion,
showing how light and shadow
affect each other,

the spaces we live in,
we move through,
all in our own way.
Now it's my time."

"I'm with you. Yet when I think about getting old, it seems to me that old people have it kind of tough because more and more doors are closing at the end of their lives."

"Maybe, but I think the young ones have it harder because they're struggling to replace the old ones who aren't ready to move on and make way for them. And don't you think, old or young, that a new door opens for each door that closes? You just have to keep going and dare yourself to try opening all the doors you find. One will open, sooner or later."

"What if you can't open a new door?"

"Leave it and go on."

"That story you told us about you and Greta, was that your whole story? Everything?"

"No, they're really just the highlights and those special small moments that stay crystal clear and stand out from the rest, but everything? Never. Let's face it. We couldn't remember half of it anyway."

I'm curious about what you haven't told?"

"It's only the things that don't need to be said. It's never right to tell things that are still hurtful to people. We have to respect their dignity and our own."

"But I'm your buddy, Alex. You could tell me. You know I'd never tell anyone."

"Yes, John. I know. You, especially. But I respect you too much to burden you with private hurts and regrets that are better left unsaid, and that's all they are: burdens."

John and I walked back from the pond towards the cabin.

The rest of the day was filled with happy words, some drinks, and lots of laughs. The last hours were spent packing and looking around and smiling. I was happy here. I knew I was going to miss John and Estelle and the stream, of course.

John took us to the airport. The good-bye was like the hello. We drove down the two strips of crushed rock in the lawn that led from the garage to the road. Estelle stood at the porch, smiling and waving. She looked frail. We hadn't been easy on her.

Out on the highway we soon passed the shack where the two new motorbikes were still parked out front.

We lived the scenery, sitting quietly in the car.

"It was sure nice, John. Thanks again."

"The red carpet is always out for you, Alex. You know the key's under the doormat. Anytime."

There was nothing more to say. I could hear the turning of the rubber wheels on the pavement as the car gently followed the ups and downs of the road that hugged the contours of the land, and again my eyes looked beyond the hood to the pavement and straight out to its end. We crossed the border and spent a couple of hours seeing what we'd seen when we'd first arrived. Then we seemed to miss a turn.

"John, is this the right road?"

"No, sorry. I missed the last turn."

John is the kind of guy who doesn't keep his mind on the road when he's thinking or talking, mostly thinking. It doesn't bother him to travel off on the wrong road as long as his mind eventually finds what it was looking for.

"Alex, are those stories you told us true?"

"I've willed you my stories and relived them with the telling. Nothing else matters. Frankly, I don't see why I should keep all of them to myself, leaving someone else to try and figure out what and how I did things, and then tell others how they saw me. They'd be wrong, most likely, anyway. What does it matter, John, true or not? It was fun telling it."

"Well, was it true?"

"John, you could say it was a true story, and you could say it wasn't. It doesn't matter. It was just a story, nothing more."

"That's what I figured you'd say."

We arrived at Dorval airport. Greta and John kissed good-bye. I was glad they liked each other. In those last few minutes what I really wanted to say was how much I loved him and how much he meant to me, but in the end I just patted his cheek and smiled. I felt awkward when I saw John standing alone where we left him. It wasn't the way I wanted to say good-bye—just patting his cheek. Then we were swallowed up in the activities of…

> ***Leaving In An Airport***
> *Among strangers,*
> *milling,*
> *gathering up luggage,*
> *throwing smiles and good-byes*
> *as we headed towards the waiting plane.*

After we settled into our seats, I asked Greta what she'd thought of him.

"Now I understand why you said he's your best friend. He's wonderful."

"I wanted you to meet him to understand him. I knew it didn't make much sense when I'd told you how little time we'd actually spent together. I could have talked my head off and not convinced you, but now that you've met him, you know it's true. It happens here and there in life. We've met off and on, a few days here and there, over the years. When you're young and meet someone somewhat like yourself—the same way as you and I did—someone who fits, you weld into each other, quick and deep. But I think you have to be young to weld into each other deep enough to make it stick."

"Why didn't you tell John your story was all true?"

"I thought that keeping him guessing at the end made it a better story."

"Do you think John and Estelle fit together?"

"Yes, very well. They've had a long time to work at it. I think it wasn't all that easy. They're both smart and watch out for their rights in the territories that they've negotiated from each other. I think she needs him and loves him. I believe she thinks he isn't all that smart, or as smart as he makes out. And John respects her for knowing his tricks and ways."

"But, Alexander, I have the impression that he's very smart."

"Yes, he is. But I suspect he's made a few mistakes along the way, like losing money in the stock market, and she hasn't quite forgiven him for it. She wouldn't have risked what he did. I suspect he can't quite get away from puttering around in the market. It's part of the make-up he inherited from his dad. His dad lost a lot of his wife's money breeding expensive horses. John's mother told me that once, and laughed and laughed. She could laugh then because it had happened such a long time before."

"I think John will only go so far gambling in the market."

"Yes, his dad risked much more than John ever would. John learned by watching his father."

"They need each other, don't they?"

"Yes, like you and I. And John needs that place, not because he is dumb, but because he is smart. Otherwise it would be tough for him to go on. Estelle is smart too because she goes along with it. Even though she thinks it's dumb, she knows he needs it. She knows the cabin is his place to get old in, the cure for his tiring blood. It reminds me of how his dad raced smelly boxers. John's mother went along with it though she thought it was dumb. She knew then what Estelle knows now. That's what should happen between two people who are going along the same road together, like a couple out pulling a cart, with give and take, trying to understand each other while each does his own part as well as he can."

"You and I are similar to them, yet somewhat different. We are all doing our part by dealing with whatever life gives us, trying to make it turn out as well as possible."

"That's the most important thing—trying your best with whatever life gives you—whatever it is. Then it doesn't matter if you fail, as long as you've done it from your heart."

"I can understand how that makes failing easier to accept."

"Yes, and that's why doing things with your heart—with every fiber of your being—is so important."

"I agree. You become a better person when you give your best throughout your life, and in the end, you have more fun too. Don't you think?"

"Yes."

www.alexandermunzel.com